complete
knitting skills

DEBBIE TOMKIES

Search Press

A QUARTO BOOK

Published in 2013 by
Search Press Ltd
Wellwood
North Farm Rd
Tunbridge Wells
Kent TN2 3DR

ISBN-13: 978-1-84448-901-5

QUAR.QRK

Conceived, designed and produced by
Quarto Publishing plc
6 Blundell Street
London N7 9BH

Senior editor: Katie Crous
Copy editor: Lindsay Kaubi
Art director: Caroline Guest
Art editor: Joanna Bettles
Designer: Emma Clayton
Illustrator: Kuo Kang Chen
Picture research: Sarah Bell
Proofreader: Claire Waite Brown
Photographers: Simon Pask &
   Phil Wilkins
Films by: Simon Pask
Film 'hands': Debbie Tomkies
Voiceovers: Meghan Fernandes

Creative director: Moira Clinch
Publisher: Paul Carslake

Colour separation by Modern Age Repro
   House Ltd, Hong Kong
Printed in China by 1010 Printing
   International Ltd

10 9 8 7 6 5 4 3 2 1

Contents

❶ The technique is demonstrated by 1 film

2 The technique is demonstrated by 2 films

Foreword

. . . .

I learnt to knit as a child on my Grandma's knee, and I was captivated from the outset by the exotic balls of colourful yarn in my local yarn store and by the excitement of being able to create my own unique garments. One of the challenges I've faced along the way is finding all those useful techniques and tips that make knits look better, shortcuts that save time and ideas that enhance my designs.

So I've written this book to help you find everything you need to know quickly and easily, in one convenient place. Whether it's essential knitting skills, more advanced techniques for experienced knitters or tips and tricks to make your knitting easier and more enjoyable, you'll find it all here. And, to make learning even more accessible and fun, key techniques are also available to watch online. View the films on your computer, tablet or smartphone; pause and revisit as often as you like.

The final chapter of this book is by no means the least important. Containing useful information on connecting with other knitters, taking advantage of new technology to expand your hobby's horizons and putting your skills to good use for good causes, you can find out how to take your knitting beyond the needles by becoming part of a growing and rewarding knitting community.

Debbie Tomkies

About this book

Discover an extensive range of techniques that will get you out of the starting blocks if you're a novice, and will extend your knowledge and ability into the realm of expertise if you're a more seasoned knitter. Follow the chapters for a logical progression, or skip around for specific details. However you use this book, don't forget to access the accompanying online films.

The films

Follow techniques on the move using your smartphone to access the online tutorials quickly via QR codes, or via the Internet on your laptop or netbook. It's like having your very own knitting tutor sitting right next to you!

The techniques that have an accompanying film tutorial are marked in the Contents (pages 4–5) with a ❶ symbol, and more complex subjects are dealt with using two tutorials. Throughout the book you'll find the QR code for scanning with your smartphone on the opening page for the relevant technique. Simply download a free app to scan, if needed, or you may prefer to type the URL address into your web browser to link you to the relevant web page. All the films come with expert commentary to guide you through the essential stages of the technique.

Browse all 27 film clips

Want to see a complete list of all 27 films, with live links to each? Then scan the code, right.

No QR scanner? No problem!

Want to view all the films in this book on your laptop or desktop computer? Then go to: http://www.searchpress.com/video/cks/9015/

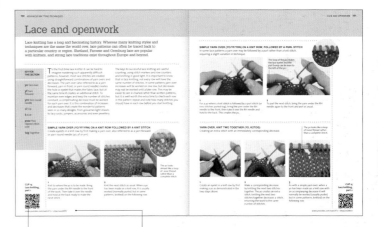

Scan the QR code for instant playback on your smartphone.

Type the URL address into your web browser to be taken to the relevant web page.

The camera angle is set up as if it's your own hands you're watching, making it easy to copy the movements of the knitter. Knit as you watch, using the pause and rewind functions in your browser where needed.

A helpful zoom at crucial stages makes sure that you can see the exact stitch being made.

A worked example shows you the end result so you know what you're aiming for.

CHAPTER 1: Equipment and yarn, pages 10–29

Starting to knit need not be expensive, and this chapter explains the essential items you'll need and the extras you may wish to purchase, as well as showing you some of the luxury options available.

The book
CHAPTER 2: Getting started, pages 30–83

Nothing is taken for granted, and this chapter covers not only the basics – casting on and casting off, knit, purl, etc. – but also key skills such as understanding knitting terms and concepts, and following patterns and charts.

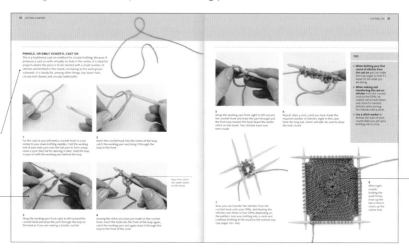

Essential beginners' and alternative methods are explained in full.

Clear, zoomed-in step photography takes you through the main stages.

The end result is shown for reference.

Chapter 3: Finishing, pages 84–109

A good knit can be turned into a great knit with some simple tips on finishing and making up – find them in this chapter, which is packed with useful information on achieving professional results.

CHAPTER 4: Taking it to the next level, pages 110–159

Whether you're adapting an existing pattern, trying to decide on the best method for the job or looking to add a decorative edge or practical pocket, this chapter will show you how.

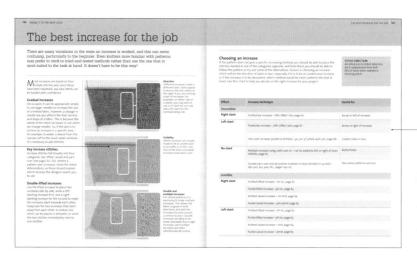

Different methods are shown in use, so you can compare how they work in practice.

This chapter includes summaries of your options and at-a-glance guides to picking the best one for the job.

CHAPTER 5: Advanced knitting techniques, pages 160–217

Perhaps there's something you always wanted to try, or something you need to come to grips with in order to knit that gorgeous pattern – look no further! From working in the round to entrelac and Fair Isle, you'll find it here.

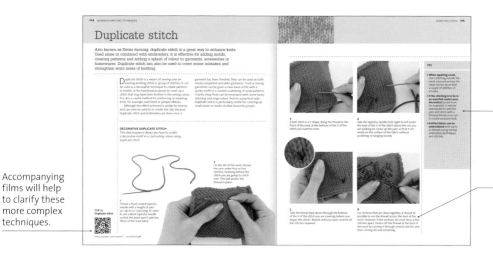

Accompanying films will help to clarify these more complex techniques.

Expert advice helps take your knitting beyond the page.

Clear written instructions are given that break down the stitch into digestible segments.

CHAPTER 6: Knitting SOS, pages 218–235

An error in your knitting need not be a disaster. Learn how to avoid mishaps and how to fix common problems when they do arise with minimum fuss.

CHAPTER 7: The knitting community, pages 236–245

Knitting has come full circle, and knitting in public is once again a popular group activity. If you would like to connect with other knitters or want to knit for others, here are some ideas for getting involved.

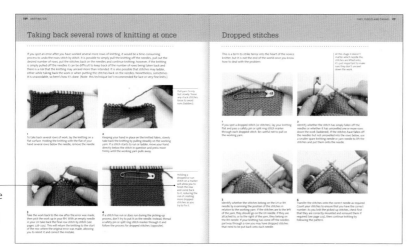

Notes alongside the steps stress the most important details.

equipment
and yarn

Spoilt for choice, the modern knitter has no problem finding all the necessary tools and materials; the trouble is being able to decide on which ones would best suit your project, and budget. Read the following pages to make sure you're familiar with all the options and their uses before you start spending your cash.

Needles

The right tools are an important part of any project, and knitting is no exception. Fortunately, getting started with good-quality materials need not be expensive and, with a few basic tools, you will be creating wonderful projects in no time.

To begin your knitting journey, all you will need to get started is a pair of knitting needles, some yarn, a tape measure, and a pair of scissors. A suitable pair of knitting needles is your first requirement.

Needle types

Knitting needles are available in a wide range of materials, shapes and sizes, from practical plastic or metal to wood, bamboo and even glass! When it comes to choosing your first needles, try as many different types as you can. Ask friends who knit or visit a local yarn shop. Try needles of different lengths, shapes and materials if you can. Remember that you may need at least two pairs for your first project, so consider your budget when making your first purchases. If your budget limits you to buying inexpensive plastic or metal needles, that's fine; you will still be able to complete any knitting project. You can often pick up needles from charity shops, on upcycling websites such as Freecycle, Craig's List or Freegle.

Single-pointed pairs of needles
Widely available and commonly used, single-pointed needles are sold in pairs and have a point at one end and a knurl, knob or other stopper at the other end to prevent the stitches sliding off. Use these needles for knitting flat fabrics.

Double-pointed needles
These needles have points at both ends and are sold in sets of four or five needles. Often referred to as DPNs, they are used for knitting tubular fabrics, for example, socks, jumper sleeves and seamless jumpers (also called knitting in the round). Extra-long DPNs can be used with a knitting belt or sheath for traditional Fair Isle knitting.

Circular needles
A circular needle comprises two short, single-pointed needles, joined to each other by a flexible cord. The cord may be permanently attached but sets are also available with interchangeable needles (tips) and cords of different lengths. Circular needles are versatile because they can be used for knitting flat fabrics as an alternative to single-pointed needles, or for knitting tubular fabrics in place of DPNs.

Needle lengths

The most common lengths for standard single-pointed needles are 30cm (12in) and 35cm (14in) and these will suit most knitters. For small projects (toys, accessories, etc.) and for working with children, shorter needles of around 15–20cm (6–8in) are available.

12.5cm (5in), 19cm (7½in) and 25cm (10in) DPNs
Choose the length you find most comfortable to work with, bearing in mind that the more stitches you have and the thicker the yarn, the longer your DPNs will likely need to be.

Extra-long, 40cm (16in) DPNs
Very long needles are used for some traditional Fair Isle techniques, where the needles are stuck into a leather belt or wooden sheath worn around the waist. This isn't a commonly used technique today but was once popular in Europe, and allows for fast knitting.

Circular needle tips and cords
The tip of a circular needle refers to the actual needle; the cord joins the two needles together. Tips are normally short, around 10cm (4in). Cords range from 20cm (8in) to 150cm (60in). The length of the cord should be chosen to give a circumference slightly smaller than that of the tube being knitted.

The following sizes are given in length and UK/Canadian/ Australian and European needle sizes, with US needle size in brackets.
1 Knitting needle holder **2** Rosewood, 35cm (14in) long, 000/10mm (size 15) **3** Birch, 35cm (14in) long, 000/15mm (size 19) **4** Wooden, 25cm (10in) long, 0/8mm (size 11) **5** Bamboo, 35cm (14in) long, 2/7mm (size 10½) **6** Metal circular, 75cm (29½in) long, 7/4.5mm (size 7) **7, 8 & 9** Birch DPNs, 12.5cm (5in), 19cm (7½in) and 25cm (10in) long, 6/5mm (size 8) **10** Metal DPNs, 19cm (7½in) long, 11/3mm (size 2) **11** Kids' aluminium, 19cm (7½in) long, 8/4.5mm (size 6) **12** Aluminium, 30cm (12in) long, 8/4mm (size 6) **13** Aluminium, 35cm (14in) long, 8/4mm (size 6) **14** Plastic, 40cm (16in) long, 2/7mm (size 10½)

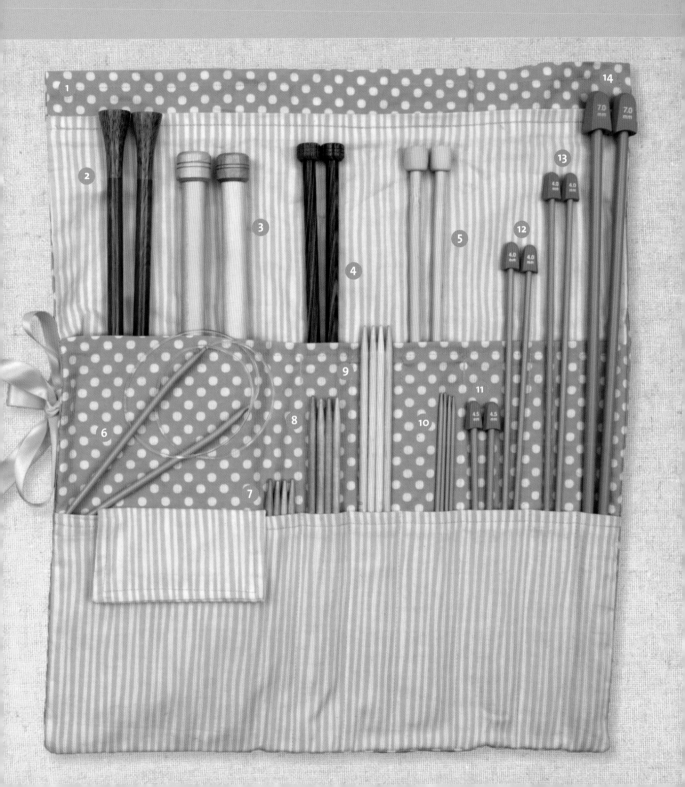

Decorative gift needles,
23cm (9in) long, 4.5mm
(size 7)

Rosewood square needles,
4.5mm (size 7)

Needle shapes

Round
This is far and away the most common needle shape on the market; easy to use and available in all formats, sizes and materials.

Square
Many knitters with dexterity problems report that these needles are a much easier shape to grip and manipulate. Worth a try if you find traditional round needles uncomfortable. Square needles are currently not available in all materials and are more expensive than round, but prices will no doubt become more competitive with time.

Hexagonal
A newcomer to the knitting market, these needles are at the upper end of the price scale but are pretty and comfortable to use. The shape also makes them less likely to roll off the table! They are currently only available in wood.

Needle materials

Plastic needles
Plastic needles are inexpensive and are readily available in a wide range of sizes. Plastic needles are the first choice for many knitters, beginners and experienced alike. Flexible and light in use, you can buy a pair at a time or choose a pre-packaged set with a range of sizes.

Bamboo
Bamboo needles are flexible, lightweight and warm to the touch, making them popular with knitters who have arthritis or rheumatism. Budget bamboo needles can split with use, so buy the best pair within your budget. They can be lightly sanded with emery paper if they develop rough spots over time.

Wood
There are many beautiful wooden needles on the market and many knitters find these the most comfortable to work with because they are warm, light and easy on the hands. Like bamboo they can break but can be sanded with care.

Metal
Many knitters prefer metal needles because they are virtually indestructible. They are the needles of choice for many lace knitters because they have the sharpest points for fine work. The smooth finish also makes them a popular choice for knitting at speed. Prices vary significantly for metal needles.

Glass
Glass needles are a luxury choice: they are lovely to use and very beautiful. They are more durable than you may imagine since most are made from Pyrex, although naturally they are best kept away from the rough and tumble you may subject your normal needles to. Not as wide a range of sizes, particularly small sizes, but now available in single-pointed, double-pointed and circular formats.

Interchangeable
knitting needle kit

TIPS

- **Build your needle collection gradually,** buying needles only as you need them for each project. It will save you money and you can try different needle types until you find the ones that are most suited to you and work best with the project you are working on.

- **Look after your needles** by keeping them in a needle roll or case, or store them flat in a sturdy plastic tube. Check wooden and bamboo needles for snags and gently file with emery paper as required. Clean plastic and metal needles with warm, soapy water and dry thoroughly. Other needles can be carefully buffed with a lint-free cloth to remove oils, perfumes and marks.

Accessories, gadgets & gizmos

In addition to your knitting needles, there are a few items that you will find very useful, and a small number that are essential.

In the majority of cases, you will already have what you need at home. There are, of course, lots of gadgets and accessories that you may wish to purchase as you progress.

Essentials

Pen, pencil and notepaper
These essential knitting bag items are useful for marking off where you are in a pattern and making notes about patterns and any alterations you may have made. If you are designing your own knits, jot down any thoughts, ideas and inspiration for this and future projects.

Scissors
Choose small scissors with sharp points because these will allow you to cut neatly and in the right place. It is worth investing in good-quality scissors, since inexpensive ones may snag your knitted fabric. Keep them in a pouch or case to avoid accidents.

Yarn needles
Referred to variously as yarn needles, bodkins and darning needles, you will need a small selection of these to sew up your knits. Blunt or round-ended needles are useful for sewing up seams where it is important not to split the yarn. Choose a size appropriate to the yarn.

Knitting needle gauge
A good needle gauge will enable you to identify the size of any knitting needle and is useful for converting between different measurement systems (for example, metric, imperial, US, Australia). Also handy if you are given needles, or buy them secondhand, because the numbers may have worn away with use.

Sewing or tapestry needles
Needles with sharper points, such as the type used for needlepoint or tapestry, are useful for sewing in ends where you need to split the yarn. Sewing needles can also be used for adding buttons, zips and other accessories. Select a size to suit your thickness of yarn. If you are planning to add beads, you will need a beading needle, because even regular sewing needles are too thick for most beads.

1 Tape measure
2 Notepad and pencil
3 Split-ring stitch markers **4** DPN point protectors **5** Bobbins

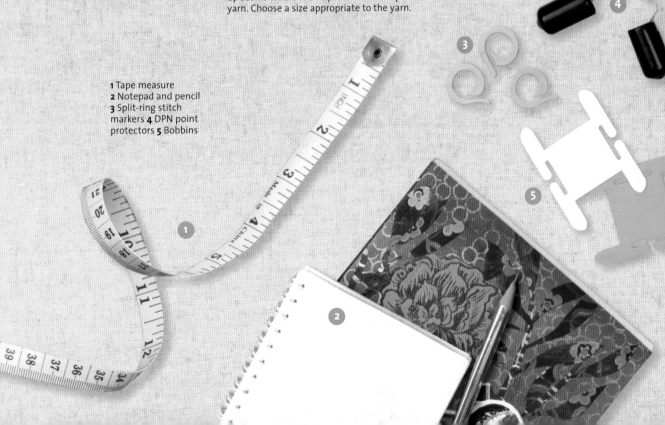

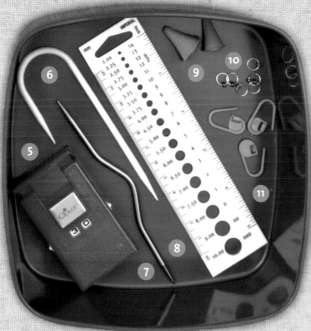

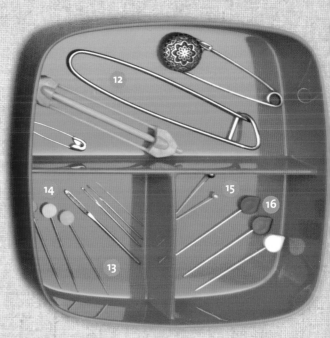

1 Decorative washi tape for marking charts 2 Sewing scissors 3 Emergency mini crochet hooks – simply attach to your knitting bag 4 Thread 5 Row counter 6 & 7 Cable needles 8 Needle gauge 9 Point protectors 10 Ring markers 11 Split-ring stitch markers 12 Stitch holders 13 Sewing needles 14, 15 & 16 Pins

Smooth, contrasting thread
You will find that 10g ('/₂oz) or so of smooth thread (cotton is a good choice) in a contrasting colour to your knitting will have many uses. For example, it is useful for holding stitches, marking key stages in your knitting, indicating the location of pattern repeats and for specific techniques, such as provisional cast on and lifelines.

Tape measure and ruler
Use a tape measure for body measurements and for measuring anything that isn't flat. A ruler is useful for measuring stitches and rows for gauge swatches. It also doubles as a handy marker for keeping your place on knitting charts.

Pins
Pins are used to hold your knitting together when assembling. Choose large-headed pins where possible so that you can see them easily. A selection of longer pins for longer seams and shorter pins for smaller areas will be useful. Special T pins are available for blocking knits. These have a T-shaped head, making them easier and safer to use vertically (as opposed to flat to the knitting).

Optional extras

Stitch holders
Available in several lengths to accommodate different numbers of stitches, stitch holders look like large safety pins. A safety pin can be used for a small number of stitches, but be careful not to snag the yarn on the hinge. Alternatively, stitches can be transferred onto a piece of contrasting thread.

Row counters
Pen and paper are perfectly adequate for recording your knitting progress, but there are also lots of handy row counters on the market. These range from simple plastic click mechanisms, and barrels that sit on the end of your needles, to clever apps to download onto your smartphone.

Stitch markers
Ranging from inexpensive plastic to beautiful, handmade beaded sets, stitch markers denote key points in your knitting, for example, marking the end of a round or pattern repeat. Choose a size slightly larger than your needles, checking that they slide easily and that any beads won't catch in your work.

Split rings
These are similar to stitch markers but with an open end, allowing them to be inserted and removed anywhere at any time. Useful for marking key points in your work when you need to leave the marker in the work and return to it later.

Cable needles
Also called cable pins, cable needles are short, double-pointed needles that are straight, hook-shaped, or with a kink in the middle. They are used when creating cables as a means of temporarily holding a small number of stitches. Choose a size the same as, or slightly smaller than, your main knitting to avoid stretching your cable stitches.

Point protectors
Flexible plastic or rubberised point protectors keep your work on the needles when you are not knitting. They also stop points from poking out of workbags and avoid damage to the points of the needles.

Crochet hooks
A selection of crochet hooks will come in handy for adding edgings and beads, and for picking up dropped stitches.

Bobbins
Used in place of hand-wound 'butterflies' to hold small amounts of yarn, usually for intarsia or Fair Isle work.

The language of yarn

Knitters around the globe may share a love of knitting, but they have many and varied ways of describing the yarns they work with.

It is really more correct to use the term 'yarn' to describe all the different types of 'string' we knit with. Of course 'wool' is a term many knitters associate with any type of knitting yarn, regardless of the fibre from which it is made. Strictly speaking, however, the term 'wool' only applies when the actual fibre content of the yarn is processed sheep's fleece. It is therefore more correct to use the term 'yarn' to separate it from the idea of fibre content, which describes the raw material, or materials, from which a yarn is made.

A further aspect of any yarn description is its quality. This may be described in different ways depending on the country of origin of the yarn (or indeed of the pattern or the designer). In this context quality doesn't usually refer to how good the yarn is – that would generate a lengthy debate among any group of knitters!

Yarn glossary

There are myriad technical words in the world of yarn. Here's a rundown of some of the key terms and their meaning in the context of knitting.

Yarn
The basic material used to create a knitted fabric. This includes the many commercially produced yarns available from yarn stores and other shops, but also includes handspun or handmade yarns, yarns made from wire, plastic, strips of fabric or other materials.

Fibre content
Yarn fibre could come from an animal (for example, sheep, alpaca, camel, goat), from a plant (for example, cotton, hemp, linen, nettle, bamboo, soy), or from a manmade source (for example, acrylic, polyamide, wire, plastic). Regenerated fibres such as viscose, tencel and rayon are made from wood pulp. Recycled fibres may include fabric or even plastic bottles. The choice of fibre content will influence the use, handle, appearance and suitability of a yarn for particular projects.

Yarn quality
A broad term used to describe the nature of the yarn. This will often incorporate, among other things, yarn weight, yardage, how many plies the yarn has and yarn count.

● **Weight** In the context of yarn quality, weight refers to the thickness of the yarn, not the actual weight of the ball/skein. Terms to describe yarn weight vary and there is (rather confusingly) some overlap with plies and yarn count. US terminology, for example, includes fingering, sport, worsted and bulky. Equivalent UK terms refer to the thickness of a yarn by ply – 2-ply, 4-ply and so on.

● **Plies** This refers to the way a yarn is made. Yarn starts out life as one strand, referred to as a singles thread or singles. It is then plied (either by twisting or by folding) with one or more other threads to create a thicker yarn. A 2-ply yarn is made from two strands, a 4-ply from four strands, and so on. Depending on the thickness of the original strand this determines the thickness of the finished yarn and therefore its quality. Traditionally, in the UK, a 2-ply would describe a fine (lace weight) yarn but, of course, if the yarn begins life as a single, thick strand, a 2-ply of this yarn could be much thicker, so arguably using plies to describe yarn thickness can be misleading.

● **Yardage/metreage** This is a useful guide when deciding the amount of yarn needed for a project. Some fibres are heavier than others so there are fewer yards per ounce with, for example, a silk than a cashmere yarn. However, 92m (100 yd) of fingering quality silk should knit the same number of stitches as 92m (100 yd) of fingering quality cashmere, making this a useful measure when substituting yarns.

● **Yarn count** This term is closely linked to yarn thickness and plies. The yarn count is the number of yards of yarn in a given weight (actual weight) of finished yarn. Rather unhelpfully there are many systems for arriving at a yarn count, including worsted count, linen count, cotton count, Yorkshire count and tex.

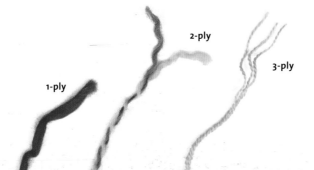

1-ply 2-ply 3-ply

1 100% silk 2 100% bamboo
3 100% Aran wool 4 100% merino wool 5 100% baby merino wool 6 Organic cotton
7 69% silk, 31% stainless silk
8 Mercerised cotton
9 Naturally dyed crisp linen lace
10 Ribbon ball yarn 11 70% super kid mohair, 30% silk
12 50% merino wool, 50% cotton 13 Chunky alpaca

Choosing and substituting yarn

At some time, most knitters will find the perfect pattern only to discover that the recommended yarn has been discontinued, or is one that they don't like or can't wear due to allergies. Other times, a great pattern can be made even better by incorporating a small amount of a luxury or novelty yarn, or an expensive yarn can be substituted with a more economical choice.

Charity shops can be a rich source of fabulous vintage patterns and pattern books. You may even be lucky enough to be given an old pattern collection. Not surprisingly, the yarn used in these patterns has often been discontinued, which means that an alternative yarn has to be found. Although this may seem a little daunting, substituting yarns is quite straightforward and can be great fun, too.

Yarn substitutions fall broadly into three categories:

Like for like
If a pattern calls for a pure wool yarn in a fingering weight but you can't buy the stated yarn in your country, you simply need to replace it with a yarn that is as similar as possible. This can be done relatively easily.

All change
It may be necessary to change a yarn completely, for example, using a cotton yarn instead of wool if you have allergies. A complete change is perhaps the most challenging substitution, but by following some simple guidelines it can be achieved successfully and with fantastic results.

Spicing it up
A plain pattern can often be enhanced, or a vintage pattern updated and customised, simply by including a small amount of a different yarn. Knowing how to choose two yarns that work well together is also very useful if you don't have enough of the main yarn to finish a garment.

Shopping for a different yarn
If you are buying yarn to match a pattern, it may not be possible to make tension squares. Fortunately, most ball bands should give details equivalent to a tension square, showing the stitches/rows to the centimetre/inch usually worked in stocking stitch and using a specified needle size. There may also be a recommended range of needle sizes for the yarn. While not as accurate as producing your own tension squares, using a yarn that has a range of needle sizes and a tension measurement close to that stated in your pattern should give a good tension match.

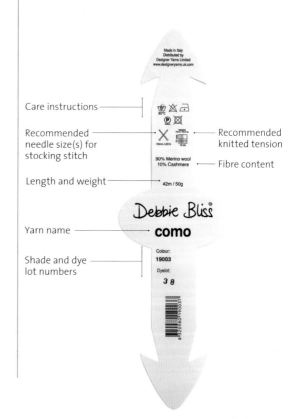

Care instructions

Recommended needle size(s) for stocking stitch

Length and weight

Yarn name

Shade and dye lot numbers

Recommended knitted tension

Fibre content

Made in Italy
Distributed by
Designer Yarns Limited
www.designeryarns.uk.com

90% Merino wool
10% Cashmere

42m / 50g

Debbie Bliss®
como

Colour:
19003
Dyelot:
3 8

A ball band supplies the knitter with a wealth of information.

Using your stash

If you want to use up existing yarn from your stash, or use handspun yarn, you may not have much information to go on. In this case, follow the instructions below.

Begin by choosing a yarn that looks similar to the pattern yarn. Wrap the yarn closely around a ruler until 2.5cm (1in) has been covered. Count how many times the yarn is wrapped around the ruler to give you the wraps per inch (WPI). Use the chart to decide the closest yarn type to your yarn. If this is the same as the pattern yarn, you are well on the way. If not, you may have to consider using a different yarn.

Yarn weight symbol and category names	0	1	2	3	4	5	6
Types of yarns in category	Fingering 10-count crochet thread	Sock, fingering, baby	Sport, baby	DK, light worsted	Worsted, Afghan, Aran	Chunky, craft, rug	Bulky, roving
Knit tension range in stocking stitch to 10cm (4in)	33–40 sts	27–32 sts	23–26 sts	21–24 sts	16–20 sts	12–15 sts	6–11 sts
Recommended needle in metric-size range	1.5–2.25mm	2.25–3.25mm	3.25–3.75mm	3.75–4.5mm	4.5–5.5mm	5.5–8mm	8mm and larger
Recommended needle in US-size range	000–1	1–3	3–5	5–7	7–9	9–11	11 and larger
Wraps per inch (WPI)	16–18 WPI	14 WPI	12 WPI	11 WPI	8–9 WPI	7 WPI	6 or fewer WPI

Gauging tension

Once you have found a potentially suitable yarn, knit a tension square exactly according to the pattern instructions. Wash and block the square (see page 86) before measuring (see page 39) since yarns react differently to washing and this may affect the finished tension and therefore size and texture.

If your washed square matches the tension, you can use this yarn. If it is close, try again with smaller/larger needles. If you need to go up or down more than three needle sizes to achieve the right tension, think carefully about using this yarn because you may not get the desired effect.

Incorrect tension
If there are too few rows or stitches than the pattern suggests, as shown above, your knitting is too loose. Make another swatch with smaller needles. Conversely, if you find that you have more rows or stitches, then the tension is too tight and you should switch to a larger needle.

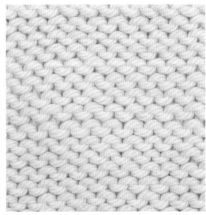

Correct tension
In this case, you are safe to proceed to knitting the real article.

How much yarn? (Yardage)

Even though two yarns knit to the same tension, you may need differing weights of yarn to make the same design. This is because the density of the yarn, the fibre composition, the tightness of twist and the texture all affect the weight. A worsted-quality cashmere, for example, may have as much as 200m (218yd) in a 50g (1³/₄oz) skein, a pure wool 100m (109yd), but a cotton chenille may only give 50m (55yd) per 50g (1³/₄oz). Because it is the length that primarily determines the amount of yarn needed, 50g (1³/₄oz) of cashmere will go further than 50g (1³/₄oz) of wool and considerably further than 50g (1³/₄oz) of cotton chenille.

25g cashmere DK
This cashmere swatch is the largest. With lots of air trapped between the fibres, there are more yards of yarn in 25g.

25g wool DK
Wool yarn is light and has lots of air trapped between the fibres, but not as much as cashmere, so there are fewer yards per ball.

25g cotton DK
Cotton is a dense fibre and so has fewer yards per ball. It produces the smallest of the three swatches.

If your yarn has no yardage information

Weigh one ball. Wrap your yarn once around a book, measure it and note the length. Wrap snugly but without stretching the yarn because this would distort your calculations. Wind off the complete ball by wrapping it around the book. Count the number of times the yarn is wrapped around the book and multiply this by the length you noted above to give the number of metres/ yards per ball. Compare this to the total metres/yards per ball as stated in the pattern. If they are similar, you should need the same weight of yarn as stated in the pattern. If your yarn has more metres/yards per ball, you should need fewer balls. If there are fewer metres/ yards in your ball, you will need more balls than in the pattern.

Example: Metric
Weight of ball/skein: 100g
One wrap of yarn around niddy noddy = 1.5m
Total number of wraps in skein = 250
Total metreage in 100g skein = 1.5m x 250 wraps = 375m.
This equates to a sock/4-ply yarn.

Example: US imperial
Weight of ball/skein: 4oz
One wrap of yarn around niddy noddy = 1.64yd
Total number of wraps in skein = 240
Total yardage in 4oz skein = 1.64yd x 240 wraps = 395yd
This equates to a sock/4-ply yarn.

If you have a partial skein or ball and need to compare to a ball band for a full-sized skein/ball

Simply add this step:

Example: Metric
Weight of ball/skein: 85g
One wrap of yarn around niddy noddy = 1.5m
Total number of wraps in skein = 212
(Each wrap is the same length but because there is less weight of yarn there will be fewer wraps)
Total metreage in 85g skein = 1.5m x 212 wraps = 318m
Total metreage in 100g skein = 318m/85g x 100g = 374m

Example: US imperial
Weight of ball/skein: 3oz
One wrap of yarn around niddy noddy = 1.64yd
Total number of wraps in skein = 180
(Each wrap is the same length but because there is less weight of yarn there will be fewer wraps.)
Total yardage in 3oz skein = 1.64yd x 180 wraps = 295yd
Total yardage in 4oz skein = 295yd/3oz x 4oz = 395yd

If your pattern does not state the length of yarn required

There are various charts available online to help you calculate the yardage (try www.lionbrand.com), or try blogs and other online knitting communities (see pages 238–239) for advice.

Substituting yarn

For those occasions when you want to completely change the yarn used in the pattern (for example, using a man-made fibre instead of cashmere, if you are working to a budget) the basic principles are the same, but there are some additional considerations to bear in mind. Most of these things are simply common sense, but you may find it useful to consider the following when choosing your yarn:

Yarn composition and structure

Yarns vary in many ways. Silk, for example, has virtually no stretch but its weight gives it lovely drape. Wool is generally springier, lighter and less dense but isn't particularly 'drapey'. Man-made yarns are often less expensive than their natural counterparts, and may be easier to look after; however, they may not be as breathable or feel as luxurious as natural yarn. Try to handle and sample as many yarns as you can and you will soon be able to select alternative yarns with confidence, and even to exploit different yarn characteristics to create exciting new effects.

This cotton swatch has been knitted on 4mm (size 6) needles, the recommended size for this thickness of yarn. However, it has more drape and is softer than an equivalent wool yarn knitted on the same needles. This is because the cotton has no elasticity and so has a flowing handle rather than a springy, bouncy feel like wool.

Will this yarn be suitable for your purpose?

Once you have found a yarn that knits to the right tension, consider whether your tension square has the right drape and feel for its intended use. Is the fabric hard or soft? Are there big holes between stitches or are the stitches densely packed together? How easy was it to make your tension square?

Each yarn generally works best on a small range of needles (see the yarn weight chart on page 21); if your needles are too small the fabric will be hard and unforgiving, too large and it will be loose and holey. Of course, you can use this deliberately: a summer shrug worked in fine yarn on large needles will create an ideal open fabric, whereas a backpack may need smaller needles than usual to make the fabric stronger and more durable.

Handle your tension square as you would handle the finished item. If you are making a rug, stomp on it and wash it in the machine to be sure it will be durable; for a lacy stole, check for softness and drape.

Mohair yarn worked in stocking stitch (30 stitches x 70 rows) has been knitted on the recommended needles (4mm/size 6), producing a neat and even fabric.

The same mohair yarn knitted on larger needles (6mm/size 10) to create a more open, looser stitch (20 stitches x 35 rows).

Yarn texture, stitch patterns and style

The pattern you will be using to create your design will add another dimension to the overall look and feel of your finished item. A very fluffy mohair yarn on a complex Aran pattern, for example, may not do justice to either the yarn or the pattern. A smooth yarn will show off cables and similar stitches much more effectively.

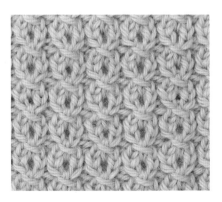 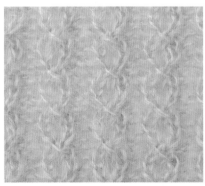

This eyelet cable has been knitted in sportweight yarn using 3.75mm (size 5) needles. The eyelet holes are clearly visible and the overall look is chunky.

The same eyelet cable worked in fine mohair using 5mm (size 8) needles is delicate and pretty, but the patterning is much softer and less distinctive.

Experimenting

A great way to experiment with different yarns is to incorporate a small amount of a fancy yarn into an otherwise simple pattern. The same principles apply as for completely changing a yarn, but there is the added fun of deliberately playing with the different characteristics of the yarns to achieve interesting effects. For example, knitting stripes of a springy yarn with a non-stretchy one produces a lovely rippled effect; using two inelastic yarns with different characteristics can create lovely tones and textures; and motifs may be worked in a fancy yarn – for example, a furry or boucle yarn for a teddy bear design.

To see how your yarns will work together, begin by checking that the two yarns knit to the same tension. Next, knit a sample square combining the two yarns in similar proportions to your intended design. If you like the effect, use the information given on page 23 to estimate how much yarn you will need (bearing in mind that one yarn may go further than the other) and have fun!

This simple hat design is brought to life by using three types of fibre with similar tension but different properties: lustrous silk for sheen, cotton chenille for texture, and pure wool for warmth and body. Note how the different fibres cause a rippling effect in the fabric.

TIPS

- **When combining yarns,** don't make your sample square too small; you need to get an idea of the effect over a wide area.

- **Yarns with little elasticity** may not be suitable for larger garments, such as coats and jumpers, because the lack of 'bounce' means that they often sag or droop over time. To check, knit a large swatch and hang it from a line for a time to see the effect of gravity on the swatch.

- **If you are using an inelastic yarn on a cuff or neckline,** try using a size larger needles and knit a shirring elastic with the yarn to give it stretch.

- **To add interest and 'lift,'** try combining a high-lustre yarn with a matt yarn.

- **Yarn too thin for your pattern?** Two strands of a 4-ply yarn, for example, can often be combined to produce a DK-equivalent. Just remember to allow for this when calculating yarn quantities.

- **To find out more about discontinued yarns,** ask your local yarn shop, which may have details. If you know the manufacturer's details, they should have records. There are also a number of websites that provide information on a wide range of yarns.

Care

Last but not least, take a few minutes to think about how you will look after your finished item. Always wash tension squares, particularly where two or more yarns are used because they may wash differently or colours may run. A busy new mum may not have time to hand wash baby knits, so a machine-washable yarn may be needed. A glitzy party wrap may need gentle hand washing but, because it won't be worn as often, this may not be as important. See pages 108–109 for more information.

Recycling and repurposing

Reusing yarn from a partly finished project is simple, and recycling yarn from finished projects, providing the garment hasn't felted or matted, is a great way to pick up some lovely yarn at a reasonable price (or even for free!).

Partly finished projects, or UFOs (unfinished objects!), are found at the back of a knitter's closet or at the bottom of a knitting bag more often than we care to admit. Rather than leave perfectly good yarn languishing unused, it's a straightforward matter to unpick it, recycle the yarn and put it to a new use. If you can't use it, consider a swap with a friend, or donating to a good cause. And recycling yarn needn't stop there. If you find a hand-knitted item in good condition in a charity shop, often the yarn can be reused. Knits with a small amount of damage can also be saved if there is enough yarn left once the damaged section has been removed. So, if you see that perfect shade of cranberry in an old jumper, it may be a great opportunity for repurposing.

Finished knits

Garments that have been commercially knitted are not easy to unpick for reuse. The yarns used are often very fine and the machine seaming is difficult to unpick, so it is best to avoid commercially knitted garments and choose hand knits.

Condition of the yarn

Is the yarn generally in good condition? If it is felted or matted, unpicking and reusing is likely to compound any existing yarn damage. Small areas of damage, such as a stain, can be dealt with providing there will be enough yarn left after removing the damaged yarn. A wool garment that hasn't been well stored may well have moth damage. This yarn is probably best consigned to the bin.

TAKING A HAND KNIT APART
Begin by unpicking any seams so that you have a series of flat pieces. Work in the following order: Start with the neckline or collar, followed by the shoulder seams, then the sleeves so that they are separate from the body of the garment. Move onto the side and sleeve seams, finishing with any edgings, pockets or button bands.

Start here

Shoulder seams are next

And, finally, the sleeves

IDENTIFYING THE CAST-OFF EDGE AND UNRAVELLING

When unravelling a knitted fabric, it is easiest to start with the cast-off edge since this edge will unravel in a steady, uninterrupted series of stitches. If you find that it is necessary to unravel stitches individually, almost to the extent that you are unknotting the yarn, try working from the opposite end of the fabric.

1

Identify the cast-off edges by looking for the distinctive chain of stitches running along the edge. Usually, these will be at the tops of the shoulders, on the sleeves and on the back and front neck. Be aware, however, that the garment, or parts of the garment, may have been knitted from the top down, in which case you will need to unpick from the bottom edge.

2

Unless you can see where the end of the yarn has been sewn in, snip one thread of the cast-off chain, close to one end, and begin unwinding the individual pieces.

3

As you unravel the yarn, wind it into a ball. Once you have unravelled each piece, you should have a series of balls of yarn of varying sizes. The next stage is to wind the loose balls into skeins (see page 28).

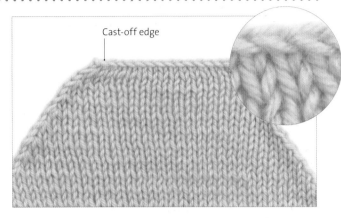

Cast-off edge

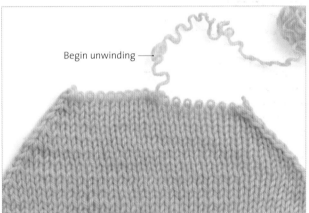

Begin unwinding

Gather the yarn

TIPS

- **Use sharp scissors with a fine point** to avoid cutting into the main part of the knitting.

- **On finer yarns,** a sewing seam ripper can be used, with care.

- **Keep any short pieces of yarn,** since these may come in handy for sewing up your new project.

Yarn pre- and post-straightening

STRAIGHTENING RECYCLED YARN: SKEINING AND SOAKING

Recycled yarn balls need to be wound into skeins for washing and straightening out any kinks. Use a niddy-noddy, chair back, large book or a pair of hands to wind the yarn around. Remember not to wind too tightly or you won't be able to remove the yarn. Soak the skeins in warm water with a small amount of wool wash. As soon as the skeins are wet, remove them, rinse in lukewarm water, squeeze out any excess water by rolling in a clean towel and hang to dry. If the yarn is still crinkly, hang a light weight from the skein, heavy enough to pull out the kinks but not so heavy that it stretches the yarn (see Weighting Skeins, below).

1 Around a chair back
Wrap the yarn around the back of a chair to form the skein, making each skein about 100g (4oz). Tie the ends together when finished.

2
Tie each skein in three or four places with small pieces of spare yarn. Fasten off the ends of the yarn by tying the start of the yarn to the end or by tying around the skein.

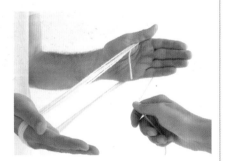

Around a friend's hands
Try winding a yarn around a friend's outstretched hands. Tie the loose ends together and then tie the loose ties as shown in step 2 above.

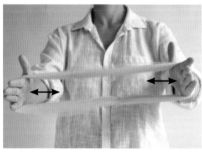

Between both hands
Hold the yarn between both hands. Move your hands quickly together and then out again to bang out all the knots and tangles. Gradually, a smooth skein of yarn will be formed.

FIGURING HOW MUCH RECYCLED YARN YOU HAVE

Once your recycled yarn has been straightened, it's time to begin planning a new project. If you have a ball band, you can look for a suitable pattern for your recycled yarn. If not, before you wind your skein into a ball, measure one wrap around your niddy-noddy or book and count the number of times the yarn is wrapped around.

Working out yardage (or metreage)

1 Multiply the number of wraps by the length of each wrap to give the total metreage (yardage) in your skein.

2 Work out the metreage (yardage) in 100g (4oz) of yarn by dividing the total metreage (yardage) by the length of each wrap and multiplying by 100 (4).

3 Match this information to the stated yarn in the pattern and you should be able to use your yarn for the pattern.

Example:

- One wrap = 1.5m (1.64yd)
- Number of wraps = 250
- Weight of skein = 85g (3oz)
- Total metreage 1.5m x 250 wraps = 375m (Total yardage = 1.64 x 250 = 410yd)
- Meterage per 100g = 375m/85g x 100g = 440m (Yardage per 4oz = 410yd/3oz x 4oz = 547yd)

This equates approximately to a sock/ 4-ply yarn.

WEIGHTING SKEINS

Empty shower gel containers with hooks are very handy for weighting skeins. Fill with a little water at a time and hang on the bottom of the skein until it is weighted just enough to even out the kinks.

Making your own yarn

There are lots of creative ways to make your own yarn from items found around the house. Old sheets or curtains can be cut into strips to make great knitted rugs and bags. Dye them first in the washing machine using an appropriate all-purpose dye to brighten up the colour.

Old wool blankets also make great yarn for bags and rugs. Stitch any short strips together to make a longer ball and knit using extra-large needles.

Instead of throwing away old carrier bags, cut these into strips to make strong, colourful bags. Avoid using biodegradable bags or your knitting may disintegrate over time! Thinner strips of plastic bags can be knitted into body-scrubbing mitts or pan-scouring cloths.

Video and audio tape can be knitted into ornamental flowers or other three-dimensional objects, such as pots and vases.

Eco knitting with plastic bags
Cut lightweight plastic bags into strips of fairly equal width (a spiral cut makes a continuous strip).

Thinking outside the box
Nothing is exempt from the avid repurposer: old T-shirts (above) and newspapers (below) can enjoy a new lease of life as yarn.

Repurposing fabrics
Tear lightweight cotton fabrics into strips about 2cm (³/₄in) wide. Join the strips with simple knots, or overlap the ends and sew them together. Use 8mm (size 10) needles or larger.

getting
started

Mastering just a handful of key techniques will get you knitting in no time. Find them all here, clearly explained and supplemented with online films for some extra guidance.

How to read knitting patterns

Knitting patterns may look complicated and intimidating, but once you get to grips with the basic structure, following a pattern is no more difficult than cooking with a recipe.

Always read the pattern through before beginning a project and, as a general rule, knit the pieces in the order presented in the pattern, since there may be a specific reason for doing so.

Sizing (1)

A pattern will normally begin with sizing and will usually provide two distinct measurements: one is 'actual size', the other the 'to fit' measurement.

Actual size refers to the physical dimensions of the garment when it is knitted and will include extra centimetres (inches) to allow for 'ease'. The amount of ease will vary depending on the garment's intended fit. A skinny jumper, for example, will have less ease than a long jacket.

Because it can be difficult to know how much ease is built into a garment, pattern writers will also provide a 'to fit' measurement. This refers to the body measurements of the wearer. Several measurements may be given, for example, sleeve length and length of neck to shoulder but, because these measurements can be adjusted during knitting, it is best to select your size based on the 'to fit' chest measurement.

Schematic

A schematic is an outline drawing showing where key measurements should be taken. This is particularly useful for garments such as hats, or garments with unusual features such as dropped waistlines, where it is important to measure at the right place to achieve the desired finished size.

Materials and equipment (2)

Here you will find essential information about the yarn used to knit the pattern, plus details of any additional items you may need, such as zips and buttons. The needles used for the project will also be listed, but bear in mind that you may need to change these depending on your tension.

For best results it is advisable to use the yarn stated in the pattern. If you intend to substitute for an alternative yarn see pages 20–25. When buying yarn, make sure you buy enough to complete the garment. Yarn is dyed in batches and there can be differences between batches (also called dye lots), so it is important to check that all the balls come from the same dye lot number, which is on the ball band.

Tension (3)

Tension, also referred to as gauge, is a crucial part of any pattern. Correct tension is the key to making a garment that fits as the designer intended. See page 22 for instructions on checking your tension.

Abbreviations (4)

To make sure that patterns are a manageable size for printing, pattern writers use certain conventions and abbreviations. Many of these will take a similar format, but each pattern will have a section that covers any abbreviations used and will detail any special instructions that may be unique to that design. It is worthwhile reading through the pattern and any abbreviations or special notes before starting, even if you are a seasoned knitter. This is particularly important when using patterns that have been translated because terminology can differ between countries.

Assembly

Also referred to as making up, this part of the pattern explains how to prepare your pieces for sewing up – for example, whether to block the pieces, pin them, etc. – and how to sew the various parts together. It is advisable to follow the order given. This is because some patterns will ask you to sew up certain seams (for example, one shoulder seam), then do something else such as add a neckband, before going on to sew up other seams. Depending on the pattern, you may be advised to use a certain stitch or technique. If not, refer to pages 87–97 for suggestions.

wide-neck lace sweater

This lavish lace sweater with an elegant scoop neck is worked in a combination of *finest silk and mohair* yarn in beautifully blended colors for a truly indulgent experience.

MATERIALS
Rowan Kidsilk Haze. Shades 595 Liqueur and 606 Candy Girl. 9 (9, 9, 10, 10) x 25g balls (229 yds, 210m per ball) in each color. Use two strands of yarn (one of each color) throughout.

1 pair size 3 (3.25mm) and 1 pair size 6 (4mm) needles.

GAUGE
2 patt repeats (20 sts) = 3½" (9cm) wide using 2 strands of yarn on size 6 (4mm) needles, or needles required to obtain this gauge.

PATTERN
BACK
Cast on 104 (112, 124, 132, 144) sts using smaller needles and 2 strands of yarn.
Work 6 rows in k2, p2 rib.
SMALL, LARGE, AND XX LARGE SIZES Dec 1 st at beg of last row – 103 (123, 143) sts.
MEDIUM AND EXTRA LARGE SIZES Inc 1 st at beg of last row – 113 (133) sts.

Change to larger needles and lace patt as follows.
Row 1 (RS) * K3, p1, yo, s1, k1, psso, k1, k2tog, yo, p1, repeat from * to last 3 sts, k3.
Row 2 * P3, k1, p5, k1, repeat from * to last 3 sts, p3.

Row 3 * K3, p1, k1, yo, s1, k2tog, psso, yo, k1, p1, repeat from * to last 3 sts, k3.
Row 4 * P3, k1, p5, k1, repeat from * to last 3 sts, p3.
These 4 rows form lace patt repeat. Cont in patt until work measures 13¾" (35cm).

Shape armhole
Bind off 3 (4, 5, 6, 7) sts at beg of next 2 rows.
Dec 1 st at each end of next and every other row until 91 (97, 103, 107, 111) sts remain. Cont without shaping until work measures 20½ (21, 21¼, 21½, 22)" (52 (53, 54, 55, 56)cm).

Shape neck
Row 1 Patt 29 (31, 33, 34, 35), bind off 33 (35, 37, 39, 41) sts, patt 29 (31, 33, 34, 35).
Work on these 29 (31, 33, 34, 35) sts for first side of neck.
Row 2 Patt.
Row 3 Bind off 5 sts, patt to end.
Rows 4–9 Repeat rows 2 and 3 three times – 9 (11, 13, 14, 15) sts.
Row 10 Patt.
Row 11 Bind off.

Second side of neck
Rejoin yarn to rem sts at neck edge and work rows 3 to 11 as given for first side of neck.

SIZES

	SMALL	MEDIUM	LARGE	XL	XXL
To fit bust	32–33"	34–36"	37–40"	41–42"	43–46"
	(81–84cm)	(86–91.5cm)	(94–102cm)	(104–107cm)	(109–117cm)
Actual size	35" (89cm)	38.6" (98cm)	42" (107cm)	45.6" (116cm)	49" (124cm)
Back length	21.6" (55cm)	22" (56cm)	22.6" (57cm)	22.6" (58cm)	23.6" (60cm)
Sleeve seam	19.4" (49cm)	19.4" (49cm)	19.4" (49cm)	19.4" (49cm)	19.4" (49cm)

GARMENT SIZING See page 124
ABBREVIATIONS See page 126

UNDERSTANDING PATTERN CONVENTIONS

Parentheses: sizing (5)
Parentheses can be used to indicate points in a pattern where you are required to do different things depending on the size of the garment. For example, 'cast on 100 (120, 140, 180)' means that if you are making the first size you cast on 100 stitches, the second size cast on 120, the third 140 and so on. It's helpful to photocopy the pattern and mark the relevant numbers/instructions for your size. If the instructions only give one number, this number is used for all sizes.

Parentheses: repeats
Parentheses may also be used to indicate sections where the instructions are to be repeated a number of times. For example, 'k1,(p1, k3) 3 times' means k1, p1, k3, p1, k3, p1, k3.

Asterisks (6)
Asterisks are used in a similar way to parentheses to indicate sections of a pattern that are to be repeated. These can be repeats within a row, a repeat of several rows, or even a repeat of a large section of a garment. For example, 'k1,*p1, k3, rep from * to last st, k1' means k1, p1, k3, then repeat just the p1, k3 as many times as required until

you reach the last stitch of the row. The last stitch is then knitted. This can also be described as 'k1, *p1, k3*, rep from * to * to last st, k1' and means that you should repeat the section between the two asterisks.

Where a pattern has two parts that are similar, for example, a jumper back and front, the pattern may say 'FRONT: Work as far back until **'. The front is knitted in the same way as the back until the double asterisk shown on the back section is reached.

Watch for multiple asterisks and make sure you work to the

correct number of asterisks. If you see what appears to be a stray asterisk, it will become relevant later in the pattern.

Asterisks and parentheses may be used in the same line of a pattern. So, '*k1, (p1, k3) 3 times, rep from * to end' means k1, p1, k3, p1, k3, p1, k3, then repeat k1, p1, k3, p1, k3, p1, k3 until the end of the row. Different shaped parentheses, for example [ ] or ( ), may also be used in combination. Treat matching parentheses as a pair, working the stitches within the matching pair as with asterisk/parentheses combinations.

Following charts

Charts are a way of depicting pattern information in a graphic form. They are mainly used to depict the more complex parts of a design, for example, a Fair Isle or lace design. Many knitters and designers find them helpful because it is possible to see the pattern structure at a glance.

Charts may be written using symbols or by using different colours to represent different stitches or colours. Symbols are more commonly used for lace, cables and other stitch patterns, whereas coloured charts are generally restricted to Fair Isle and other colourwork designs.

Charts are read from the bottom to the top following the direction of the knitting. Each square represents a stitch and each horizontal line of squares a row of knitting.

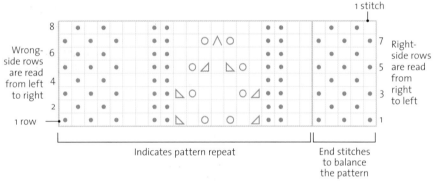

Wrong-side rows are read from left to right

Right-side rows are read from right to left

1 stitch

1 row

Indicates pattern repeat

End stitches to balance the pattern

Symbol-based chart

The symbols represent an instruction and have been designed to resemble the appearance of the knitting. Before you start knitting, familiarise yourself with the symbols and techniques of the chart you are going to work from, making a note of them for quick reference if desired.

Colour-based chart

Colour charts are read in the same way as symbol-based charts, with each square representing a stitch of knitting. As most colourwork uses stocking stitch, stitch symbols are replaced with coloured squares, each colour representing a different yarn colour.

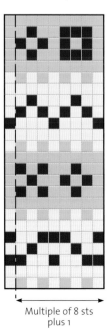

Multiple of 8 sts plus 1

Key

Each chart is accompanied by a key; always read the key before you begin because there is no standard set of symbols and designers and publishers follow different conventions when producing charted patterns. Take particular care to note any symbols that have a double use. For example, a blank white square will often be used to depict a knit stitch on a RS row and a purl stitch on a WS row. In other words, this would produce a series of stocking stitches. Purl stitches worked on a RS row may then have a separate symbol (often O), so don't worry if you see what are apparently two instructions for a single stitch type. A key might look something like this:

□	k on RS, p on WS
⊡	p on RS, k on WS
⃥	k tbl on RS, p tbl on WS
⊿	k2tog
◺	skpo
⊿	p2tog
⋀	s2kpo
↗	k3tog
⬉	sk2po
⋔	m1
⋔	m1p
⋔	m1L
⋔	m1R
O	yarn over needle

Anatomy of a chart: chart components and what they mean

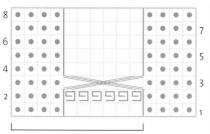

10-stitch repeat

Multiple of 4 sts

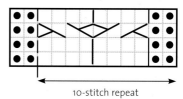

10-stitch repeat

Squares and spans

Each square of a chart represents one stitch of knitting. Combinations of stitches, such as cables or decreases, may span over a number of squares. This means that these stitches are worked as a unit.

The chart above would read as follows:
Row 1 (RS) P4, *k6, p4, rep from * to end.
Row 2 K4, *p6 wrapping yarn twice around needle for each st, k4, rep from * to end.
Row 3 P4, *cr6, p4, rep from * to end.
Row 4 K4, *p6, k4, rep from * to end.
Row 5 As row 1.
Row 6 As row 4.
Row 7 As row 1.
Row 8 As row 4.
These 8 rows form the pattern.

No stitch

To make charts easier to produce, where a stitch is decreased – and so does not exist for the remainder of the section – a black or greyed-out square is often used to depict 'no stitch'.

In this example using blackberry stitch, the chart is read straight across, ignoring the greyed-out squares. So the equivalent written pattern would read:
Row 1 (RS) P.
Row 2 [(K1, p1, k1) in 1 st, p3tog] to end.
Row 3 P.
Row 4 [P3tog, (k1, p1, k1) in 1 st] to end.
These 4 rows form the pattern.

Pattern repeats

Where a pattern is repeated several times across a row the designer will normally chart the pattern section just once (the pattern repeat). Any odd stitches at the beginning or end of the row are shown at either side of the pattern repeat and the section to be repeated is bordered with a bold line or clearly demarcated in another way.

This chart, for example, would read:
Row 1 (RS)P2, [k8, p2] to end.
Row 2 K2, [p8, k2] to end.
Row 3 P2, [c4b, c4f, p2] to end.
Row 4 As row 2.
These 4 rows form the pattern.

MULTIPLE CHARTS
It is rare for a chart to show an entire garment due to the size of chart this would require. Therefore, where there are several areas of pattern in a piece, there will be several small charts. You will be instructed on which chart to follow at the appropriate part in the text.

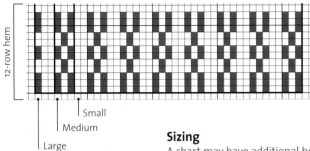

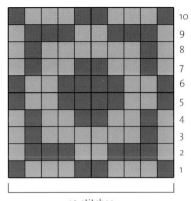

10 stitches

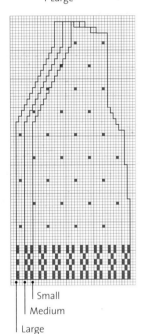

Sizing

A chart may have additional boxed-out or demarcated sections to depict the different instructions for different sizes. Follow the correct section for your size. Here, if you were making the small size of the left front (knitted flat as a separate piece) you would work the first three rows as follows:

Row 1 (RS) *P1, k1, p1, k2 rep from * to end.
Row 2 *p2, k1, p1, k1 rep from * to end.
Row 3 As row 1.

The medium size would read:
Row 1 (RS) *P1, k1, p1, k2 rep from * to last 3 sts, p1, k1, p1.
Row 2 K1, p1, k1, *p2, k1, p1, k1 rep from * to end.
Row 3 As row 1.

And the large size would read:
Row 1 (RS) *P1, k1, p1, k2 rep from * to last st, p1.
Row 2 K1, *p2, k1, p1, k1 rep from * to end.
Row 3 As row 1.

Colour charts

Usually used for colourwork, each coloured square represents a different colour yarn. Because the colours on the chart may not match the ones you are using, make notes on the chart representing your own colours.

Row numbering

To save printing space and to make patterns easier to visualise, designs where alternate rows are all identical may not be shown on the chart. This will be clear from the row numbering (usually printed vertically up the side of the chart) where only every other row will be numbered. Alternatively, the key may have instructions to treat every alternate row as, for example, a purl row.

Knitting direction – flat knitting vs circular knitting

Charts are used for both flat and circular knitting (see pages 40–41). The key difference in following these charts is in the direction of knitting and the order in which to read the chart.

Flat knitting

Rows are normally worked starting at the bottom right corner and read from right to left for the first row. The next row then starts at the left and is read from left to right.

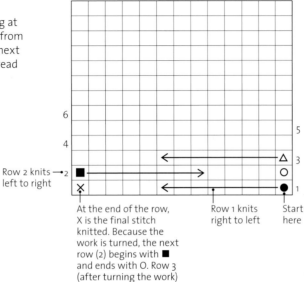

Row 2 knits left to right

At the end of the row, X is the final stitch knitted. Because the work is turned, the next row (2) begins with ■ and ends with O. Row 3 (after turning the work) begins with Δ.

Row 1 knits right to left

Start here

Circular knitting

With projects knitted in the round, all rows (rounds) are read in the same direction, usually starting at the bottom right corner and reading from right to left. This may seem confusing, but if you visualise your knitting as you hold it, a flat piece is knitted from the right-hand edge to the left, swapped back into the left hand and knitted from left edge to the right. By contrast, with a circular knit you are always knitting in the same direction, usually from right to left, and the work never swaps hands.

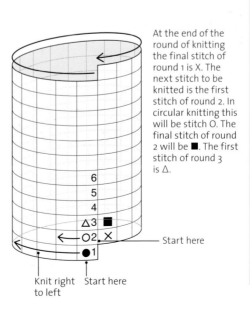

At the end of the round of knitting the final stitch of round 1 is X. The next stitch to be knitted is the first stitch of round 2. In circular knitting this will be stitch O. The final stitch of round 2 will be ■. The first stitch of round 3 is Δ.

Start here

Knit right to left   Start here

Tension

A knitter's best friend, but also, arguably, the part of a project that knitters like the least – tension. Mention tension swatches (or tension squares) to most knitters and wait for the groans! But, while they may seem like an annoyance that only serves to keep you away from your precious knitting project, they can save a lot of disappointment.

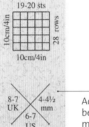

Yarn manufacturers will often give a guide to the appropriate tension for the yarn on the ball band. The number of rows and stitches to a given measurement, together with the needle size and the stitch used, will be given.

Additional information may be included, such as the manufacturer's recommended range of needle sizes for the yarn.

Tension is simply the size (length x width) of a knitting stitch knitted on a specific size of needle using a specified technique. Because stitches form the basis of a knitted fabric, it stands to reason that if your stitches are larger or smaller than the ones knitted by the designer (usually if you knit more loosely or tighter), you may not produce a piece of knitting the same size as the one the designer knitted. If you doubt that this is the case, ask three of your knitting friends to each make a square using the same needles, rows and stitches and compare the finished sizes. They will almost certainly be different.

But does this matter? Small differences over a small square may not seem significant, but if your stitches are just an eighth bigger than the designer's, for every 100 stitches the designer casts on, your work will measure the equivalent of 12 stitches larger. On a shawl with 400 stitches, that's the equivalent of an extra 50 stitches without your having cast on a single extra stitch. Equally, if your square is smaller than the designer's, your garment will be correspondingly smaller – and the greater the difference, the smaller the garment will be.

So, on balance, as much as a tension swatch seems like an obstacle designed to prevent you from getting stuck into your project, knitting one is a worthwhile exercise.

Non-matching tension

There are occasions when it is not possible to match both the number of rows and the number of stitches simultaneously. With one set of needles your rows are correct but you have too few stitches. However, when you go up a needle size, the stitch numbers are correct, but there are too few rows.

Because we all knit differently, it is quite common to find that you can't exactly match the tension stated in a given pattern. If, having tried a couple of needle sizes, you find that you can't match both stitches and rows, it is generally advisable to ensure that the number of stitches is correct, even if this means that the number of rows is different from the pattern. Where the number of rows is different from the stated tension, you may need to work either fewer or more rows to achieve the correct dimensions. If the pattern gives measurements – for example, 'knit until the work measures Xcm/ in' – the number of rows isn't usually important, although you may not end in the same place on the pattern repeat. Where the pattern requires a specific number of rows, calculate what the length will be based on the stated tension. Compare this to the length if you used your own tension and aim to work more/fewer rows to match the original length. If it is a close measurement over a small length this may not be necessary, but over a long length, adjustments will be needed. Aim to adjust length in areas where there is no shaping, if at all possible. If adjusting rows in an area where stitches will be picked up, you may need to adjust the number of stitches being picked up accordingly.

MEASURING TENSION

Knit your swatch exactly according to the pattern, bearing in mind that you may be asked to work in a pattern stitch or in a simple stockinette stitch. Knit the swatch 10 or so stitches larger and work an extra 10 rows more than the stated tension. This allows you to measure in the centre of the swatch, which is more accurate since edge stitches are rarely the same size as the main body of the garment and can distort your calculations.

1

Cast off, wash and block your swatch (see page 86). Ideally, leave it overnight to allow the stitches to settle. Measuring in the centre of the swatch, mark a line vertically, straight up one column of stitches, with a large-headed pin. Use a ruler to measure the stated width, usually 10cm (4in). Measure across the centre of the swatch to avoid distortions. Mark this measurement with a second pin. Count the stitches between the two pins. Include any half, quarter or partial stitches.

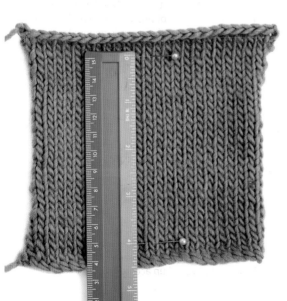

2

Starting several rows into the swatch and in the centre of the width, place a pin horizontally, straight along a row of stitches. Measure the stated length in a straight vertical line and mark this point with a second pin. Count the rows between the two pins including any partial rows. If your finished measurements match the pattern, you can start knitting with the needles you have been using. If the square is too small, repeat the process using needles a size larger. If the square is too large, try again with smaller needles.

TIPS

- **If you are working with textured yarns** it can be difficult to measure stitches and rows accurately. To remedy this, use a piece of smooth, contrasting thread and add it during knitting by inserting a lifeline (see page 229) after four or five rows. Lay a second piece of thread between the fourth and fifth stitches to mark out the edge and again after the number of stitches stated to be the correct tension in the pattern. Run these threads up the sides of the work like a running stitch by taking them to the back after two rows and bringing them forward after a further two rows, and so on. Once the stated number of rows has been knitted, add a further lifeline. Use these lines to measure your work.

- **Label swatches and keep them for future reference** in a folder or box. They may come in handy if you knit the project or use the same yarn again.

- **Swatches can be made into projects** such as coasters, mats, or small purses. They can also be sewn together to create a blanket – a wonderful history of your knitting projects!

- **If a pattern is to be knitted in the round,** make sure you knit your tension swatch in the round, since tension is often different when comparing circular to flat knitting.

- **Use the same needles as you did for your correct swatch** and remember to adjust any smaller or larger needles for ribs or bands correspondingly.

Flat and circular knitting

Historically, many garments were knitted 'in the round' on sets of four or five needles – mainly for speed, since the method results in fewer seams, and knitters were paid piecework for their labours. In the mid-nineteenth century it began to be replaced by 'flat knitting'. It is likely that this change was influenced by a desire to make knitted fabric that could be more easily shaped and seamed to replicate tailored garments.

CHECKING YOUR TENSION
If a pattern is to be knitted in the round, make sure you knit your tension swatch in the round, because tension is often different when comparing circular to flat knitting.

The tube effect
As the vest above shows, knitting in the round avoids the need for side seams, making a neater finish, especially when using a continuous pattern like stripes.

Knitting that is worked in a tube rather than in a flat panel is known as knitting in the round, or circular knitting. Certain countries and cultures have retained circular knitting, but for a time it fell out of favour in countries such as the UK. The reason for this is not known – and there are early examples of flat knitting from Egypt and elsewhere – one assumes that certain knitted items, such as shawls and wraps, rugs and carpets, blankets and so on, would always have been knitted flat.

Fashion doubtless played its part in the change, since certain styles are more achievable on flat fabrics. The knitted equivalent of a sewn dart is created in a knitted fabric by the use of short rows. This technique is not easily adapted to knitting in the round if darts are to be placed at waist or bust lines, because the work needs to be turned at regular intervals.

Garments knitted in the round would often be cut or steeked (see pages 136–141) at necklines and armholes. However, raglan and similarly shaped sleeves are not well suited to this technique, so even a garment knitted predominantly in the round will have these sections knitted flat. V-necks and other neckline shapes may also be very wasteful of yarn if steeked, so this part of a jumper would generally be worked flat.

Certain knitting techniques lend themselves more readily to flat knitting. Intarsia and knitted motifs, for example, can be knitted in the round but are much easier to work on flat pieces. Similarly, any pattern that is not readily suited to stranding or weaving in

CIRCULAR KNITTED SHAPES

Circular knitting can be adapted to make seamless tubes of all sizes, or shaped to make cones, rounded domes or flat circles.

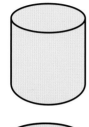

Straight tubes
Straight tubes may be made to any size using circular needles for large sizes and sets of DPNs for smaller sizes.

Tapered tubes
Tapered tubes may be increased (or decreased) at one side (e.g. for a sleeve), or evenly all around at intervals.

Shallow cones
A shallow cone (e.g. for a jumper yoke) is usually worked with evenly spaced shaping.

Domes
A dome (e.g. for a hat) is also shaped, decreasing more sharply towards the centre top.

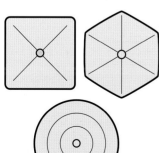

Flat medallions
Flat medallions may be worked from the centre outwards in various geometric shapes.

(see pages 192–196) is likely to be both wasteful of yarn and unnecessarily heavy.

To recreate a knitted piece based on a sewn garment, it is possible to use a paper pattern and knit flat pieces to the shape of each pattern piece. While this requires skill in knit design, it is far more easily achieved than designing a similar project to be knitted in the round.

Another factor in the change from knitting in the round to knitting flat may be comfort. Traditionally, knitters earning a living from their work would knit on the move, standing up; with their knitting needles stuck in a knitting belt or sheath so that they could free up their hands easily for other activities. When knitting became more of a sitting-room pastime, perhaps long needles and knitting sheaths were impractical and it was more comfortable and ladylike to knit smaller pieces rather than have the bulk and weight of an entire jumper in one's lap.

Knitting in the round

As already mentioned, circular knitting is a useful technique for avoiding seams and creating fabrics that require minimal assembly. Popular items for circular knitting include socks, mittens, gloves and hats; however, larger garments such as jumpers, jackets and tops may also be knitted this way. Many traditional garments, such as ganseys and Fair Isle jumpers, were knitted in the round because, with practice, it is quicker, and in Fair Isle knitting in particular, floats (the yarn not in use being carried between colour changes) can be dealt with more neatly using seam-free knitting.

Until the early 1920s, knitting in the round was done on a set of either four or five double-pointed needles. In the 1920s a Norwegian company applied for a patent for the Flexiknit, believed to be the first circular needle in commercial production. This circular needle comprised two short metal needles joined by a metal wire cord. Improvements in materials, smoother joins and more flexible cords have meant that knitting in the round has been embraced by a new generation of enthusiastic knitters, as well as by those who grew up using regular needles. See pages 162–169 for step-by-step guides to knitting in the round.

Holding the work

Ultimately, how you hold your yarn and needles is about what you find to be the most comfortable, so use this section as a guide, but don't feel compelled to follow the instructions to the letter.

KEY FOR THIS SECTION

RH Right hand

LH Left hand

TIPS

- **It is useful to practise several techniques,** since this will enable you to vary your position, giving muscles and arms a rest.

- **When knitting colourwork,** the ability to use both the left and right hands to hold the yarn is invaluable, because one hand can hold each colour without the irritation of untangling yarns every row.

There are probably as many ways to hold yarn and needles as there are knitters, and there is no 'wrong' way if it allows you to make a neat knitted fabric comfortably and enjoyably.

Broadly speaking, ways to hold the needles fall into three categories: the knife and fork, curled and the pen. Needles may be held at waist level, tucked under the arm, or – less commonly today – tucked into a knitting sheath or belt. Yarn may be held in the right or the left hand (or even both for some techniques, see pages 197–199). Yarn may be manipulated by using the left-hand needle, the right-hand needle, or both. How you hold your needles will also depend on whether you are working flat or in the round.

The way these styles evolved owes as much to fashion as it does to practicality. Early knitting was a practical business. Garments were needed for wearing or to raise a valuable income, so speed and efficiency were of the essence. For early knitters, who would knit standing up and on the move, long needles and the knitting belt or sheath were developed. Supporting the work and the needles, this left one hand free to manipulate the yarn (or stir a pot or rock a crib) with minimal interruption. Needles were held like a knife and fork with the needle under the hands, or fingers were curled around the needle.

When knitting evolved into a pastime for genteel ladies, style became more important. To distinguish themselves from working knitters and to appear more elegant, lady knitters would hold the needles like a pen.

Knife and fork style
This knitting style lends itself to both flat and circular knitting. It is quick and efficient, the fabric isn't bunched up, and the thumb doesn't poke into it and distort the work. If the needle is tucked under the right arm, only the left needle has to move and the LH needle can be used to push the loop of the stitch onto the RH needle rather than inserting the RH tip into the loop on the LH needle. The LH can push the RH needle through the loop.

Curled
Similar to the knife and fork but the hands are more curled around and below the needles. This can give more support to the needles and may be more comfortable on the wrists. Suitable for both flat and circular knitting.

Tucking the needle frees up the right hand.

Pen style
The needles sit between the thumb and index finger, the RH needle resting on top of the hand. This method can be used for both flat and circular knitting. Arguably, this style is slower and less comfortable than the other two because the work can bunch up between the crook of the thumb/index finger and the tip of the needle. Moving the thumb below the work can distort and damage the knitting.

To tuck or not to tuck?
The RH needle can be tucked under the right arm or into a knitting belt/sheath. This is a speedy method because the right hand has more freedom to move quickly. However, tucking is not suitable for knitting on circular needles or short double-pointed needles. For this reason, knitters who normally tuck but want to knit in the round may need to adapt their needle and yarn holding style to accommodate knitting on short, unsupported needles.

Holding the yarn – right hand
This method is common throughout the UK, parts of Europe and the USA. It's suitable for all needle positions and knitting styles. The yarn may be wrapped in a variety of ways to achieve an even tension.

Holding the yarn – left hand
Believed to have originated in Germany and often referred to as continental knitting, this style is also used in certain other parts of Europe. Holding the yarn in the left hand is also used in the USA and was latterly popularised by Elizabeth Zimmerman among others. Suitable for all knitting styles and needle positions, although arguably easier with the curled and knife and fork styles.

Casting on

Casting on marks the beginning of the knitting process and provides the basis for the initial stitches from which your knitted fabric will be formed. Choosing the right method for casting on will give your knits a professional look and ensure that they stand up to wear and tear without losing their shape.

There are many different methods of casting on; however, they can be broadly categorised into two types, collectively referred to as single-needle and two-needle methods. Many knitters will only ever use one, or possibly two, different methods of casting on for all of their knitting, and you can knit virtually any project using just one of the two basic methods.

When you are working from a commercial pattern you may find that the pattern designer has recommended a cast-on technique. If the pattern does not specify a technique, one of the two basic methods should be fine; however, if no specific guidance is offered, or if you are designing your own patterns, it is worth taking a few moments to think about your project and what type of edge you will need.

Depending on the project, you may begin by casting on as few as two stitches or, in the case of something like a fine shawl, anything up to several hundred stitches. For some projects you will need an edge that has good elasticity and will withstand lots of stretching. Sock cuffs are a good example of this. A fine shawl, on the other hand, may require a cast-on edge that is barely visible in order to preserve the drape and delicate look of the piece. In other cases, you may cast on using a temporary or provisional method. This allows cast-on stitches to be undone to expose the first row of live stitches on the needle. This method is often used when an edging is to be added at a later stage, or when two pieces of knitting are to be joined together. Where this type of edging is needed a cast-on method will normally be specified in the pattern. For more information on choosing the right cast on, turn to pages 116–121.

MAKING A SLIPKNOT
The slipknot forms the first stitch and is used to begin most cast-on methods.

COUNTING CORRECTLY
Your cast-on row is not normally included when counting the number of rows worked.

CLIP 1
Long-tail cast on

www.youtube.com/watch?v=syFlfyR0Jpg

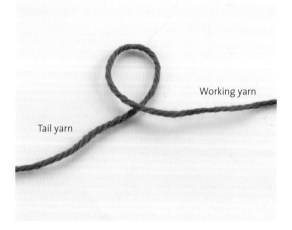

Working yarn

Tail yarn

1
Make a circle of yarn by folding the working yarn over the tail yarn. The circle should be 1–2cm ($^3/_8$–$^3/_4$in) in diameter.

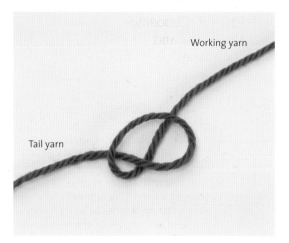

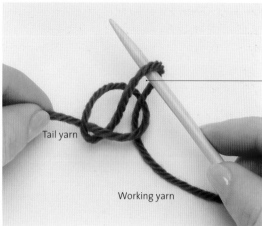

Keep your loop fairly small to prevent pulling the tail yarn through.

2
Take the working yarn (on the right-hand side) under the loop as shown.

3
Holding the circle firmly in either your LH or RH, use your knitting needle to dip into the circle and pull the working yarn through the circle and back towards you. Take care not to pull the tail completely through the circle.

The loop sits securely on the needle, but can still be moved.

4
Gently draw the loop away from the two yarn ends until a knot begins to form. At this stage, don't tighten the knot.

5
Draw one end of the yarn tight to secure the knot, and then draw up the other end of the yarn so that the loop is snug on the needle, but not so tight it can't slide along it.

CLIP 2
Two-needle cast on

www.youtube.com/watch?v=teKXfMNCP5w

THE LONG-TAIL, OR THUMB, CAST ON
This is a popular casting-on method with many variations; versatile and straightforward, it gives a reasonably elastic edge.

GENEROUS TAIL LENGTH
The tail yarn needs to be long enough to allow you to make all of your cast-on stitches. Don't worry about there being too much yarn left over – you can use any spare tail yarn for sewing up.

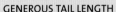

1
Measure your yarn so that you have a yarn tail three times as long as the edge you are casting on. Make a slipknot in the yarn at this point, place it on your needle and draw it up so that it is snug but not too tight. Hold the needle with the slipknot and the tail in your RH and the working yarn in your LH.

2
Holding the working yarn taut with your LH fingers, hook your left thumb under the working yarn from back to front. While tensioning the yarn, insert the tip of the needle into the front of the loop on your thumb.

For a neat cast-on edge, maintain an even tension between your tail and working yarns. Don't pull your stitches too tight because you won't be able to work into them later.

3
Using your RH, bring the tail yarn up under the needle from right to left, taking it between the thumb and the needle, over the top of the needle and holding it to the right.

4
Lift the loop on your thumb over the tip of the needle, remove your thumb and draw up the working yarn. You now have two stitches on your RH needle (the slipknot counts as one stitch). Repeat steps 2–4 until you have made the number of stitches specified in your pattern.

KNITTED, OR TWO-NEEDLE, CAST ON

This is another all-round popular method of casting on. It is not very elastic but it gives a nice, firm edge.

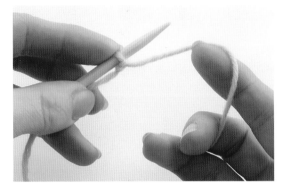

Hold the working yarn evenly tensioned around your RH fingers.

1
Make a slipknot – leaving a tail around 15cm (6in) long – and place it snugly on the LH needle. Hold the tail yarn around the fingers of your LH with an even tension. The tail isn't used to make the stitches but can be used for sewing up later.

2
Insert the tip of the RH needle from front to back into the slipknot. Wrap the working yarn around the RH needle by bringing it up under the needle from right to left, taking it between the two needles, over the top of the RH needle, and holding it to the right.

Draw the stitch up so that it is snug but not too tight.

3
Maintaining an even tension on the working yarn, use the RH needle to catch the working yarn (see detail) and draw it through the loop between the needles. Opening out your hands and elbows, as though opening a pair of shears, will help you to see the working yarn and will make drawing the loop through easier.

4
Insert the tip of the LH needle into the loop on the RH needle from front to back. Slide the loop onto the LH needle and draw the stitch up. Two stitches cast on (the slipknot counts as stitch one). Repeat steps 2–4 until you have made the number of stitches required.

Alternative cast ons

Here are some further cast-on methods, which are not as commonly used as the preceding ones, but that still have their use.

BACKWARD LOOP, OR TWISTED, CAST ON (SINGLE NEEDLE)
Suitable for soft edgings and lacy pieces, where a light, understated edge is needed. This technique also forms the basis of some other methods, for example, tubular cast on (see opposite). The first row of this cast on is quite loose and can be a little difficult to work so check the number of stitches after the first row to ensure that none have been dropped.

Insert the needle front to back.

1
Make a slipknot and place it on the RH needle. Holding the needle in your RH and the working yarn in your LH bring your left thumb (or index finger if preferred), behind, under the yarn and forward, looping it over the thumb.

2
Where the yarn loops over the thumb, insert the RH needle from front to back under the front of the loop and over the top of the back of the loop.

3
Carefully remove your thumb and draw the loop tight. Repeat steps 1–2 (except for the slipknot) until the desired number of stitches is made.

Because the cast-on stitches are just looped around the needle and not knitted, this loose cast on gives a soft edge, ideal for lacy scarves.

Tubular cast on gives a neat, professional and almost invisible finish.

TUBULAR CAST ON (SINGLE NEEDLE)

This method, also known as an invisible cast on, uses a piece of contrasting waste yarn and a single needle. It is a provisional type of cast on because it requires spare yarn that is later removed. It provides a great edging for ribs, although it is not as robust as the alternate cable cast on (see page 55). You may need to work it on a needle a couple of sizes smaller than is used for the main pattern.

Making the change to the main yarn colour.

1
Using a piece of smooth, contrasting-colour yarn, cast on half the number of stitches needed for the main piece using the backward loop method (see opposite). (For an odd number of finished stitches, halve the number and round up; for example, for 31 stitches cast on 16 loops).

2
Change to the main yarn colour and work 1 row p, 1 row k, 1 row p, 1 row k. Below the contrasting yarn you will see a series of 'bumps' made in the main yarn (see detail). These bumps are picked up in this row, increasing the stitches.

This swatch shows the blue waste yarn that is partly unravelled to reveal a subtly cast-on edge.

3
To create a k1, p1 rib, *p1, then with LH needle lift the bump of main yarn below the contrasting yarn, place it on LH needle and k tbl, repeat from * to last stitch. For an even number of stitches, p1 then lift the final stitch in main yarn at the edge; place on LH needle and k tbl; for an odd number, p the final stitch.

4
Check you have the correct number of stitches, then turn and continue to work in k1, p1 rib. Remove the waste yarn by unravelling stitches carefully after you have worked several rows and gently pulling free.

This cast on uses waste yarn and a crochet hook and so requires basic crochet skills.

PROVISIONAL, OR TEMPORARY, CAST ON (SINGLE NEEDLE)

This cast on is worked with spare yarn in a contrasting colour but of a similar thickness to the main yarn, a single needle and a crochet hook the same size. It is an ideal way to seamlessly join two pieces of knitting. For example, a scarf that starts in the centre of the neck is worked first in one direction down to the lower edge. The cast-on edge is then undone and the stitches placed on a needle. These stitches are used to knit the other half of the scarf, which allows you to make a scarf with a balanced pattern and matching lower edges.

The provisional cast on is also useful when you want to add an edging later. For children's garments, when extra length may be required in the future, start with a provisional cast on, initially ignoring the ribbing. When the piece is complete (before sewing up), undo the provisional cast on, place the stitches on a needle and complete the rib from the top down. As the child grows, the rib can be unravelled back to the provisional cast on, extra length added as required and the ribbing redone.

1
To make a crochet chain, place a slipknot on a crochet hook the same size or one size larger than your main needle. Hold the hook in your RH and the working yarn in your LH.

2
Wrap the working yarn around the hook, taking it from back to front. Maintain the tension on the slipknot with your thumb and first finger to keep the slipknot at the bottom of the hook.

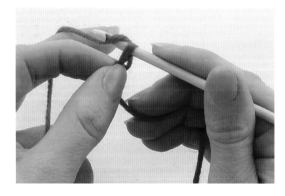

3
Catch the working yarn with the tip of the hook.

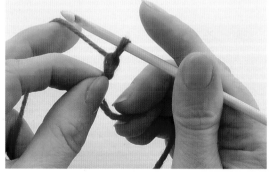

4
Draw the working yarn through the slipknot on the crochet hook. One chain made. Repeat steps 2–4 until the desired number of chains has been made.

After the main fabric has been knitted, the crochet chain is removed to reveal the live stitches, which are then put onto a needle for knitting.

- **Don't unravel all of the chain** at once, work one stitch at a time.

- **You may find that you have one stitch fewer/ more** than you should when you pick up your live stitches. This may be explained in your pattern but if not, add or decrease one stitch so that you have the correct number.

- **Use a nice, smooth yarn** for your crocheted chain because it makes it easier to unravel.

- **If your cast-on edge is always too tight,** try going up a needle size for the cast-on row only. Likewise if it is too loose, try a size smaller needle.

- **If you are unsure which cast-on method to use,** make small samples before beginning. Try starting on a wrong-side row rather than a right-side row to see how this affects the look.

- **For provisional cast ons,** be sure to use a smooth yarn of roughly the same weight as the main yarn in a clearly contrasting colour to make it easier to undo later.

Hold the chain and yarn firmly to stop the slipknot and loop from sliding off the needle.

You may find it helpful to use the LH to help the loop of the crochet bump over the working yarn to form the new stitch.

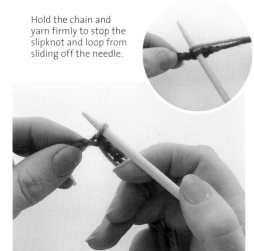

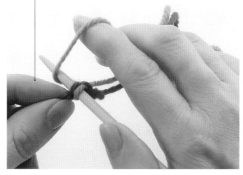

5
Holding a knitting needle the same size as for the main fabric in the RH, insert the needle into the first bump at the back of the crochet chain and loop the working yarn over the needle. Hold the loop firmly with the RH and draw the loop through the crochet bump.

6
With the working yarn, make a knit stitch in the normal way into the next bump on the back of the crochet chain.

7
Repeat step 6 until you have cast on the desired number of stitches. When you are ready to unravel your provisional cast on, simply return to the crocheted chain, loosen the end and pull back the chain. As you do so, the live stitches will be exposed. Place each live stitch on your knitting needle as you unravel the chain.

PINHOLE, OR EMILY OCKER'S, CAST ON

This is a traditional cast-on method for circular knitting. Because it produces a cast on with virtually no hole in the centre, it is ideal for projects where the piece is to be started with a small number of stitches and knitted in the round, increasing as the work grows outwards. It is handy for, among other things, top-down hats, circular-knit shawls and circular tablecloths.

1
For this cast on you will need a crochet hook in a size similar to your main knitting needles. Fold the working end of your main yarn over the tail yarn to form a loop. Leave a 15cm (6in) tail for darning in later. Hold the loop in your LH with the working yarn behind the loop.

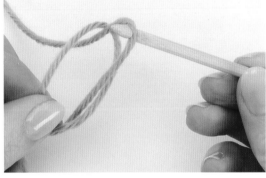

2
Insert the crochet hook into the centre of the loop, catch the working yarn and bring it through the loop to the front.

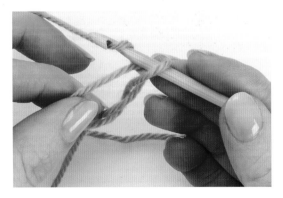

3
Wrap the working yarn from right to left around the crochet hook and draw the yarn through the loop on the hook as if you are making a double crochet.

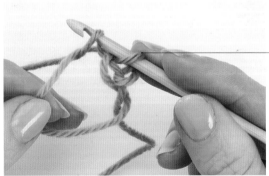

Your first stitch sits lower down on the hook.

4
Leaving the stitch you have just made on the crochet hook, insert the hook into the front of the loop again, catch the working yarn and again draw it through the loop to the front of the work.

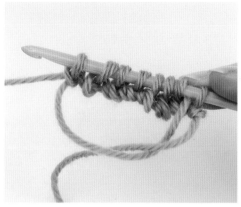

- **When knitting your first round of stitches from the cast on** you can make the loop larger so that it's easier to see what you are doing.

- **When making and transferring the cast-on stitches** from the crochet hook to the DPNs, be careful not to twist them, and check for twisted stitches when joining the stitches into a circle.

- **Use a stitch marker** to denote the start of each round when you join your knitting into a circle.

5
Wrap the working yarn from right to left around the crochet hook and draw the yarn through just the first loop nearest the hook (leave the earlier stitch on the hook). Two stitches have now been made.

6
Repeat steps 4 and 5 until you have made the required number of stitches, eight in this case. Note the long tail, which will later be used to draw the hole closed.

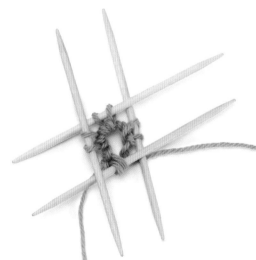

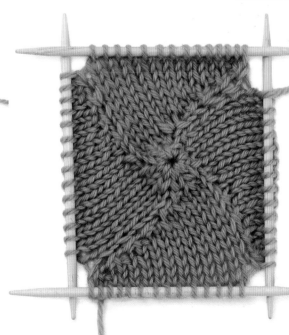

8
After eight rounds, holding the work firmly, draw up the tail so that it closes up the centre hole.

7
Now you can transfer the stitches from the crochet hook onto your DPNs, distributing the stitches over three or four DPNs depending on the pattern. Join your knitting into a circle and continue knitting in the round in the normal way (see pages 162–169).

CAST-OFF CAST ON

This crochet chain cast on is a good choice when you need a cast on that matches a standard chain cast off. You will need a crochet hook the same size as the main knitting needles.

1
Place a slipknot on the crochet hook and hold in your RH (see detail). With the needle in your LH and the working yarn in your RH, lay the crochet hook over the top of the needle. Take the yarn under the needle to the back and around the crochet hook from right to left.

2
Pull the hook through the loop. Leave the new loop on the hook and draw it out slightly if necessary. Flick the working yarn off the needle so that it lies under the needle, between the needle and the hook.

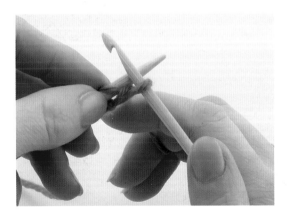

3
With the loop still on the crochet hook, take the working yarn back under the needle and repeat steps 1 and 2.

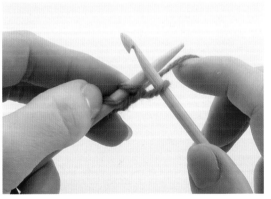

4
Repeat steps 1 and 2 until one less than the desired number of stitches has been cast on. The loop on the crochet hook is then transferred to the needle as the final cast-on stitch.

Cable and alternate cable cast ons are useful for ribbing: they are firm yet elastic.

CABLE AND ALTERNATE CABLE CAST ONS (USE TWO NEEDLES)

These methods of casting on can be used for both k1, p1 rib and wider ribs. They are also nice as decorative edgings.

1 Cable cast on

Make the first two stitches as you did for the knitted cast on (see page 47).

2

Holding the yarn to the back, insert the RH needle between the first and second stitches. Knit this stitch, drawing out the loop to the front and placing the new stitch on the LH needle (see detail). Repeat until the desired number of stitches has been cast on.

1 Alternate cable cast on

Work steps 1 and 2 as for cable cast on, above. Take the yarn to the front of the work as if to purl. Insert the RH needle from back to front, between second and third stitches on the LH needle (see detail).

2

Work as for normal purl stitch but do not transfer the new stitch to the RH needle. Instead, return to the LH needle. One purl stitch cast on. Continue to cast on by repeating step 2 of the cable cast on for knit stitches, steps 1 and 2 of the alternate cable for purl stitches.

NOTES

- **When you are working k1, p1 ribbing,** if the last cast-on stitch was k, the first stitch of the new row should be k; if the last stitch was p, the first stitch should be p. Due to the way stitches are cast on, all knit stitches on the first row should be worked into the back of the stitch. For stocking stitch and other patterns, work the new row according to the pattern.

- **Note how alternating p and k avoids a line,** the cast on undulating to follow the rib pattern instead, staying firm yet springy.

- **For a k2, p2 rib,** cast on two stitches knitwise and two purlwise, repeating as required.

The knit stitch

The term 'knitting' encompasses all the stitches and processes associated with making fabrics using sticks and string. We talk about learning to knit and so on whenever we talk about the craft. So it can be a little puzzling when we talk about the knit stitch.

KEY FOR THIS SECTION

RH Right hand

LH Left hand

The knit stitch is in fact a specific stitch in its own right. It is the first stitch that most knitters learn and once you have mastered it a whole world of patterns and projects opens up to you. Armed with just the knit stitch you can begin to create beautiful, exciting projects.

The knit stitch forms the basis of many of the more complex knitting stitches and patterns and is a fundamental part of many techniques – colourwork, lace knitting and cables to name just a few.

You may also have heard the term 'garter stitch' used to describe knit stitches. Garter stitch is simply a pattern stitch where all the stitches are made using the knit stitch. Every stitch and every row is made using the knit stitch. This creates a distinctive, attractive fabric with a familiar ridged appearance. It is a reversible fabric, making it useful for items where both sides may be visible. It is also one of the few stitch patterns that gives a square fabric – each stitch has the same height and width. So, a fabric that is 20 stitches wide and 20 rows tall will be square.

1
Hold the yarn in your RH. Insert the tip of the RH needle into the front of the next stitch from the previous row, entering the stitch from left to right. The RH needle goes beneath the LH needle.

2
Bring up the yarn around the back of the RH needle. Keep the yarn slightly tensioned but not too tight.

CLIP 3
The knit stitch

www.youtube.com/watch?v=UxY7ryHd11Q

The knit stitch is versatile and can be worked on virtually any size needle with any yarn. Here 4mm (size 6) needles and DK yarn have been used. Very large needles and chunky yarn will make a quick, easy scarf.

Try to keep the working yarn close and parallel to the RH needle. This will help prevent it slipping off the needle as you bring the RH needle through the opening.

3
Take the yarn over the front of the RH needle from left to right so the yarn is on the RH side. The yarn should be wrapped snugly around the needle, but not too tight.

4
Open out the hands slightly as though opening a pair of shears. You should see a small opening in the work with the wrapped RH needle behind. Angle the RH needle and bring the tip towards you through the opening.

The stitch is smooth on the front of the work with a bump on the back.

5
With the tip of the RH needle now in front of the LH needle, you should see a loop of yarn on the LH needle behind the RH tip. Carefully slide this loop of yarn off the LH needle. This completes the new stitch. Keep the working yarn to the right.

6
The completed knit stitch is now on the RH needle. Draw up the working yarn so that the stitches are even, not too tight or floppy.

The purl stitch

The purl stitch is the second stitch that all knitters need in their repertoire. Armed with this stitch and the knit stitch, a vast range of patterns and design opportunities opens up to even a novice knitter.

Combining rows of knit and purl stitches allows you to create smooth knitted fabrics, but it is also possible to produce an extensive range of beautiful, textured patterns by combining the stitches within a row. Alternating knit and purl stitches are also the basis of most rib patterns.

When working the knit stitch you will have noticed that the stitch that faces you is flat, while on the reverse of the fabric the same stitch has a bump or ridge. When every row in a fabric is knitted with the knit stitch, alternating rows of smooth troughs and bumpy ridges are created and the result is a bouncy, ridged fabric called garter stitch. To create a smooth-faced fabric, you need to get all of the smooth faces of

the stitches on the same side of your knitting. To do this, you need to introduce a stitch that has the opposite characteristics of the knit stitch – bumpy on the facing side, smooth on the reverse. This role is fulfilled by the purl stitch. By working in alternating rows of purl and knit stitches it is possible to create a fabric that is smooth on one side, with all the ridges together on the reverse. This fabric is called stocking stitch, or stockinette stitch.

1
Hold the working yarn in front of the RH needle in your RH so that it lies over the top of the needle from left to right.

2
Insert the tip of the RH needle from right to left up into the front of the first stitch on the LH needle. Keep the working yarn to the front of the work in your RH.

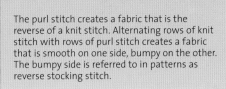

The purl stitch creates a fabric that is the reverse of a knit stitch. Alternating rows of knit stitch with rows of purl stitch creates a fabric that is smooth on one side, bumpy on the other. The bumpy side is referred to in patterns as reverse stocking stitch.

Hold the working yarn at an angle to the needle.

3
Wrap the working yarn under and around the tip of the RH needle going from right to left.

4
Tension the yarn slightly and hold it at a slight angle to the left of the RH needle.

The stitch is bumpy on the front of the work and smooth on the back – the opposite to knit stitch.

5
Pivot the RH needle and move it away from you, behind the LH needle. There should be a loop of yarn on the RH needle and the original loop on the LH needle.

6
Slide off the loop on the LH needle. That's one purl stitch made. To continue in purl, keep the yarn to the front of the work and repeat steps 1–6 as required.

Increases

The purpose of increases in knitting goes beyond simply making something larger. Increases are also used to add shape, contour and structure to knitted pieces. Curves, pleats, darts, edgings or decorative stitches may all involve increases in one form or another.

CLIPS 5a & 5b
Bar increase and Lifted increase techniques

When knitting even the simplest garment or accessory, understanding how shaping affects the look and feel of the finished fabric is the key to success. The right shaping technique, whether it is intended to be discreet and unobtrusive or showy and decorative, can really set your pieces apart and give them a designer look.

A woven fabric must be cut and sewn to alter its shape, but simply using different needle sizes and stitch patterns can shape knitted fabrics. Many designers exploit these unique attributes to create fabulously contoured garments and accessories.

However, this technique does have its limitations, so knitters also need to learn some alternative methods for adding shape or for making a garment larger. This is usually achieved by adding extra stitches at strategic points in the work. Increases also play a vital part in the creation of many decorative stitches. Lace in particular relies on increases to create its delicate patterns of holes and eyelets.

Most increases are based on four simple stitches and, once these have been mastered, any new stitch can be tackled with confidence.

Bar increases

This increase leaves a little bar stitch at the front of your knitting. It can also be referred to as 'knit into the front and back of the stitch'.

KNITTED BAR INCREASE (KFB/ KF AND B/ KTW)

1
Knit into the front of the stitch in the usual way.

2
Without dropping the stitch from the LH needle, lift the RH needle over from front to back (see detail) and knit again into the back of the same stitch. Drop the two stitches off the LH needle.

Increases may involve adding a single stitch, a series of stitches, or a large number of stitches at once.

PURLED BAR INCREASE (PFB/ PF AND B/ PTW)

1
With the yarn held to the front as is usual for a purl stitch, insert the tip of the RH needle into the back of the next stitch by bringing the RH needle from back to front through the back of the stitch.

2
Purl this stitch as usual but without allowing the loop on the LH needle to drop off.

TERMINOLOGY
As with all things knitting, cultural and regional differences mean that one knitter's yarn over is another knitter's yarn forward, while to you it may be a yarn over needle. Where a pattern uses increases, check the abbreviations, because these should explain which type of increase the designer wants you to use. If the pattern is not specific, you should be able to place the stitches needed in one of these categories and, from there, follow the pattern or try out some of the alternatives.

Make sure the yarn is to the front of the work.

3
Keep the yarn to the front and bring the RH needle in front of the LH needle and purl into the front of the same stitch. This time allow the stitch to drop off the needle.

NOTES

Changing needles
Using larger needles will increase the size of the knitted fabric. However, it will also affect its feel, density and drape because the entire stitch will increase in size. To achieve an increase in a specific area – for example, widening a sleeve from the cuff to the armhole – extra stitches must be added rather than relying on making each stitch larger.

Key increase stitches
Increase stitches fall broadly into four categories: bar, lifted, raised and yarn over.

Need an invisible increase?
The bar increase is done by knitting or purling twice into the same stitch. This method produces a good, all-around increase, which is easy to work and doesn't leave any risk of a hole or a loose stitch. However, the bar is visible, so if you need an invisible increase, the lifted increase may be a better choice. Two bar increases can be paired around a central stitch for decorative effect, for example, to highlight an area of shaping such as a raglan sleeve.

Lifted increases

Also referred to as knit below or row below, lifted increases can be slanted to the right or left for excellent, almost invisible increases. However, because it draws up the stitch from the previous row, it is best suited to instances where increases are four or more rows apart.

KNITTED RIGHT-SLANTING INCREASE

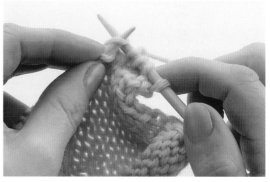

1
To create an increase that slants to the right, insert the tip of the RH needle from front to back going under the right leg of the stitch below the stitch about to be worked.

2
Knit into this loop, then knit the next stitch as usual.

KNITTED LEFT-SLANTING INCREASE

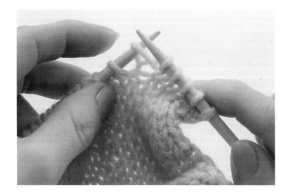

Gently draw the loop open if it is difficult to work the stitch.

1
For an increase that slants to the left, insert the tip of the LH needle from back to front, into the left leg of the stitch on the row below the stitch that has just been worked.

2
Draw out the loop slightly. Knit into the back of this loop and knit the next stitch as usual.

The lifted increase is a good
choice of method for sleeve seams
and areas where discreet shaping
is required, because it forms a
smooth surface.

PURLED RIGHT-SLANTING INCREASE

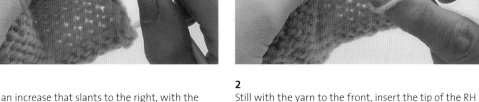

Hold the yarn
firmly to prevent
the stitch from
sliding off the
needle.

1
To create an increase that slants to the right, with the
yarn to the front, insert the tip of the LH needle from
front to back into the stitch below the one just completed
on the RH needle.

2
Still with the yarn to the front, insert the tip of the RH
needle from back to front into the back of the stitch on
the LH needle. The RH needle goes in front of the LH
needle as for a regular purl stitch. Purl this stitch.

PURLED LEFT-SLANTING INCREASE

1
For an increase that slants to the left, with the yarn to the
front insert the RH needle from right to left into the front
of the top of the stitch below the next stitch on the LH
needle. The RH needle goes in front of the LH needle.

2
Purl into this stitch, taking care not to let the stitch on the
LH needle drop off. Purl the next stitch as usual.

Raised increases

A raised increase is also referred to as the strand increase (particularly in UK patterns) or as make one (m1), and is made using the strand between two stitches. It can be slanted right or left. It can create a small hole but if the stitch is worked as shown below, this problem can be minimised.

. . . .

KNITTED RIGHT-SLANTING INCREASE

Increase by knitting into the front of the stitch.

1
For an increase that slants to the right, insert the tip of the LH needle from front to back under the connecting yarn between the stitches on the LH and RH needles. Hold the loop on the LH needle.

2
Insert the tip of the RH needle from front to back into the front of the loop you have just put onto the LH needle. Knit this stitch.

. . . .

KNITTED LEFT-SLANTING INCREASE

Increase by knitting into the back of the stitch.

1
For an increase on a knit row that slants to the left, insert the tip of the LH needle from front to back under the connecting yarn between the stitches on the LH and RH needles. Hold the loop on the LH needle (see detail).

2
Knit into the back of the strand on the LH needle.

A raised increase is formed independently of the neighbouring stitches and can therefore be placed exactly where it is needed.

PURLED RIGHT-SLANTING INCREASE

Purl into the back of the stitch for a right-slanting increase.

1
For an increase on a purl row that slants to the right, with the yarn to the front, use the LH needle to pick up the strand between the two needles and insert the needle from front to back. Hold the loop on the LH needle.

2
Still with the yarn to the front, insert the tip of the RH needle from back to front through the back of the loop on the LH needle. Purl this stitch.

PURLED LEFT-SLANTING INCREASE

Purl into the front of the stitch for a left-slanting increase.

1
For an increase on a purl row that slants to the left, with the yarn to the front, insert the LH needle from back to front under the strand between the LH and RH needles. Hold the loop on the LH needle.

2
With the RH needle in front of the LH needle, insert the RH needle tip up into the front of the loop on the LH needle and purl this stitch.

The hole created by the yarn over can be seen clearly after working a couple of rows. It is the placing of these holes that creates decorative lace patterns.

Yarn-over increases

This type of increase has a number of names including yarn forward (yf), yarn round needle (yrn), with yarn in front (wyif) and yarn over (yo)/yarn on needle (yon). Because the yarn is wrapped around the needle and not worked, this increase can be placed exactly where it is needed.

YARN-OVER INCREASE ON A KNIT ROW

1
Work a yo on a knit row by bringing the yarn forward from back to front between the needles.

2
Then take it around the RH needle to the back, ready to knit the next stitch.

3
As the next stitch is knitted, the loop created by the yo can be seen on the RH needle.

YARN-OVER INCREASE ON A PURL ROW OR BEFORE A PURL STITCH

1
With the yarn forward as for a purl stitch, take the working yarn around the RH needle, going from left to right over the top of the RH needle, under the RH needle, between the two needles and up to the front.

2
Purl the next stitch as normal.

3
As for the yo knit stitch, a purled yo can be seen on the RH needle. The hole can be seen clearly after a couple of rows have been worked.

Multiple increases

If you need to increase several stitches in one go, you would usually do this by casting on those stitches. T-shaped garments, shrugs and other, similar styles, particularly those worked from side to side, often require many stitches to be added in the space of just one or two rows. In these circumstances the extra stitches needed are normally cast on at the beginning of a row. For these garments, the backward loop (see page 48) or cable cast on (see page 55) give a neat finish.

Casting on extra stitches can create a simple T-shape. Stitches can be added, as here, on both knit and purl rows.

CABLE CAST ON (PURL ROW)

1
With your knitting in your LH, insert the RH needle from front to back between the first two stitches.

2
Make a knit stitch (see detail), then return the stitch to the LH needle.

3
When the required number of new stitches has been made, work the whole row to the end as usual, including the newly made stitches (which will be worked first).

Decreases

In addition to being a means of making a knitted fabric smaller, decreases are used to shape necklines, armholes, pockets, buttonholes and many other key design features.

KEY FOR THIS SECTION

k2tog Knit two together

ssk Slip, slip, knit

sl Slip

k Knit

psso Pass slipped stitch over

p2tog Purl two together

p Purl

ssp Slip, slip, purl

sts Stitches

tog Together

Shaping isn't limited to the purely functional aspects of knitting design. Interesting effects can be achieved by restructuring knits with shaping. For example, something as simple as making a blanket square from two triangles rather than in one single piece is an easy way to create a surprisingly different look without affecting the finished shape. Shaping is also an essential part of sculptural knits such as knitted toys and other three-dimensional pieces.

Whether you are working to a commercial pattern or to your own design, it can be fun to play around with different ways of decreasing stitches and, even if you are following a commercial pattern, it is useful to understand why a particular decreasing method has

been chosen and to observe the effect achieved when the pattern is completed. If you are planning to design or adapt your own pattern, you may like to try different decrease methods by making swatches beforehand and seeing how they work together. Attention to small details such as decreases can really make a difference to the look of your garment.

Depending on the type of decrease you choose, you may get a finish that is barely noticeable or one that is intentionally bold for decorative effect. A decrease will normally slant either to the right or left.

CLIPS 6a & 6b Knit-two-together decrease and Slip-slip-knit decrease

KNIT-TWO-TOGETHER: RIGHT-SLANTING DECREASE (K2TOG)
This is a straightforward way to decrease a stitch and slants to the right.

Hold the working yarn firmly to avoid stitches slipping off the needle when knitting the two stitches together.

1
When you're at the point where you want to make your decrease, insert the RH needle from front to back into the next two stitches on the LH needle.

2
Wrap the yarn as usual for a knit stitch and knit the two stitches as if they are one stitch.

Use the direction
of decreases as a
stylistic feature to
emphasise shaping.

SLIP, SLIP, KNIT: LEFT-SLANTING DECREASE (SSK)

The ideal pairing for a k2tog is a slip, slip, knit (ssk). It gives a neat, left-sloping stitch.

1
Insert the RH needle into the next stitch as if to knit (knitwise), then slip it onto the RH needle without knitting it. Repeat with the next stitch on the LH needle so that you have two slipped stitches on the RH needle. The stitches should only be slipped one at a time.

2
Insert the tip of the LH needle from right to left up into the front of the two slipped stitches (the RH needle is behind the LH needle).

3
K2tog by knitting into the back of both of them. That's one stitch decreased.

SLIP ONE, KNIT ONE, PASS SLIPPED STITCH OVER: LEFT-SLANTING DECREASE (SL1, K1, PSSO)

This is another frequently used, left-sloping decrease. It is particularly popular when worked together with a yarn over in lace knitting.

1
Insert the RH needle as if to knit (knitwise) into the next stitch on the LH needle and slip it onto the RH needle without knitting it.

2
Knit the next stitch.

3
Use the tip of the LH needle to lift the slipped stitch over the knit stitch just worked and drop the slipped stitch off the RH needle.

Viewed from the right (knit) side of the work, a p2tog produces an almost invisible decrease when worked at the end of a purl row. When worked at the beginning of a purl row, a slip one purl one, pass slipped stitch over decrease is more visible from the right side.

PURL TWO TOGETHER: RIGHT-SLANTING DECREASE (P2TOG)

This decrease slants to the left (to the right when seen on the knit side of the work).

PURL-ROW DECREASES
Decreases on purl rows are less noticeable when seen from the purl side and there is little difference in direction.

1
With the yarn forward, insert the tip of the RH needle into the front of the first two stitches on the LH needle, taking the needle from right to left. The RH needle should be in front of the LH needle.

2
Wrap the yarn as usual for a purl stitch and p2tog.

SLIP ONE, PURL ONE, PASS SLIPPED STITCH OVER: RIGHT-SLANTING DECREASE (SL1, P1, PSSO)

This decrease slants to the left when viewed from the right (knit) side of the work.

Hold the yarn tensioned with the index finger to make lifting the slipped stitch easier.

1
For this stitch, slip the next stitch knitwise (not purlwise) onto the RH needle.

2
Purl the next stitch, then lift the slipped stitch over the purled stitch and drop off the RH needle.

. . . .

SLIP, SLIP, PURL (SSP OR SL2, P SL STS TOG)

This decrease slants to the right when viewed from the right (knit) side of the work.

1
Purl as far as the two stitches to be decreased.

2
Slip the next two stitches one after the other, knitwise (not purlwise), onto the RH needle.

3
Return both stitches to the LH needle.

4
Insert the RH needle from back to front into the back loops of the two slipped stitches on the LH needle and purl the two stitches as one (ssp/sl2, p sl sts tog).

Joining in a new yarn

There are a number of methods for joining two balls of yarn. Because yarns vary in their texture, thickness and structure (smooth, fluffy, slippery and so on), choosing the right join can be important.

Joins can be made at almost any point in a piece of knitting. A join may be needed when you run out of yarn and simply need to carry on knitting in the same yarn, or when changing colours or changing from one yarn type to another in a textured garment.

Where possible, a join should be made in an unobtrusive part of the knitting and also at a point where it will be secure and unlikely to unravel if placed under strain. Some yarns, such as Shetland and other 'fuzzy' wools, have a natural tendency to grip to one another, so more joining options are available for them. Smooth cottons, bamboo, silk and similar yarns have no natural grip, so it is important to use a join that will be permanent but at the same time remain subtle. Certain fabrics, such as fine shawls, will show

joins more readily, and thick yarns may need to be thinned to reduce bulk where the new yarn is introduced. Joining at a row end, where the join is likely to be hidden within the seam, is often a good choice. Splicing (also referred to as wet-/spit-splicing) or a Russian join is a good choice for 'grippy' wools and can be carried out anywhere in a row. Where there are many joins, for example with colourwork, it is often best to vary the location of the colour changes if possible, to avoid the joins stacking up on top of one another and causing a thickened section.

ROW END

This is a simple method that works well for seam edges, but is not necessarily the neatest edge for a neckline or front edge, particularly when working with a fine yarn. It is an excellent join for stripes where a new row is always begun with the new colour and a complete stripe of the new yarn is to be made.

**CLIPS 7a & 7b
Joining in at the row end and Joining in, overlapping method**

www.youtube.com/watch?v=Yjs4ErG5LUg

1
At the end of the row before the colour change, knot the old and the new yarns together. At the start of the next row, start knitting with the new yarn.

2
During assembly, carefully undo the knot, weave in the ends and trim.

. . . .

OVERLAPPING METHOD

This method has the advantage of being possible to work anywhere in a row, but it can cause a bulky patch where the two yarns are worked together. This is not an issue with fluffy or slubbed yarns (unless the slubs come together in the same place). However, with a smooth pattern or a fine yarn, the join can be seen and may well spoil the overall look.

Shown here in two colours for clarity, this technique is used only where joining in a yarn of the same colour.

1
Lay the new yarn over the old, with its tail end facing the working end of the old yarn. Overlap the two yarns by around 20cm (8in) and hold them together.

2
Work only with the old yarn for approximately 8cm (3¼in), then knit with both the old and new yarns held together. You will have a tail sticking out from the stitches on the RH needle and several stitches worked with two strands of yarn.

3
Once around 10cm (4in) has been worked using both yarns together, drop the old yarn and continue to work in the new yarn only. Trim the old yarn to a tail of around 10cm (4in) to allow for darning in later.

SPLICING (WET-SPLICE OR SPIT-SPLICE)
This technique is suitable for wool and similar yarns with natural grip and a tendency to felt when rubbed together. It can be done almost anywhere in the knitted fabric and creates a smooth join with no knot. It is only suited to joining two yarns of the same colour because the two are knitted together for several stitches.

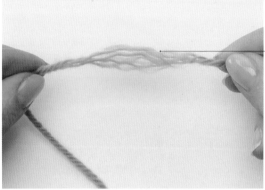

Join the two untwisted ends.

1
Take the end of the tail yarn and untwist the plies for about 3–5cm (1¼–2in). Do the same with the new ball of yarn.

2
Lay the two untwisted ends over each other so that they overlap with the ends pointing away from each other. Intertwine the untwisted ends into each other as smoothly as possible, like interlocking fingers.

The two yarns merge to appear as one.

3
Dampen your thumb and forefinger and gently roll the joining area so that the yarns begin to felt together. Start at the centre and work out towards the cut ends.

4
Keep working the yarn until the two ends are almost invisible.

TEMPORARY KNOT METHOD

This method places a temporary knot in the two yarns that is later undone and left for darning in. In this technique, the temporary knot holds the two yarns together but doesn't allow the stitch where the yarns join to stretch or spread. When the knot is undone, placing a single knot in the yarn holds the stitches either side in place without causing any puckering or holes. Because the yarns are woven in opposite directions, the stitches remain firm but not pulled. Weaving in the ends rather than knitting with two yarns eliminates bulk at the join. Joins can also be made anywhere in the row.

1
When you reach the point at which the yarns are to be changed, tie the old and new yarns together with an overhand knot. Leave a tail on each of about 15cm (6in) to allow for weaving in later.

2
You should aim to keep the knot to the wrong side of the work and adjust its positioning as required to achieve this.

3
When assembling, carefully undo the knot. Then, place a single knot in the two yarns.

4
Draw up the single knot gently until it is more or less flat with the knitted fabric.

5
Weave in the two loose ends, working in opposite directions to the direction of the yarn in the knitting. Working on the wrong side of the fabric, the new yarn should be woven in to the right and the old to the left. Weave the ends back on themselves for a couple of stitches, then trim close to the fabric.

RUSSIAN JOIN

This is a stitched join, which is good for joining two yarns of the same colour and can be worked almost anywhere in the knitting. A smooth join with no knot, however, may not be suited to very bulky yarns due to the doubling of the yarn at the loop.

A fine needle will more easily split the yarn.

1
Thread as fine a needle as possible onto the tail of the old yarn.

2
Take the threaded needle back along the yarn tail, working into the centre of the ply twist. Depending on the fineness of the yarn and how grippy it is, thread back through the yarn for around 3–4cm (1¼–1½in).

Keep the loop small so it is less likely to pucker when pulled taut.

3
Leaving a small loop of yarn, pull the tail completely through and take it off the needle.

4
Thread the tail of the new yarn onto a fine needle and pass it through the loop of the old yarn.

5
Sew the new yarn back through itself as you did with the old yarn, for about 3–4cm (1¼–1½in). Gently pull the tail through and off the needle.

Although two colours have been used here for clarity, this technique is used to join two yarns of the same colour.

6
Working at both ends, carefully draw the tails tighter until the two loops disappear, and continue knitting as usual.

Casting off

When a piece of knitting is complete, it is important to finish it off correctly to ensure that the stitches don't unravel. Like casting on, a well-chosen cast off can make a big difference to the appearance and suitability of the fabric for its purpose.

KEY FOR THIS SECTION

k Knit

p Purl

k2tog Knit two together

yo Yarn over

Cast-off stitches can offer edgings that are firm, elastic or temporary for joining to other pieces. Two pieces of knitted fabric can also be cast off together and effectively seamed at the same time.

Casting off is essentially a way of removing blocks of stitches in one go. Casting off fulfils two essential purposes: ending a piece of work by removing all of the stitches on the needle at once; and removing a number of stitches at one time to achieve certain shaping effects. Just as you may need to add a large number of stitches at once, you may also need to remove many stitches at one time. To do this you can

cast off stitches or, if you intend to use the stitches later (for example, in a neckline), place the stitches on a stitch holder. Casting off can also be combined with seaming by using a special technique known as the three-needle cast off.

As with casting on, consider the look you want to achieve and the purpose and location of your cast off in the piece. In some cases it may be desirable to have a cast off that is soft, flexible, and barely visible. For other projects a bold, decorative cast off may be a good choice.

STANDARD (CHAIN) CAST OFF
This is a popular cast off and a good all-purpose method. It is neat and forms a chain of stitches across the top of the work. It can be worked on either a knit or purl row.

Try to keep an even tension for a neat chain.

1
Work (knit) two stitches as usual. Use the tip of the LH needle to lift the first stitch worked (knitted) on the RH needle.

**CLIP 8
Casting off**

www.youtube.com/watch?v=arEf3Xu_TVU

Only one stitch
remains on the
RH needle.

2
Take the first stitch over the top of the second stitch and drop it off the RH needle. One stitch cast off.

3
Work (knit) the next stitch. The second stitch you worked (knitted) is then lifted over this stitch and dropped, leaving only the third stitch on the needle. Two stitches cast off.

4
If you are casting off all the stitches, when you reach the final stitch cut the yarn, leaving a 30cm (12in) tail, pass the tail yarn through the stitch and draw up firmly. Use the tail yarn for making up later or darn in neatly. If you are not casting off all the stitches, continue knitting to the end of the row.

This cast off creates a neat line of chain-like stitches, which is firm but not very elastic.

COUNTING CORRECTLY
In patterns where a set number of cast-off stitches is required, this refers only to the number of stitches lifted and dropped off. The stitch left on RH needle does not count as one of the cast-off stitches.

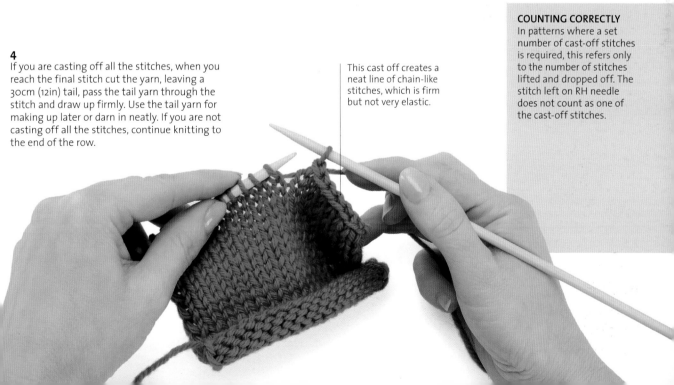

SEWN-STYLE CAST OFF USING KNITTING NEEDLES

The sewn-style cast off is a great choice for a strong but elastic finish on cuffs, especially toe-up socks. This cast off is usually made using a tapestry needle; however, this version achieves the same result using knitting needles rather than a sewing needle.

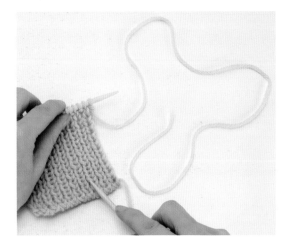

1
Cut your working yarn leaving a tail at least three times the length of the edge being cast off.

2
Knit the first two stitches on the LH needle as if to k2tog, but leave both stitches on the LH needle.

3
Use the RH needle or your fingers – whichever you find easiest – to pull the tail yarn through the stitches from right to left, still keeping them on the LH needle. Draw the yarn up, but not too tightly.

4
Purl the first stitch with the tail yarn, leaving it on the LH needle, and use the RH needle or your fingers to pull the tail yarn through from left to right. If you are knitting a flat fabric, drop this stitch off the needle. For a fabric knitted in the round, for the first stitch only, slip the stitch to the RH needle. On subsequent rounds drop the stitch as for knitting flat fabrics.

5
Repeat steps 2–4 until all but one stitch has been cast off, leaving just one stitch on the LH needle. For flat fabrics, pass the tail yarn through this stitch and draw up the yarn for a neat finish. If working in the round, follow the instructions in Working in the Round, right.

WORKING IN THE ROUND
When you reach the last two stitches you will have the final stitch of the round plus the first stitch of the round (the one you slipped across during setup). Work the last stitch and this stitch as left then slip it off the needle and draw up the yarn for a neat finish.

Casting off in this way retains the continuity of the rib, giving a neat, unobtrusive finish.

The sewn-style cast off is stretchy but not too loose, making it a good choice for sock tops. It matches the tubular cast on.

· ·

EXTRA-STRETCHY CAST OFF

Getting the balance right between a nice, elastic cast off and an untidy, floppy edge can be challenging. This method is straightforward and effective, and it is a good choice, especially for sock cuffs. The steps shown here demonstrate how to work a super-stretchy cast off on a k1, p1 ribbed cuff.

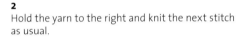

The reverse yo creates an extra stitch at the start of the cast-off row.

1
Because the first stitch is a knit stitch, begin by making a reverse yo, taking your yarn around the needle in the opposite direction to usual (see page 66). The working yarn comes from the LH needle, under the RH needle, goes from right to left over the top of the needle, and finishes by going under the RH needle from left to right.

2
Hold the yarn to the right and knit the next stitch as usual.

3
You will have two stitches on the RH needle – the yo and the stitch just knitted. Lift the first stitch (the reverse yo) over the stitch just knitted.

4
Before the next (purl) stitch, make a yo as usual and purl the next stitch.

With all the stitches cast off you will see just how stretchy this casting-off method really is.

Adding the yarn overs is what makes this cast off so stretchy.

5
You now have three stitches on the RH needle, the stitch left from step 1, the yo and the purled stitch, both from step 2. Insert the LH needle into both the stitch from step 1 and the yo. Lift these two stitches over the purl stitch. One stitch remains on the RH needle.

6
On the next and any subsequent knit stitches make a reverse yo by going from right to left over the front of the RH needle, taking the yarn between the needles, under the RH needle and holding it to the right.

Lift the yo together with the worked stitch.

7
Knit the next stitch. You will have three stitches on the RH needle, the purl stitch from step 4, the reverse yo and the stitch just knitted.

8
Using the tip of the LH needle, lift both the reverse yo and the purl stitch over the stitch just knitted.

finishing

It's often said that the way a project is finished will determine the overall quality of the item – often said because it's true. Spending a little time learning the final steps will help to produce that much-coveted professional polish.

Blocking and pressing

Blocking (also called dressing) is a means of finishing your knitting so that it is straightened out, the stitches are set and enhanced and the knitting is restored to its intended shape and size. Most knits benefit from blocking and this is normally done as part of the assembly stage.

You can buy special mats for blocking, although children's foam play-mats are an inexpensive alternative that you may be able to pick up secondhand – wash off any sticky marks or stains before you use them though!

You will need a flat, clean surface into which you can stick pins, and that won't be damaged by water or steam. Your bed or even a clean, carpeted floor can be used, or clean fibreboard covered with a clean sheet. If you are using your floor, remember that there may be a couple of hours' drying time, as you'll need to leave the pieces where they are while they dry.

If you knit shawls, look out for special kits for dressing shawls that include blocking wires, fine wires that are threaded through the edges of the knitting, as well as measures and other useful items.

Traditional wooden jumper and shawl frames have been used for many generations in the Scottish Highlands and are also now available to buy. These offer a way to dress a completed garment as opposed to blocking the pieces separately before sewing up.

Most knits can be wet blocked or steamed. For wet blocking, gently wash the piece and then roll in a towel to remove excess water before pinning to your blocking surface. When steam blocking, pin the dry knitting to the blocking surface. Check the finished size measurements on your pattern and use this as your guide when pinning.

HOW TO PIN PIECES

Carefully pinned pieces will result in a professional final finish. Once pinned, if you are wet blocking, the piece can be left to dry, but if you're steam blocking you will need to hold a steam iron or wallpaper steamer over the piece. Keep the steamer moving over the fabric until it is damp, then leave to dry.

Use good-quality, fine, rustproof dressmaking pins, and carefully pin the edges of the piece to its correct size and shape. Start by pinning the corners. Next pin halfway along the edges. Continue, placing pins at regular intervals along each edge. Use plenty of pins to avoid distorting the fabric.

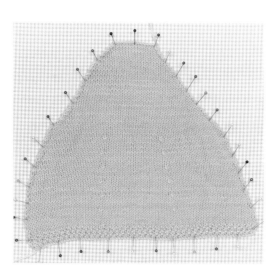

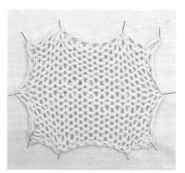

Incorrectly pinned
See how the stitches are pulled and distorted.

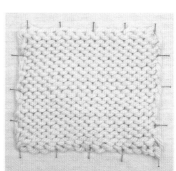

Correctly pinned
Taut swatch retaining its natural shape. If the edge has points, pin out each point.

Seaming (assembling)

There are many types of seams and stitches for joining knitted and crocheted fabrics. Some produce arguably better results than others, whereas some are simply a matter of personal taste.

**CLIP 9
Backstitch
seaming**

www.youtube.com/watch?v=CyUAfYzpLPA

It is tempting, in your enthusiasm to complete a project, to sew it up using just one type of stitch for all seams. However, spending a little time choosing the right seam for the right purpose will yield dividends and give your work a truly professional look.

To produce professionally finished knits, it is not necessary to learn a large number of techniques. The key is in selecting the best technique for the purpose. Knits can be joined using a very small repertoire of stitches. When selecting a seaming stitch, factors to consider are the location of the seam, how much strain the area will be under when worn, and whether the fabric needs to be elastic or firm. Comfort is also a consideration. Sock toes, for example, need a smooth but robust seam and babywear would also benefit from smooth, flat seams. Areas that will be under high strain, such as the attachments for bag handles, may need a stronger, less elastic seam such as backstitch. Often patterns will specify a particular seaming technique, and it is sensible to use this as a starting point; however, with experience, you will be able to evaluate your own knits and select the best seam for the purpose.

BACKSTITCH

This is probably the stitch for sewing knitting and crochet seams that you will be most familiar with. It's a good all-arounder, strong, and simple. It can be a little bulky in some circumstances, particularly on babywear and very fine work, where grafting or other techniques can be a better choice.

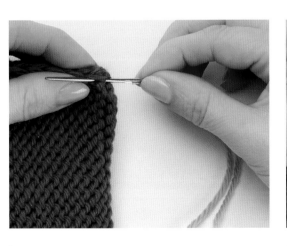

Contrasting yarn is used here for clarity; normally you would use the same colour of yarn as your knitting.

1
Begin by placing the two pieces with right sides together. Secure the yarn (RH end for right-handers, LH end for left-handers) with two small stitches on top of one another.

2
With the yarn at the back of the work, bring the needle up, from the back to front of the work, a short distance to the left of the first two securing stitches.

Each stitch should cover approximately 1–3 rows of knitting, depending on the fineness of the fabric.

3
Reinsert the needle at the end of the previous stitch from the front to the back of the work.

4
Bring the needle up again slightly to the left of the last stitch.

Fasten off firmly to make sure that the seams don't come undone. Check that the seams aren't puckered or too loose.

5
Take the yarn back down through the fabric at the end of the last stitch.

6
When the seam has been completed, make a couple of tiny stitches on top of one another, thread the yarn carefully back through the seam a little way and fasten off.

OVERCASTING (OVERSEWING OR WHIP STITCH)

This is a simple seaming technique. It does not produce a seam as firm as backstitch, but it is flatter and less bulky for areas that won't be subject to a lot of stretching and strain.

Contrasting yarn is used here for clarity; normally you would use the same colour of yarn as your knitting.

1
Place the two edges to be overcast together. Usually, right sides are placed facing one another, but if this is not appropriate for the pattern – for example, for a decorative stitch – it will be made clear in the instructions.

2
Secure the yarn at the start of the seam by sewing two small stitches on top of one another, through both thicknesses of the fabric. If you are right-handed, work from right to left. Left-handers may prefer to work left to right.

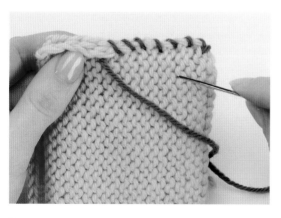

Although this seam may look untidy on the reverse, when viewed from the RS of the work and stitched in a matching colour, it should be almost invisible.

3
Overcast as shown, working the stitches firmly but not so tightly as to pucker the work.

4
At the end of the seam make a couple of tiny stitches, thread the yarn carefully back through the seam and fasten off.

LADDER STITCH

To join two pieces of stocking-stitch fabric, a classic backstitch is generally a good option. However, there is an alternative technique called ladder, or mattress, stitch that works particularly well on straight side seams, because it less bulky than backstitch.

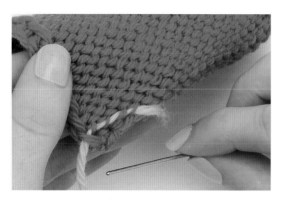

1
If you don't have a piece of tail yarn to work with, cut a piece of matching yarn, thread it onto a yarn needle, and run the yarn horizontally through five or six stitches along the WS edge of the knitting. If you do have a length of tail yarn to work with, ignore this step.

Make the first stitch as near to the corner of the work as possible to avoid mismatched seam edges.

2
Turn the work so that the right sides are facing you. Hold the work in your left hand with the Vs of each stitch running horizontally from right to left. Insert the yarn needle under a stitch on the piece of knitting closest to you (the front piece), as close to the corner of the work as possible.

3
Draw the yarn up and take the thread into the corner of the piece furthest away from you, going from front to back.

Use a blunt needle for this technique, to avoid splitting the yarn of the knitted fabric as you sew.

4
Draw the yarn up again. As you look at the knitting, the knitted stitches run from right to left. If you look carefully you will see a strand of yarn, almost hidden, at the base of the V of each stitch. Insert the yarn needle from right to left under this strand, on the front piece of fabric.

Draw up the yarn every 5 or 6 stitches and check that the seam is smooth and flat.

5
At this stage, draw the yarn up but leave it a little loose. Take the yarn needle under the strand at the base of the V on the back fabric.

6
Repeat steps 4 and 5 until five or six stitches have been worked. Note how the stitches form a 'ladder' of stitches along the seam. Draw the yarn up so that the edges meet neatly but without puckering.

7
Continue in this way until the seam has been completed. Finish with two small stitches. Cut the yarn, leaving a short tail for darning in later.

This stitch produces excellent, almost invisible seams on stocking-stitch fabrics. Because it is sewn with the RS facing, it is easy to match up rows of stitches, making it a good choice for stocking-stitch stripes and other colourwork patterns.

SHOULDER SEAMING (FAKE GRAFTING)

Use this method for a smooth, almost invisible seam when joining shoulder seams. This technique gives a look similar to grafting (see pages 94–97).

Work to the very edge of the fabric to avoid an untidy edge.

1
With the RS of work facing, place the shoulder seams together. Thread the tail yarn, or a new piece of yarn, onto a yarn needle, anchoring if necessary by running under several stitches on the WS of the work. Bring the needle from the WS to the RS and take it under both legs of the stitch nearest the RH edge of the lower piece.

2
Working from right to left, take the needle under both legs of the corresponding stitch on the top piece, lining up the stitches with the bottom piece.

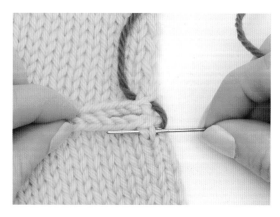

Although worked from the RS of the fabric, as the stitches are sewn they cover the cast-off edges creating a neat, smooth seam.

3
Draw the thread up and make the next stitch by going under both legs of the V on the next stitch on the lower piece.

4
Continue working across the edge – making sure that your tension matches the tension of the knitting – to create a row of sewn stitches that look like knitted stitches. When you reach the end, fasten off neatly on the WS of the work.

JOINING A HORIZONTAL EDGE TO A VERTICAL EDGE

This technique may be required if you are setting in a sleeve where is it necessary to join the vertical armhole stitches to the sleeve cap. In this case, a combination of the ladder stitch and the shoulder seam join is required.

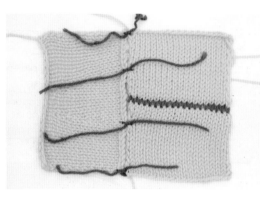
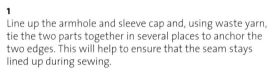

1
Line up the armhole and sleeve cap and, using waste yarn, tie the two parts together in several places to anchor the two edges. This will help to ensure that the seam stays lined up during sewing.

2
Starting at the RH sleeve edge, work a fake grafting stitch (see opposite) on the (horizontal) sleeve cap and a ladder stitch on the armhole (vertical) edge. To keep the seam even, it may be necessary to go under two or three bars on the vertical edge for each stitch on the horizontal edge.

Combining ladder stitch along the vertical edge with fake grafting along the horizontal edge maintains a neat, straight line along both sections, giving a smooth, attractive join.

3
Work a ladder stitch (see pages 90–91) on the vertical armhole edge.

Grafting

Grafting is a technique used to join two pieces of knitting to give a virtually invisible finish. Also referred to as Kitchener stitch, it is used for sock toes, shoulder seams, alterations and joins where normal sewing would be unsightly or too bulky. Grafting can take practice; however, once you have mastered the basic principles, you will quickly get the hang of this useful joining method. It may be used where there are an equal number of live stitches to join together on either side. Live stitches are ones that are still on the needles or on a holder and have not been cast off or finished. In effect, grafting replicates a row of knitted stitches, creating an extra row of stitches between two pieces of knitting to join them together.

Unlike many other joining techniques, grafting is carried out on the right side of the work. Usually, it is worked on the knit (right) side of a stocking-stitch fabric. It is also possible to use grafting when repairing knits, particularly when replacing worn heels, elbows or worn patches in garments. Grafting is usually done while the knitting is on the needles but some knitters find it easier to put the stitches on a piece of waste yarn and work with the knitted pieces flat.

The following sequences show grafting with the work on the needles, working on the knit side of stocking stitch.

Two pieces of knitting are joined together by an extra row of stitches on the knit side.

SETTING UP
To join two flat pieces of knitting you need to transfer the stitches onto two double-pointed needles, one for each piece. Here, pink yarn is used to show clearly the stitches, but you would use the same colour yarn as your knitting, in practice.

CLIP 10
The grafting technique

1
Take the two pieces of knitting and place the stitches for each piece on separate needles.

2
Leaving a yarn tail long enough to weave through all the stitches (about four times the length of the seam), cut off the working yarn and thread it onto a tapestry needle.

www.youtube.com/watch?v=NahPapkHwDo

3
Hold the needles alongside one another in your LH with the WS of the work together. The working yarn should be on the back needle to the RH end. (Note that if you are working with two flat pieces you will have two working yarns, one for each piece. Trim one of the two yarns, leaving about 20cm/8in for darning in later, then cut the second yarn as described in step 2 and use this as your working yarn.) Hold the tapestry needle in your RH, ready to make your stitches.

Use a blunt-ended needle to avoid splitting the stitches as you work.

FOUNDATION STITCHES
Grafting begins with two foundation stitches, which are worked just once.

Take the tapestry needle below the work to avoid the yarn looping over the top of the needles.

1
Pass the tapestry needle through the first stitch on the front knitting needle as if to purl. Draw the yarn up. Leave the stitch on the needle.

2
Pass the tapestry needle through the first stitch on the back needle as if to knit. Draw the yarn up. Be careful to take the yarn below and behind the front knitting needle, making sure it isn't looped over the front knitting needle. Leave the stitch on the needle.

STITCH SET

Next follows a series of paired stitches that are worked into the stitches on the front and back needles alternately, two on the front, two on the back.

Note that you should have gone through this stitch twice – purlwise in foundation step 1 (see page 95), then here, knitwise.

NOTES
The following may be helpful as a reminder. After the foundation stitches, the steps are as follows:

Front knit, slide, front purl.
Back purl, slide, back knit.
Repeat.

1
Bring the yarn to the front of the work and pass it through the first stitch as if to knit.

2
Slide this stitch carefully off the needle.

3
Take the yarn through the next stitch on the front needle as if to purl. Draw the yarn up. Don't slide this stitch off the needle just yet.

Again, note how this stitch has been worked into twice before being taken off the needle – knitwise in the foundation and purlwise here.

4
Pass the yarn through the first stitch on the back needle as if to purl.

5
Slide this stitch carefully off the needle.

6
Take the yarn through the next stitch on the back needle as if to knit. Don't slide this stitch off the needle just yet.

7
Repeat the stitch set until you reach the last stitch. To finish, take the yarn through the final stitch on the back needle as if to purl. Slide this stitch off the needle and fasten off neatly.

Picking up stitches

Professional finishing can be the difference between a garment fit for the catwalk and one destined for the back of the wardrobe. The key features of a well-finished garment are the edgings, bands and necklines: these are commonly made by lifting, or picking up, the stitches along garment edges and knitting into them.

The beauty of this technique is that by using existing stitches there is no need for seaming or sewing up, which gives a neater result. Picking up stitches allows knitted edges to travel in a different direction to the main knitting. Contrasting yarns and interesting stitch combinations can also be incorporated into a picked-up edging, allowing designers to add stylish features and originality to an otherwise simple design.

Picked-up edges, when used as a base for fasteners such as buttonhole bands or cords, have a practical function because they give a garment extra stability, shape or structure. Stitches may also be picked up around armholes in order to knit sleeves from the armhole to the cuff, along sock heel flaps, to create fingers in gloves, and more besides. Key features of a garment can be emphasised by the use of a picked-up edging.

Many knitters find picking up stitches particularly challenging and are often frustrated by the appearance of the edgings on their knits. However, there are some straightforward techniques that can solve this problem and, with a little practice, it is possible not only to achieve a great finish but even to add customised edgings and finishes.

PICK UP AND KNIT ALONG A STRAIGHT, VERTICAL EDGE

The principles for picking up stitches along a vertical edge can be applied to most fabrics. If the designer intends the knitter to pick up stitches along an edge, the pattern will normally have plain stitches along the edge of the main fabric to make this process neater and easier.

Remember to allow for any adjustments you may have made to the length of a garment. If you have knitted extra or fewer rows you may well need to pick up more or fewer stitches than stated in the pattern.

**CLIP 11
Picking up stitches**

www.youtube.com/watch?v=5XNs0XSXVh4

Use large-headed, contrasting-coloured pins that can be seen easily against your knitting.

1
To add an edging along the straight, vertical front edge of a garment, begin by measuring the edge and dividing it into manageable sections. Mark each end with a pin. Mark the halfway point between the two pins, dividing the edge into two sections. Repeat, dividing each section until the sections are about 10–15cm (4–6in) apart.

The V-shaped knit stitches will be used as the basis for the new knitting.

2
Calculate the number of stitches to be picked up in each section by dividing the total number of stitches by the number of sections (in this case, four). Count the number of rows of knitting in each section. This will give an indication as to whether a stitch will be picked up from each row. As a rule, a stitch will be made into three out of every four rows rather than one per row. Too many stitches will make the band spread and flare out. Too few stitches will cause the band to pull in and pucker.

3
When working in stocking stitch the work, when held upright, will be made up of V-shaped stitches. Turn the work on its side and stitches will be picked up sideways into these stitches. This will produce a new knitted fabric that grows at right angles to the main knitting.

4
Holding the work in the LH with the RS facing, start picking up stitches along the edge, beginning at the end nearest to you. With a knitting needle in your RH, insert the needle under both 'legs' (see Stitch Legs, page 101) of the second V-shaped stitch on the first row of knitting. Work one stitch in from the edge of the knitting because the very edge stitch may be loose and will give an uneven result.

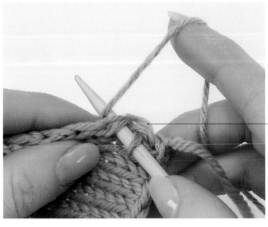

Picking up both legs of the stitch provides a firm edge, which acts as a good base for a buttonhole band or jacket edging.

5
Keeping a tail of yarn to the right (about 20cm/8in or so), wrap the yarn around the needle as if to knit and draw the loop of yarn through the V-shaped stitch. That's one stitch picked up and knitted.

6
Insert the needle under both loops of the next V and wrap the working yarn around the needle, again as if to knit, and draw the loop through the V. That's two stitches picked up and knitted.

Note that it may not be necessary to pick up a stitch in every row of the main knitting.

7
Continue in this way, checking that the number of stitches picked up and knitted in each section is the same as the number calculated in step 2. Once all the stitches have been picked up and knitted, turn the work and continue working according to the pattern.

PICKING UP STITCHES

This technique differs from picking up and knitting in that the stitches are picked up from the edge and placed onto a needle without being knitted. It can be used where stitches are picked up along an edge and the knitting is to continue in the same direction as the main fabric. In addition, it can be used in the same way as picking up and knitting in order to work stitches in a different direction. It is useful for finer knits because it gives a softer, more elastic edge, but may not be firm enough for heavier garments where a solid edge is needed, for example, on a button band.

This technique gives a softer, more elastic edge because only one leg of each stitch is lifted.

1
With RS of work facing and starting at the RH edge of the piece, pick up just the RH leg of each stitch from the main knitting and lift it onto the RH needle.

2
Once the stitches have been picked up, turn the work, join in the yarn and continue knitting.

STITCH LEGS

Stitches are described as having two legs. Imagine a cowboy sitting astride a horse: the cowboy's legs are the loop of yarn, the horse is the needle. One leg goes either side of the needle. The front (RH) leg is the half of the loop of yarn facing you; the back (LH) leg is the half of the loop going down behind the needle.

TIPS

- **If you find it difficult to pick up the stitches with a knitting needle,** use a small crochet hook to catch the loop of yarn behind the work and draw it through. Put each hooked loop onto the RH needle.

- **If you have adjusted your pattern by lengthening/shortening the garment** it may be necessary to adjust the number of stitches to be picked up and knitted accordingly. In this case, calculate how many stitches you are making per centimetre (or inch) and add/subtract the same number of stitches being picked up and knitted for each centimetre (or inch) of lengthening/shortening.

- **Check the wording of the pattern carefully:** there is a difference between picking up stitches and picking up and knitting stitches.

- **With certain fabrics, when picking up and knitting** it gives a smoother edge to work into just the RH leg of the stitch. However, the stitch should still be picked up and knitted one stitch in from the edge.

- **When working along a vertical edge** check that the stitches follow the same line of Vs for a nice, straight line.

Neat necklines and perfect bands

As with straight edging bands, successful necklines and shaped bands can really make or break a garment. With many neckline styles the techniques involved are essentially the same as those for picked-up stitches (see pages 98–101) but with a few extra tweaks to allow for the curves and angles. Some necklines, however, are stitched on.

Because many necklines benefit from having a seamless transition from the main garment, using existing stitches means there is no need for seaming or sewing up, which gives a neater result. Picking up stitches allows knitted edges to travel in a different direction to the main knitting, essential when working around curves. Picking up around a neckline ensures a good fit and can be used as the basis for a wide range of neckline styles and collars (V-necks, round or crew necks, polo necks and so on).

Certain collar types, hoods and some patterns where the designer wants to add particular stylistic features, however, are stitched on. In this case, careful attention to placing, pinning and stitching is required.

A neckline usually involves straight sections, curves and possibly diagonals all in the one piece. For this reason, necklines often need shaping as the neck develops. Because many jacket or cardigan fronts

may also have shaped edges, it is useful to be able to produce a neat band that can be stretched around a curve.

PICK UP AND KNIT ALONG A STRAIGHT, VERTICAL EDGE

Straight, vertical edgings along a neckline can be picked up in the same way as for vertical bands (see pages 98–99). Depending on the garment, however, it may be appropriate to work through just one leg of the V-shaped stitch rather than both to give a less bulky look. This is usually the leg nearest the open edge.

PICKING UP AROUND A CURVE

When picking up around a curve (or going from a straight edge to a curve) use the same technique as for a straight edge (see pages 98–101) but, as stitches are picked up, aim to pick up (and knit if appropriate) one stitch for each row of the knitting. This can be difficult to see but if the garment is held at an angle, it is usually possible to follow the line of the knitted rows and ensure that each row has a picked-up stitch.

CLIP 12
**Picking up
stitches along
a neckline**

www.youtube.com/watch?v=5iNI2s304NY

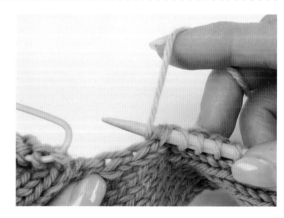

1
When the work begins to curve, holding the work with RS facing in the LH, insert the tip of the RH needle one stitch in from the edge of the garment. For a pick up and knit, loop the working yarn around the RH needle and draw it through to the front.

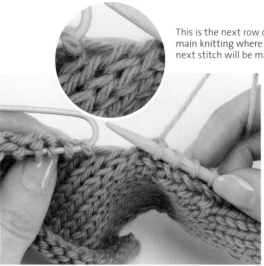

This is the next row of the main knitting where the next stitch will be made.

Make a note of where the extra stitches are either by counting or by placing a marker either side of the extra stitch.

2
Repeat this process, picking up and knitting one stitch for each row of knitting in the main garment.

3
Where the garment turns at right angles (usually where the bottom of the neckline is reached and the stitches go along the front neck), it may be necessary to pick up an extra stitch (sometimes two stitches) on the turn, in order to prevent a hole. On the next row decrease to remove the extra stitch(es) and return the stitch count to the correct number.

4
The next section of a neckline may require stitches to be transferred from a stitch holder (for example, on a round or crew neck). In this case, place the stitches on a needle with the RH edge to the front of the needle.

5
Knit across these stitches.

Working up the curve, use the rows of the main knitting to guide the positioning of your picked-up stitches. Pick up extra stitches, if necessary, and decrease on the following row.

6
Continue around the curve that forms the second part of the front neck, usually up the RH edge as viewed from the front.

Aim for a smooth transition from curve to straight edge, and check for gaps or puckering.

7
Work up the RH facing edge as for a straight edge, aiming to pick up and knit along the same line of stitches in order to maintain a neat edge.

- **Even if the rest of the garment isn't worked in the round,** a neckline may be, since it avoids a seam in the neckband. Your pattern will tell you if this is the case.

- **Check your pattern** to see which seams you need to sew up before making the neckline, because this can vary from pattern to pattern.

- **If you feel you need to pick up more or fewer stitches than stated in the pattern** to avoid holes or to avoid the knitting flaring out, don't be overly concerned. Sometimes, particularly if you have made adjustments elsewhere or if your row tension isn't exactly the same as the pattern (see page 39), this may be necessary. A little more attention may simply be required to ensure that any pattern in the neckband still matches up. For example, to avoid two adjacent purls or knits in a k1, p1 rib, add or remove one stitch.

8
At the shoulder it may be necessary to add an extra picked-up stitch, in this case to take the knitting smoothly over the shoulder seam. Again, this can be adjusted by decreasing on the next row.

9
Continue picking up and knitting around the neckline until all the stitches have been made.

Once the stitches are all picked up, check for any holes, puckers or untidy edges. If necessary, take back the work to ensure you get this stage right.

Fastenings

Knitted items may be closed with zips or a range of drawstrings and ties. When correctly attached, zips provide a neat fastening with no bulky layers. Ties and drawstrings provide a decorative effect, and buttons can be either functional or decorative.

Zips

As long as care is taken when assembling a garment, zips can be very effective. If needed, use a woven tape to help stabilise the knitted fabric when sewing the zip in.

Choose the weight of zip to suit the knitting. Lightweight, dressmaking zips will suit lightweight knits. For bulky knits you may prefer a heavyweight zip, or you can make a feature of a brass jeans zip (short lengths only). Zips range from 15cm (6in) to 76cm (30in), although you can buy other speciality sizes. The zip should never be longer than the knitted edge; otherwise it will stretch the knitting. It is better to choose a slightly shorter zip and leave a few rows of knitting unattached at the end than to choose one that is too long. It is better still to purchase the zip and then make the opening in the knitting to the length required. Choose a colour to tone with the knitting. If in doubt, a darker shade will usually look better than a lighter shade.

ATTACHING A ZIP

Zips should be sewn in place by hand. The vest front shown below is finished with a garter-stitch border, although a border is not necessary – a zip can be placed directly between any two knitted edges. A two-stitch garter selvedge or a single-crochet edge will give a neat finish.

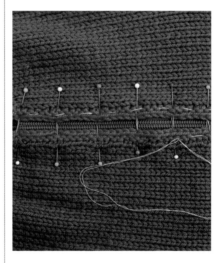

1
With the RS of the knitting facing you, place one edge just touching the zip teeth. Knitting should not be stretched. Pin in place with pins at right angles to the edge. Use a sharp sewing needle and contrasting sewing thread to tack the zip in place. Tack the top end of the zip out of the way (see step 4). Pin and tack the other knitted edge in the same way. (Make sure any patterning or stripes match up exactly.)

2
With the WS up, overcast (oversew or whip stitch) the outer edge of the zip to the WS of the knitting (see page 89). Pink thread is used here for clarity, but you should use thread to match the knitting yarn.

DECORATE YOUR ZIP PULL

You can purchase special decorative zip pulls or make your own with beads, as on the pull shown in step 4 (see opposite). Avoid decorating a zip with pompons, tassels or anything that is likely to catch in the teeth.

3
With the RS up, backstitch close to the knitted edge: this garter-stitch border is backstitched just below the cast off; on a side edge, backstitch one-half of a stitch in from the edge. Remove the tacking.

4
On this V-neck, the fabric tags at the top of the zip are tucked sideways, beneath the knitted edge. On a round-necked garment, you may prefer to fold the tags back at a right angle.

Ties and drawstrings

Garments can also be fastened with one or more pairs of ties, made from I-cords, twisted cords, plaits, crochet or purchased ribbons. Drawstrings are usually threaded through rows of eyelets. They may be used to secure a purse or to shape the waistline or the neckline of a garment.

The drawstring for this purse is an I-cord, threaded through a row of eyelets and finished with contrasting pompoms (page 212).

This edge-to-edge jacket is tied at centre front with braided ties made from embroidery floss, finished with tassels and beads.

Buttons

Search for buttons that are appropriate for your design, perhaps by visiting vintage shops, markets or online stores to source interesting and unusual examples. You can also buy kits that allow you to cover buttons to match your knitted garments. See also pages 150–153.

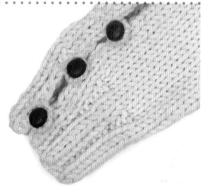

Add interest to a cuff by using more than the required number of buttons.

Hooks and eyes

An interesting alternative to buttons, hooks and eyes now come in a variety of sizes and finishes, from metal to plastic, and can be used with knitted tapes to fasten a garment.

Care of knitted items

Take time to clean your knitted items properly – after all, you've taken the time to knit them. Different fibres require different treatments: nowadays, ball bands should carry all the necessary information you need.

Consider saving a ball band from each yarn used in a project for future reference, or try sewing care labels into your garments, to help you keep track of aftercare requirements.
- If an item is stained, spot-treat the stain before washing.
- Test any process on a tension swatch that includes all the yarns used for a project.
- If an item needs repairing, do this before washing or dry cleaning. To be prepared for future repairs, keep a small ball of each yarn and wash it in a net laundry bag each time you wash the item, so the colours will always match.
- Fasten all buttons or other fastenings before washing. Pocket openings and front bands may also be tacked closed so they cannot stretch out of shape during washing.

Hand washing
Wash and rinse the work carefully by hand, and lay it flat on a towel or a mesh drying screen. Pat the garment out to match the original measurements. Turning the garment over before it is completely dry will speed the drying process. When dry, the item may be lightly pressed. Always consult the instructions on the ball band(s) for the correct temperature setting.

Machine washing
Many modern yarns are now labelled 'machine-washable' or 'superwash'. The ball band should tell you the maximum machine temperature to use. Dry as for hand washing unless the label specifies that the yarn may be machine-dried.

International care symbols
These symbols may be found on ball bands.

Hand washing	Machine washing	Bleaching	Pressing	Dry cleaning
Do not wash by hand or machine	Machine-washable in warm water at stated temperature (86°F / 30°)	Do not bleach	Do not press	Do not dry clean
Hand-washable in warm water at stated temperature	Machine-washable in warm water at stated temperature, short spin (86°F / 30°)	Bleaching permitted (with chlorine) (CL)	Press with a cool iron	May be dry cleaned with all solutions (A)
	Machine-washable in warm water at stated temperature, cool rinse, and short spin (104°F / 40°)		Press with a warm iron	May be dry cleaned with perchlorethylene, fluorocarbon or petroleum-based solvents (P)
			Press with a hot iron	May be dry cleaned with fluorocarbon or petroleum-based solvents only (F)

Dry cleaning

Most modern yarns may also be dry cleaned. Take care to remove any trims, such as buttons or ribbons, if these are not dry-cleanable. After cleaning, remove any plastic wrapping and hang the garment for a few hours in a well-ventilated place, away from direct sunlight: use a mesh drying screen, or a padded coat-hanger, or lay the garment over a solid rod (not a washing line) and turn it once or twice.

Storing knitwear

Fold and store your knitwear correctly to avoid creasing, loss of shape and fading.
- Always wash or clean before storing.
- Never hang knitted garments on coat hangers since they will drop out of shape.
- Keep folded knits away from heat, damp, dust and direct sunlight. A drawer or chest is ideal.
- Do not squash folded knits; instead they should be loosely stacked.

FLUFFY YARN LOOKS FLAT AFTER WASHING?
Garments made from mohair yarns and similar blends may be lightly brushed with a teasel brush to raise the pile and restore the fluffy appearance. Angora garments will fluff up again after a couple of hours in a plastic bag placed in the freezer.

- Natural animal fibres such as wool and mohair attract moths, so you may wish to use moth prevention. Cotton fibres and synthetics do not attract moths.
- For long-term storage, place tissue paper on top of the unfolded garment and fold as shown below. Loosely wrap each sweater with more tissue paper to allow air to circulate.

HOW TO FOLD KNITWEAR

The folding methods detailed here are for light-to medium-weight garments (purple sweater) and bulky sweaters, drop-shoulder shapes and straight armhole shapes (cream sweater). Jackets may be folded in the same way after fastening the fronts together.

Folding a bulky sweater

Lay the sweater front side down on a flat surface. Fold one sleeve and one-quarter of the front towards the back so the side seam is at centre-back. Fold the sleeve downwards. Fold the other half of the sweater in the same way.

Folding a basic sweater

Lay the sweater front side down on a flat surface. Fold back each sleeve in line with the side seam.

To finish

Fold the lower edge up to meet the shoulder line. Turn over.

taking it to the
next level

Ready to go beyond the basics? Then look no further. Having myriad methods at your disposal will help you to pick the right one for the job at hand, and then there's always that little bit extra you can add to embellish a deserving knit.

Adapting to fit

In the clothing industry, garments are designed to fit a standard body. In reality, of course, very few of us share all the same measurements as this 'standard body', but designers can't design to suit every silhouette, so knitters have to be prepared to take matters into their own hands. Thankfully, with knitting patterns this is relatively straightforward.

There are two common reasons for altering a pattern. The first is out of necessity – the problem that strikes terror into any knitter's heart – running out of yarn. See pages 20–25 for suggestions on how to deal with this issue. The second is to alter a pattern for style reasons – you might like most of a garment but not one or two aspects of it, or you might have, for example, a longer than average torso or shorter than average arms. Altering a pattern has the advantage that it is pre-planned and usually takes place before knitting begins.

Understanding your pattern – measuring

With most garment patterns there will be two sets of measurements – the actual measurements and the 'to fit' sizing. You will find more information on this aspect of patterns on pages 32–33. Accurate measuring is crucial to a good fit. Fudging your measurements means your garment won't flatter your figure, so respect your size and record it accurately. It's a good idea to record your measurements somewhere that you can always refer to them, perhaps in your diary/phone/notebook or on a piece of card in your purse. Knowing your measurements means that you will buy the right amount of yarn for your patterns and you shouldn't run out of yarn three-quarters of the way up the last sleeve!

With your measurements at hand, compare these to the key measurements given in the pattern. Which areas do you want or need to adjust?

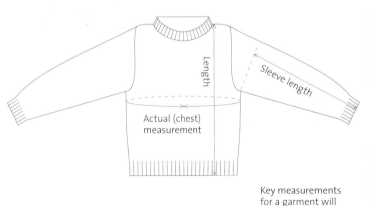

Key measurements for a garment will be shown on a schematic similar to the one on the right for the drop-sleeve, round-necked jumper above.

Sizing

To fit bust/chest	81cm 32in	86cm 34in	92cm 36in	97cm 38in
Actual measurement	92cm 36in	97cm 38in	102cm 40in	107cm 42in
Length	50.2cm 20in	56cm 22in	58.5cm 23in	59.5cm 23½in
Sleeve length	40.5cm 16in	43cm 17in	44.5cm 17½in	46cm 18in

Body length

With a simple pattern, body length can usually be adjusted by knitting fewer or more rows to make the garment the correct length. When adjusting body length, it is advisable to adjust at a straight section of the pattern.

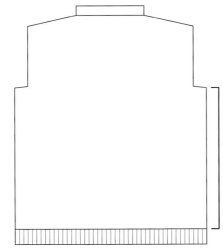

With a straight, plain fabric add length in this section.

Pattern band

If a garment has a pattern band, motif or other distinctive patterning, place any adjustment where it will be least obvious and pay attention to the balance and proportion of the garment. For example, a central motif may need to have rows added/ removed both below and above the motif to ensure it remains central on the garment. Pay attention to pattern repeats. If possible, remove or add a complete pattern repeat since these may have been designed to match the sleeve to the front.

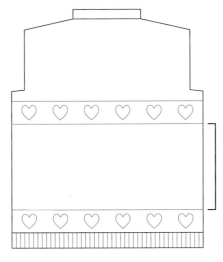

When lengthening a garment with a motif or band, make adjustments where it won't displace the motif. For example, adjusting in this section would be the best place.

TIPS

- **Make careful notes of any pattern changes** so that the front and back match.

- **Note also that any bands may need to be shortened/ lengthened** and fewer/more stitches picked up along any front edges.

- **If you are making complex changes involving pattern repeats or motifs,** consider using knitter's graph paper to chart the pattern pieces and marking changes to ensure you have matching repeats across all the pieces.

- **With simpler sleeve shapes, such as set-in or drop styles,** sleeves can be made slimmer or wider using the chart method (see page 115); however, armhole depth will also need to be adjusted. The armhole depth will be half the width of the sleeve at the top.

- **The same considerations with regard to patterning and making note of any changes** apply equally to sleeves as to body pieces.

Sleeves

Sleeves can usually be lengthened or shortened in the straight area where the shaping has been completed and before any set-in, raglan or similar shaping begins. Often this will be indicated in the pattern.

If a sleeve needs to be substantially shortened, it may be necessary to recalculate the spacing of the increases. The easiest way to do this is by using a chart (see opposite).

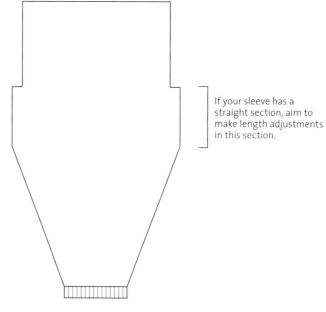

If your sleeve has a straight section, aim to make length adjustments in this section.

Necklines

Charts can be used to reshape necklines, for example, to convert a V-neck to a round neck. Bear in mind, however, the impact this may have on the overall look of the garment and the positioning of any patterning.

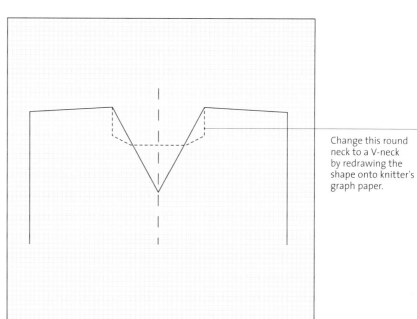

Change this round neck to a V-neck by redrawing the shape onto knitter's graph paper.

CHARTED METHOD – SLEEVE

Don't be deterred by the mathematical look of this chart. Taking it step by step, following the instructions given below, makes it a fairly simple process. All you need is knitter's graph paper, a measuring tape, a pencil and an eraser.

1
Draw the original sleeve onto knitter's graph paper printed to the correct tension. Draw a line horizontally across the start of the armhole (A).

2
Measure the desired length from here to the cuff, along the centre line of the sleeve (B). Along this line mark out the new cuff position, centring it along the centre line of the sleeve and making sure the new cuff has the same number of stitches as the existing cuff (C).

3
Working lightly in pencil, join the new cuff edges to the armhole, redrawing the sleeve shape shown by the solid line. Use this line as the basis for the new sleeve shaping and knit the sleeves from the chart.

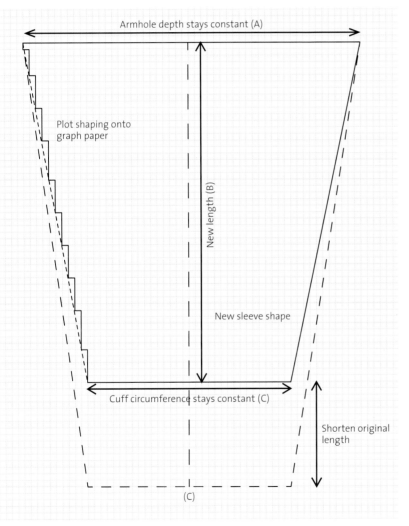

Armhole depth stays constant (A)

Plot shaping onto graph paper

New length (B)

New sleeve shape

Cuff circumference stays constant (C)

(C)

Shorten original length

– – – – – Original sleeve shaping

GENERAL CONSIDERATIONS

- **Check pieces as you knit them.** Block and measure each piece to the pattern or to your notes as you complete it. Hold it up or try it on before proceeding to the next piece. If you have a garment with a similar fit, lay it on top of the garment for a quick comparison.

- **Before sewing up,** pin or tack pieces together and try on; it is easier to unpick an individual piece than a complete garment.

- **Knit stitches are rarely square, so be sure to use knitter's graph paper** (available free on several websites) printed to the correct tension for your knitting. This will ensure any adjustments are correctly proportioned.

Choosing the right cast on

The humble cast on is an essential yet often undervalued technique. Knowing two key methods will get you started with most projects, but having an array to choose from at your fingertips will bring surefire success and professional end results.

Knitters will happily tackle any number of complex patterns and stitches, learning new ones all the time, but will often use just one, or perhaps two, cast-on methods for all their projects. But why is this so? Is it eagerness to 'get stuck in' that means this vital part of the knitting process is often taken for granted? Or perhaps there is a sense that once a method has been learned there is no need to 'fix' what isn't broken?

An unsuitable cast-on method is often not apparent until a garment is finished. It is then difficult to correct and is perhaps one reason why beginner knitters are often disappointed with their completed knits. It is also the case that beginner knitters are sometimes taught only one, or possibly two methods, so they blame themselves for an over-tight or baggy cast-on row without realizing other, more suitable, methods exist that could have solved the problem.

How to choose a particular cast on

A cast on may be chosen for practical reasons, for decorative effect or both. You must consider the nature and function of the finished article. Use this chart to help you decide on the appropriate technique for your project.

Effect	Technique	Useful for
Firm	Long-tail/thumb, page 46	Soft furnishings, soft toys
	Knitted/two-needle, page 47	Soft furnishings, soft toys
	I-cord, pages 118–121	Cast-on edge, sides of knitted fabric, cast-off edge
	Cast-off cast on, page 54	Matches standard chain cast off
	Alternate cable, page 55	K1, p1 and wider ribs, decorative edgings
	Cable, page 55	K1, p1 and wider ribs, decorative edgings
Elastic	Tubular, page 49	Ribs, sock cuffs
	Alternate cable, page 55	K1, p1 and wider ribs, decorative edgings, sock cuffs
	Cable, page 55	K1, p1 and wider ribs, decorative edgings
Invisible/seamless	Figure eight, page 117–118	Toes on socks
	Backward loop/twisted, page 48	Soft edgings on lacy pieces
	Tubular, page 49	Ribs
Provisional/ temporary	Tubular, page 49	Ribs
	Provisional/temporary with crochet hook, pages 50–51	Joining, adding edging
Decorative	I-cord, pages 118–121	Cast-on edge, sides of knitted fabric, cast-off edge
Specialist	Pinhole/Emily Ocker, pages 52–53	Circular-knitted hats, shawls, tablecloths

Alternative methods for casting on

In addition to the more familiar casting-on techniques (see pages 44–55), there is a wide variety of alternative methods. Here are just a couple.

FIGURE-EIGHT CAST ON
A figure-eight cast on is a way of making an invisible, seamless toe when knitting socks from the toe up. The name comes from the way in which the yarn is wrapped around the needles in a figure-eight. To work this cast on you will need three DPNs in the same size as for your sock, plus your yarn.

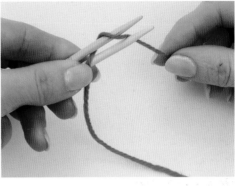

1
In your left hand, hold your two DPNs alongside one another. Hold the tail yarn firmly at the front of the bottom needle with your left thumb, keeping the tail to the left and the working yarn to the right. Take the working yarn over the bottom needle and down between the two DPNs.

2
Take the working yarn under and around the top needle from back to front, then take the working yarn back down between the two needles. You should have a loop of yarn on the top needle. This is your first stitch.

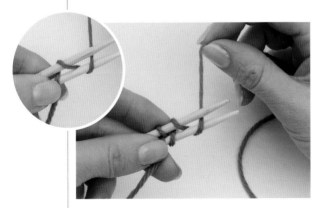

3
Now make a stitch on the bottom needle by bringing the working yarn under and around the bottom needle. Then take it from front to back and back down between the two DPNs. Repeat, making stitches on the top and bottom needles alternately, wrapping the yarn using a figure-eight motion.

4
You will need half the total number of cast-on stitches on each needle. So, if your pattern calls for eight stitches in total, you will need four stitches on each needle. You should always have an even number of stitches on each needle, finishing with the last loop on the bottom needle and the working yarn going from front to back between the needles.

- **If your cast-on edge is always too tight,** try going up a needle size for the casting on only. Likewise, if it is too loose, try a size smaller needle.

- **If you are unsure which casting-on method to use,** make small samples before beginning. Try starting on a WS row rather than a right-side row to see how this affects the look.

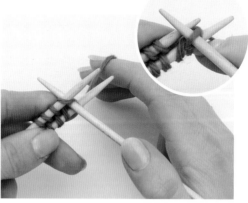

5
To knit your first row, take the working yarn and, using a third DPN, knit into each stitch on the top needle as usual. At this stage the stitches on the bottom needle may be rather loose. Use your third DPN to gently pull the loops tight, working from right to left.

6
With the loops tightened, turn the work through 180 degrees so that the bottom needle is now at the top. Take care not to flip the work over. Keep the tail yarn over the bottom needle and between the needles to stop the stitches from loosening. Knit into the back of the stitches on the top needle – you will only need to do this on these stitches, all future rounds are knitted as usual. All the cast-on stitches have now been knitted once and on the second round you can divide them onto three or four needles to continue your toe.

I-CORD CAST ON
I-cord makes a very neat edging, especially for patterns that need a firm but stretchy edge that doesn't curl. I-cord can be used on the cast-on edge, along the sides of a knitted fabric, and even on the cast-off edge. It is possible simply to knit the main fabric and the I-cord separately and sew the I-cord onto the edge during the assembly stage; however, it can be difficult to get an even edge and the sewing can create a bulky edge. A quicker, neater alternative is to integrate an I-cord into your knitting as you work. There are several methods for doing this, but this one is simple, neat, and effective. It can also be extended to work a side-edged I-cord (see page 121) and a cast off.

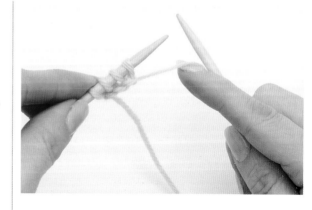

1
Cast on four stitches using your preferred method. Knit the four stitches. Do not turn the work but slip the stitches you have just knitted back onto the LH needle.

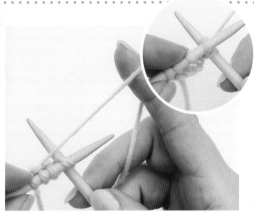

2
Knit twice into the first stitch by knitting first into the front of the stitch and then, without removing the needle from the front loop, knitting into the back of the same stitch (see detail).

3
Drop the stitch off the LH needle. You should have three stitches on the LH needle and two stitches on the RH needle.

Note how the working yarn is coming from the stitch nearest the LH.

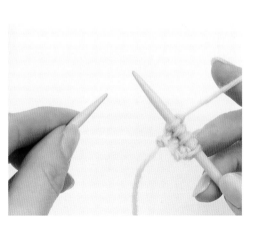

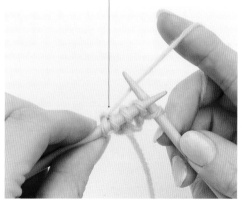

4
Knit the three stitches remaining on the LH needle as usual. You should now have five stitches on the RH needle.

5
Do not turn the work, but slip the first four stitches on the RH needle back onto the LH needle. One stitch remains on the RH needle. This is your first cast-on stitch. Repeat steps 2–5 until you have cast on one stitch fewer than the total number needed. Each time you slip the first four stitches back onto the LH needle you will leave one more stitch behind on the RH needle.

I-CORD TIPS

- **Pull the yarn tightly at the back of the work** to make sure that the I-cord rolls into a proper tube. If you can see a row of loose or baggy stitches you need to pull the yarn tighter when you knit the I-cord stitches.

- **As an alternative to knitting twice into the same stitch,** it is possible to work a yarn over before the first of the I-cord stitches. Each yarn over then creates a cast-on stitch. You could experiment with which method looks best by making a swatch using both techniques. Another method is to make a separate I-cord in the usual way, knitting the same number of rows as there are cast-on stitches in your pattern. Using the main yarn, pick up stitches (see page 101) along the I-cord. Make sure you pick up in a straight line by going into the same row of stitches in the I-cord as you pick up. This is a handy technique for an I-cord cast on in a contrasting colour or different type of yarn – you could even add beads or sequins.

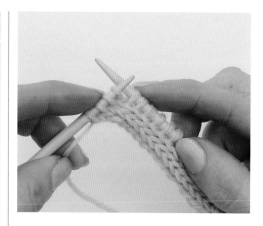

6
Unless you are continuing your I-cord around the edge of the knitting, when you have cast on the desired number of stitches (one fewer than the number required), slip the first four stitches back onto the LH needle as previously.

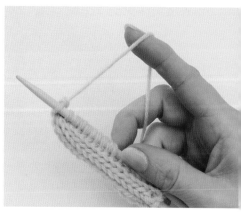

7
Knit the first two stitches together, then knit the next two stitches together. (Two I-cord stitches are now left on the RH needle, plus the cast-on stitches.)

8
Slip the first two stitches on the RH needle back to the LH needle.

9
Knit these two stitches together. The RH needle should now have the correct number of cast-on stitches because the final stitch of the I-cord becomes the last cast-on stitch. You can now turn the work and continue knitting as usual.

INTEGRATING AN I-CORD ALONG THE EDGE OF THE KNITTING

Working extra rows on just the first four stitches creates the curved edge.

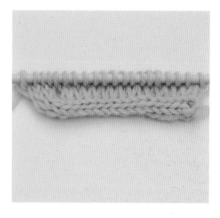

1
To continue working the I-cord along the edge of the knitting (for an integral front edge band, for example), work as on pages 118–120 up to step 7 but continue until you have made the same number of stitches as required for the pattern. Slip the first four stitches on the RH needle to the LH needle and knit these stitches as previously. Repeat this step. These two rows allow the I-cord to curve neatly around the bottom edge of the work, minimising any pulling or puckering.

2
Now turn the work so that the WS is facing you (the purl side if you are working stocking stitch, for example). Slip the first four stitches onto the RH needle purlwise (as if to purl) and purl to the end (or work according to the pattern).

3
Turn the work and knit all stitches, including the I-cord stitches.

4
Repeat steps 2–3, slipping the first four stitches on WS rows and knitting the last four stitches on RS rows. Note how the I-cord curves around the corner of the knitting and travels up the edge alongside the main knitting.

DECORATIVE EDGING

For instructions on how to make this I-cord decorative edging, see page 145.

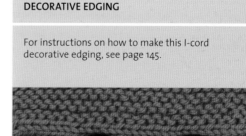

The best increase for the job

There are many variations in the ways an increase is worked, and this can seem confusing, particularly to the beginner. Even knitters more familiar with patterns may prefer to stick to tried-and-tested methods rather than use the one that is most suited to the task at hand. It doesn't have to be this way!

Most increases are based on four simple stitches and, once these have been mastered, any new stitch can be tackled with confidence.

Gradual increases

On occasion it can be appropriate simply to use larger needles to increase the size of a knitted fabric; however, a change in needle size also affects the feel, density and drape of a fabric. This is because the whole of the stitch increases in size when we change needles. So, if the aim is to achieve an increase in a specific area – for example, to widen a sleeve from the narrow cuff to the much wider armhole – it is necessary to add stitches.

Key increase stitches

Increase stitches fall broadly into four categories: bar, lifted, raised and yarn over (see pages 60–67). Where a pattern uses increases, check the listed abbreviations, as these should explain which increase the designer wants you to use.

Double-lifted increases

Use the lifted increase to place two increases side-by-side, work a left-slanting increase first, and a right-slanting increase for the second to make the increases slant towards each other. Swap over for two increases that slant away from each other. A central core stitch can be placed in between, or work the two stitches immediately next to one another.

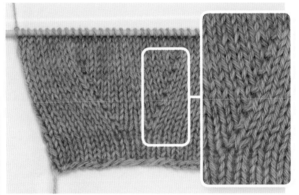

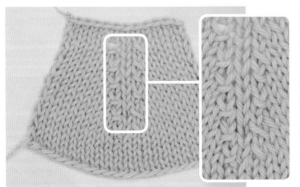

Direction

Different increases create a different look. Some appear to lean to the left, others to the right. If you are working a pair of increases, for example, on either side of a sleeve, you may wish to use a LH slant for one side and a RH slant for the corresponding side.

Visibility

Sleeve increases are usually made to be as unobtrusive as possible, so in this case, two of the least noticeable increases have been used.

Double and multiple increases

For certain patterns it is necessary to make multiple increases. This allows the fabric to grow in both directions, but with the increases focused around a central location. Double increases are likely to be more noticeable than single increases, and multiple increases are often intentionally decorative.

Choosing an increase

If the pattern does not give a specific increasing method, you should be able to place the stitches needed in one of the categories opposite, and from there you should be able to follow the pattern or try out some of the alternatives. Factors in choosing an increase stitch will be the direction of slant or lean, especially if it is to be an unobtrusive increase, or if the increase is to be decorative, which method would be most suited to the task at hand. Use this chart to help you decide on the right increase for your project.

STITCH DIRECTION
All references to stitch direction are to appearance from knit (RS) of work when worked in stocking stitch.

Effect	Increase technique	Useful for
Decorative		
Right slant	Knitted bar increase – kfb/ kf&b/ ktw, page 60	Bump to left of increase
Left slant	Purled bar increase – pfb/ pf&b/ ptw, page 61	Bump to right of increase
	Yarn-over increase (purled or knitted) – yo, yrn, yf, yfwd, wyif, yon, page 66	Creates holes in lace
No slant	Multiple increase using cable cast on – can be added to left or right of main stitches, page 67	Buttonholes
	Double yarn-over and decorative multiple increase (knitted or purled) – dyo, yo2, yo3, yo4, etc., pages 124–125	Decorative patterns and lace
Invisible		
Right slant	Knitted lifted increase – klr inc, page 62	
	Purled lifted increase – plr inc, page 63	
	Knitted raised increase – m1/m1f, page 64	
	Purled raised increase – pm1/pm1f, page 65	
Left slant	Knitted lifted increase – kll inc, page 62	
	Purled lifted increase – pll inc, page 63	
	Knitted raised increase – m1b, page 64	
	Purled raised increase – pm1b, page 65	

Further methods for increasing

In addition to the more familiar increases (see pages 60–67), here are some equally useful techniques to apply to your knitting.

DOUBLE YARN-OVER INCREASE

This is effectively a yarn-over increase 'sandwiched' between the stitches of a standard bar increase. The stitch is worked as normal, a yarn over made, then the same stitch is worked again.

1 On a knit row
K1 but do not drop the stitch from the LH needle.

2
Make a yo by taking the yarn from back to front over the RH needle.

3
Knit again into the same stitch and drop off the needle.

Working several times into the same stitch in this way will create a noticeable hole, so the technique is normally used for decorative effect.

4
When the stitch has been completed there are two extra stitches, one formed by the yo, the second by knitting for a second time into the original stitch.

TIPS

- **Shaping at the edge of a garment** is neater if worked one or two stitches in from the edge.

- **Use stitch markers** to indicate where decreases or increases start and finish. It helps with measuring when matching sections of a garment (for example, two sleeves), and with assembly.

- **If you don't want to spoil your original pattern,** for sizing and more complicated repeat patterns, photocopy your chart/pattern and use highlighter pens to indicate the size you are working to, and to mark off your rows as you work them.

Loosen the stitches a little when working multiple increases because the work can become tight and slip off the needles.

◄ **On a purl row**
P1 but do not drop the stitch from the LH needle.

2
Make a yo by taking the yarn from front to back over the RH needle.

3
Purl again into the same stitch.

4
Drop the stitch off the LH needle. Two new stitches have been made, one from the yo, the second by working twice into the same stitch.

Increasing and decreasing for decorative effects
Many stitch patterns rely on combinations of increase and decrease stitches for their decorative effect. These patterns require a balance of increases and decreases if the edges are to be kept straight! This may mean that not every row will have the same number of stitches but the pattern repeat should begin and end with the same number of stitches, because otherwise the fabric will continue to get wider or narrower.

DECORATIVE INCREASES
This multiple increase is a variant on the double yarn-over increase (see opposite) and creates an interesting effect most often used in lace and textured patterns.

For a six-stitch increase on a knit row
K1, yo three times into the same stitch, then knit into the stitch a final time and drop it off the needle.

For a six-stitch increase on a purl row
P1, yo three times into the same stitch, then purl into the stitch a final time and drop it off the needle.

Which decrease and why

When reading a pattern you may well wonder why designers choose specific shaping techniques. What influences their choice? Would it matter if you 'ssk'd' when the pattern says to 'k2tog', and if so, why?

Decreasing techniques are used in less obvious ways than simply to make an item smaller. For example, with lace stitches decreases are paired with increases to make sure the knitting stays the same size. Decreases may also change the direction of a piece, for example, with zigzags and chevron patterns. Combining decreases and increases also allows designers to create interesting effects – making a blanket square from two triangles, for example, can change the overall look without affecting the finished shape.

Making knitting smaller

The most familiar way to reduce the size of a knitted fabric is by reducing the number of stitches. In some circumstances, however, a fabric's dimensions can be altered simply by changing needle size and also by using different stitch combinations.

Choosing your decrease

Primarily, a decrease is chosen for its functionality – whether it slants to the left or the right and whether it's decorative or almost invisible. However, there are some alternative methods of decreasing, looked at here, which come to hand in certain situations.

Effect	Decrease technique
Decorative	
Right slant	Purl two together – p2tog, page 70
	Slip one, purl one, pass slipped stitch over – sl1, p1, psso, page 70
Left slant	Slip one, knit one, pass slipped stitch over – sl1, k1, psso, page 69
Invisible	
Right slant	Knit two together – k2tog, page 68
	Slip, slip, purl – ssp, page 71
Left slant	Slip, slip, knit – ssk, page 69

Effect	Alternative technique	Useful for
To make smaller, more compact stitch sizes within a pattern	Smaller needle size, page 127	Cuffs, edgings, nipping in a waistline
Making work smaller by using a different stitch pattern but without changing stitch numbers	Changing stitch, page 128	Decorative shaping, cuffs, edgings, waistline
Large-scale decrease	Cast-off decrease, page 128	Necklines; larger openings for zips, pockets, buttonholes and fasteners

Changing needle size

Many patterns use a smaller needle for a cuff or edging, changing to a larger size for the body of the garment. A smaller needle makes the stitches smaller and more compact, giving a snugger fit. Changing to a larger needle makes each stitch larger and so makes the fabric both taller and wider but without altering the number of stitches.

This technique can also be used where the designer wants to retain the same number of stitches but wants to add subtle shaping. For example, nipping in a waistline on a jumper or jacket gives a more fitted, tailored look. Decreasing stitches can do this, but changing needles may also be an option and can enhance the finished look.

Purposefully losing stitches using one of the decrease techniques on pages 68–71 breaks up this strong rib pattern, disrupting the sleek lines.

Dropping down three needle sizes decreases the width without affecting the rib pattern. Once the shaping is complete, simply return to the larger needle size.

Changing stitch

Stitch patterns affect the size, feel and shape of knitted fabrics.
To create an impression of a narrower fabric, working in k1, p1
rib gives an elastic fabric that pulls in when not under tension.
Contrast this with the same k1, p1 repeat when worked in moss
stitch over the same number of stitches. The fabric is wider and
would not achieve the desired effect of creating a narrowing of
the fabric. Similarly, garter stitch would widen rather than draw
in a fabric as it is one of the few square stitches: it is as tall as it
is wide. This is why a garter-stitch collar will stand up and out
rather than pull in, as would be the case with a rib collar.

This swatch uses 30 stitches throughout. The rib stitch (top) is much
narrower than the moss-stitch (centre) or garter-stitch (bottom)
sections. Adjusting needle size and stitch does have limitations because
it can alter the texture and drape of a fabric. More often, to create
shape, you need to change the number of stitches.

Cast-off decrease

For larger-scale decreases the simplest method is to cast off a
given number of stitches. This technique may be used to create
openings for necklines, pockets, zips or fasteners, or simply to
end the knitting. Cast-off decreases use one of the range of
cast-off techniques illustrated on pages 78–83. Use the chart
on page 126 as a guide to choosing the best method for
your project.

Decreasing methods

For gradual changes, a decreasing technique (see pages 68–71)
is normally used. Depending on the type of decrease used,
some are barely noticeable; others are intentionally bold for
decorative effect (see chart on page 126). A decrease will slant
either to the right or left.

Decreases can be
on knit or purl
sides. Here two purl
decreases have
been used.

Using an sl1, k1, psso
(left) creates a clear
left-hand slant. The
ssp (right) creates a
smooth line for an
almost invisible
increase.

A k2tog (right) is
a good choice for
a barely visible
decrease. It is usually
paired with an sl1, k1,
psso (left).

Matching decreases

As well as sloping right or left, each decrease stitch looks different when knitted. Where a pattern calls for decreases at the beginning and end of a row (for example, a raglan-sleeved jumper), each decrease has a matching 'partner'. A matching pair of decreases will look neater and more balanced, as can be seen below.

Pairing a k2tog with an ssk decrease produces two neat rows of matching ridges.

Placing two decreases around a central stitch creates a decorative effect.

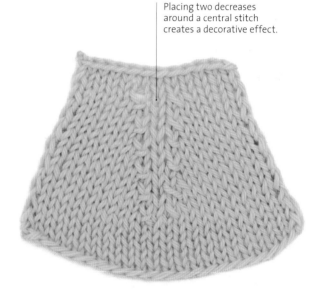

Common decreases and their matching pair

Use the chart below as a handy reminder of some of the most commonly used decreases and the slope of the stitches (slope refers to direction of stitch as the work faces you).

Right sloping	Left sloping matching pair
K2tog	Ssk (sl2, k sl st tog)
K1, sl1, psso	Sl1, k1, psso
	K2tog tbl (k2 together through back of loop)
Ssp (sl2, p sl st tog)	P2tog
P1, sl1, psso	Sl1, p1, psso
	P2tog tbl (p2 together through back of loop)

DECREASES AND ADAPTATIONS

If you are planning to design or adapt your own pattern, try different decreases and combinations by making swatches beforehand and seeing how they work together. Attention to small details such as decreases can really make a difference to the look of your garment.

Choosing the right cast off

As with cast-on techniques, it is worth spending a little time considering which of the many casting off techniques would suit your project best, to achieve that truly professional finish.

Casting off usually signals the end of a piece of knitting and it can be tempting to rush this final step in your enthusiasm to finish your project. However, if the pattern is not specific, or if you are working to your own design, you may want to sample one or two different techniques on a small swatch to decide which method will give the best result.

Alternative methods for casting off

As well as the more common cast offs on pages 78–83, there are several alternative methods that may come in useful when you're looking for a specific effect for your project. Some of these are featured on the following pages.

How to choose a particular cast off

As with cast ons, a cast off may be chosen for practical reasons, for decorative effect or both. You must consider the nature and function of the finished article. Use this chart to help you decide on the appropriate technique for your project.

Effect	Technique	Useful for
Firm	Standard chain, pages 78–79	Sturdy edge for soft furnishings, plush toys; good match with long-tail (thumb) and knitted (two-needle) cast on (pages 46–47)
Elastic	Tubular, pages 134–135	Ribs, sock and garment cuffs
	Sewn style, pages 80–81	Ribs, sock and garment cuffs
	Extra stretchy, pages 82–83	Ribs, sock and garment cuffs
Invisible/seamless	Stem stitch, page 132	Soft edges, lacy shawls; good match for backward loop cast on (page 48)
	Three-needle, page 133	Joining two pieces of knitting seamlessly
	Tubular, pages 134–135	Ribs, sock and garment cuffs
Decorative	Picot, page 131	Decorative edges that don't curl or roll
	I-cord, page 118 (for cast on)	Decorative edges that don't curl or roll
Specialist	Three-needle, page 133	Joining two pieces of knitting seamlessly

PICOT CAST OFF
This is a decorative cast off that gives a pretty frilled edge.

1
Cast on two stitches using the cable cast-on method (see page 55).

2
Knit the two stitches.

3
Cast off the next five stitches as usual. (This will cast off the two stitches you cast on, plus three stitches from the body of the knitting.)

4
Slip the stitch remaining on the RH needle purlwise (as if to purl) back onto the LH needle. Repeat steps 1–4 until all stitches have been cast off, leaving a single loop on the RH needle. Cut the yarn leaving a tail for darning in and pass the tail through the loop. Draw up the loop and darn in neatly.

- **When planning your picot cast off for knitting in the round,** you may prefer to finish the cast off with step 3. This will ensure that, because the cast off starts with a picot, it will end with a flat section so that there is an unbroken pattern of picot-flat-picot-flat – and not two picots or two flat sections together.

- **For flat knitting, if the edges are to be seamed** it may be better to begin and end on a flat section to make sewing up easier. For a scarf, however, it can give a nicer look if both edges finish on a picot. (And remember to do the same at both ends if you are working a picot cast on to match a cast off!)

- **For different effects,** try varying the number of stitches between the picots.

- **For a longer picot,** work extra stitches and more cast-off stitches.

STEM-STITCH CAST OFF

This sewn cast off is useful where an understated, soft edge is required.
It is a good match for the backward loop cast on (see page 48).

1
Use a length of yarn four or five times the width of
the edge being cast off and thread it onto a blunt yarn
needle. With the work in your LH, insert the yarn needle
into the second stitch on the needle knitwise.

2
Insert the yarn needle into the first stitch on the needle
purlwise, bringing the yarn needle underneath the loop of
yarn you have just made.

3
Slip the first stitch off the LH needle and draw up the
yarn. One stitch cast off.

When worked in
a matching yarn,
this cast off is
almost invisible.

4
Repeat steps 1–3 until all stitches have been cast off.
Fasten off by passing the tail of the yarn through the
loop and drawing up.

THREE-NEEDLE CAST OFF

This method allows you to create both a seam and a cast off in one step. It is a neat way of joining two edges where the seam needs to be smooth and even, for example when joining a shoulder seam. Although it is neater than a sewn seam it does leave a small chain ridge, so avoid using this method on toe seams (grafting is preferable for these seams; see pages 94–97). For this method you will need three needles.

If you don't have a third needle in the same size, a needle one or two sizes larger will be fine.

As you work you will see a small ridge of chain stitches forming on the WS of the work. This is normal.

1
Place the two pieces of knitting (still on the needles) with RS together in your LH (see detail). Using a third needle, insert the tip into the front of the first stitch on the front needle, then into the front of the first stitch on the back needle as if to knit (knitwise). K2tog.

2
One stitch on the RH needle. Repeat step 1. Two stitches are now on the RH needle (see detail).

Take care not to allow the stitches on the LH needle to slip off when you are casting off. Try using a small crochet hook to lift the stitch off if you find it difficult with the LH needle.

Viewed from the RS, this cast off produces a neat, almost invisible seam.

3
Using the tip of one of the needles in your LH, lift the first stitch on the RH needle over the stitch just completed. One stitch cast off.

4
Repeat steps 1–3 until only the final stitch remains on the needle. Fasten off the final stitch by cutting off the working yarn, leaving a 15–20cm (6–8in) tail. Pass the tail through the final stitch and draw it up tightly.

TUBULAR CAST OFF

Also referred to as invisible cast off, this is an ideal match for a tubular cast on (see page 49) and is a good choice for casting off a ribbed fabric. It works particularly well for casting off necklines – if not worked too tightly. For this cast off you will need three DPNs and a blunt yarn needle.

1
To work a tubular cast off on a k1, p1 ribbed fabric, work as usual until the knitting is two rows short of the desired finished length. Work the next four rows by knitting all the knit stitches as usual and slipping the purl stitches (hold the yarn at the front of the work when working the purl stitches).

2
Transfer all the knit stitches onto one DPN and the purl stitches onto a second DPN. The purled stitches should be held to the back, the knit stitches to the front. The knitting is now in two separate layers.

3 Grafting
Now, bind the stitches off by grafting the two layers together with a needle using the standard Kitchener (grafting) stitch. Pass the yarn needle (in your RH) through the first stitch on the front needle as if to purl. Draw the yarn up.

4
Pass the yarn needle through the first stitch on the back needle as if to knit. Draw the yarn up. Be careful to take the yarn below and behind the front needle, making sure it isn't looped over the front needle.

Kitchener stitch makes a near-invisible, stretchy cast-off edge, ideal for sock tops and cuffs.

Stitch set

Next follows a series of paired stitches that are worked into the stitches on the front and back needles alternately, two on the front, two on the back.

When threading the needle through the stitches take care not to split the yarn.

5
Bring the yarn to the front of the work and pass it through the first stitch as if to knit. Slide this stitch off the needle. Note that you have gone through this stitch twice, purlwise in step 1, then here, knitwise.

6
Take the yarn through the next stitch on the front needle as if to purl. Draw the yarn up. Don't slide this stitch off the needle just yet.

7
Pass the yarn through the first stitch on the back needle as if to purl. Slide this stitch off the needle. (Note how this stitch has been worked into twice before being slid off – knitwise in the foundation and purlwise here.) Take the yarn through the next stitch on the back needle as if to knit. Don't slide this stitch off the needle yet.

8
Repeat steps 5–8 until you reach the last stitch on the back needle. To finish, take the yarn through the final stitch on the back needle as if to purl. Slide this stitch off the needle and fasten off neatly.

Steeking

Even the most experienced knitter may be made nervous by the suggestion that they cut their knitting. However, although it may seem a little scary, knowing how, when and why you should cut your knitting (or 'steeking', to use the correct term) is a useful skill and it is really not that difficult.

Steeking describes the process of deliberately cutting a knitted fabric. It is best known as a means of creating jackets and cardigans from fabrics that have been knitted in the round, but it is also used to create armholes, necklines, pockets and other openings where the item is cut after the main fabric has been knitted.

Steeking has many benefits: Garments such as jackets or cardigans can be knitted almost entirely in the round in the same way as jumpers; in many cases, knitting in one piece right up to the shoulders. This makes knitting quicker as it reduces the number of seams that need to be stitched when making up. Stranded colourwork is also easier because there are far fewer ends to sew in and it is simpler to keep the stranding even because all rounds are knitted rather than alternating knit and purl rows. It is also easier to follow complex patterns when the right side of the work is always facing you.

There are a number of ways of creating a steek. The choice of steek will depend on the yarn you are using, the pattern you are following and where the steek is to be placed.

This jacket has been knitted in the round and steeked to form the open fronts, as you can see on the inside of the flaps to the right. The steeks are made using the crochet hook technique (see pages 137–139), which gives a neat finish.

CROCHET-REINFORCED STEEK

To create a steek, additional stitches are needed to form a temporary bridge between the front edge bands. The centre of this bridge is cut to form the opening. Waste yarn marks the edges of the bridge and the centre cut line. Green yarn marks the six bridge stitches, and the red yarn the cutting line.

1
A knit stitch can be visualised as a series of Vs. With an even number of stitches in the bridge, the cut will be made along a line between two Vs. The crocheted reinforcing stitches are formed by making a row of single crochets along either edge of the cut. The crocheting is done before cutting.

2
For each edge, a double crochet is made into the stitch either side of the cut. Make a slipknot and place on the crochet hook. With RS facing, starting at the bottom RH of the work, insert the crochet hook under both legs of the stitch to the left of the centreline.

3
Catch the yarn with the hook and draw it through both legs of the edging, but not the loop on the hook. Two loops on hook.

4
Wrap the working yarn around the hook and draw it through both loops on the hook. This can be either clockwise or anti-clockwise, providing you are consistent. One double crochet made. One loop on hook.

5
Insert the crochet hook under both legs of the next stitch to the left of the centreline and repeat steps 3–4. Make three double crochets for every four rows of knitting to keep the edge flat. Check periodically that the work is flat by laying it on a flat surface. When you reach the last stitch, cut off the working yarn and thread it through the final loop on the hook, drawing up firmly.

6
For the LH edge, turn the work and, starting from the top edge of the garment, work double crochets into the stitches to the right of the cutting line (as viewed with front of garment upright and facing you). Work three double crochets for every four rows, so make three double crochets, miss one row, make three double crochets and so on.

7
With both sides crocheted you should have two ridges of double crochets, one on either side of the cutting line. Pull the two sides apart gently to reveal the ladder that runs down between the two adjoining stitches and remove the red marker thread.

8
Holding the edges apart so that you can see where you are cutting; work carefully with sharp, pointed scissors to snip each ladder thread. Ensure that you only cut ladder thread by cutting each stitch individually. At the cast-on edge the cut will be through crochet chain, between two live stitches. At the top, the cut will be through the cast-off edge.

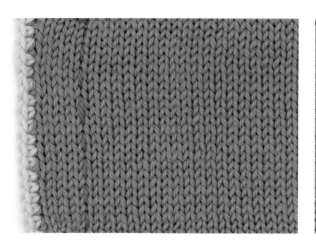

9
Stitches for the edging band are picked up along the edge of the steek as usual, following the line marked on either side by the green waste yarn. The swatch illustrated below shows stitches picked up from a moss-stitch band first, and then continued, following the line of the steek edge (marked in green yarn), finishing with the second moss-stitch band.

10
Once the bands have been completed, carefully press the steeked bridge stitches flat to the WS of the jacket. Top stitch the top and bottom edges of the steek, tucking in and anchoring any loose threads. If necessary, top stitch the steek edge to the WS of the knitting.

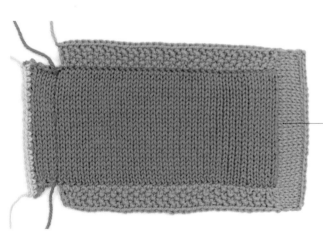

The neck and hemline bands were worked first, and stitches for the front bands picked up along the entire edge for a neat finish.

11
Viewed from the RS, one band has been completed, incorporating both of the moss-stitch bands at the hemline and neckline. The second band (left) is then worked in the same way.

TIPS

- **Use a smooth thread for your markers to make them easy to remove.** Take the yarn from the front to the back of the work every couple of rows to anchor it loosely in place and make a line of long running stitches.

- **Practice your chosen technique on a sample swatch** before making your final cut. If the steek is likely to be put under strain, apply similar strain to your swatch.

- **This technique works best on yarns that have some natural 'grip',** such as non-superwash wools, alpaca, angora and similar fibres that have some fuzziness and a tendency to felt.

UNREINFORCED STEEK

With a suitably 'grippy' yarn – usually a pure wool yarn such as Shetland – it is possible to make a bridge of steeking stitches and simply cut the fabric, allowing the natural grip of the yarn to hold the fibres in place and prevent unravelling.

A checkerboard or stripe pattern in the knitting can be used to help with placement of the steek stitches.

The edges of the steek are outlined here in magenta. The black yarn marks the cutting line.

1
An alternative way of marking the location of the steek in colourwork patterns is to work a steeked bridge using two colours from the main garment, creating a checkerboard or stripe pattern. This technique avoids long floats across the bridging stitches while clearly demarcating the borders of the steek.

2
The fabric is cut along the centreline of the steek using the checkerboard/stripe pattern as a guide, in the same way as for a crocheted steek but without any reinforcing crochet stitches.

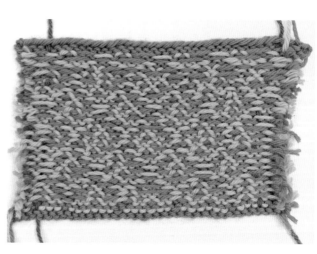

3
The cut edges are turned to the WS and folded along the magenta lines to create a neat steeked edge. If necessary, felt the folded edge slightly into the main fabric by rubbing with a little soap and hot water, then blotting and rinsing the area. In key areas such as underarms, the friction and warmth caused by wear will continue this felting process.

SEWN STEEK

With yarns that don't have natural gripping or felting tendencies, or if a steek begins to weaken due to wear or stretching, it may be advisable to reinforce a steek with stitching. This technique can also be useful where a steek may be visible (for example at a neckline) because stitching or adding a bias binding type of fabric can be neater.

A sewn steek is a good choice for yarns with little grip and fabrics knitted in a single colour where the fabric is not particularly dense, so it holds together less well when cut.

1
Create a bridge of steek stitches. Before cutting the steek, machine or hand sew one or two rows of stitches along either edge of the cutting line (see detail) using a matching cotton thread and a regular straight stitch such as backstitch.

2
Cut the steek and fold it to the WS of the fabric. Catch the edges down with fine stitching, being careful not to make the stitches visible on the RS of the fabric.

3
To neaten the steek a matching bias binding or similar fabric can be sewn in place to cover the cut edges.

Edgings and trims

Adding an interesting edging or trim is one of the quickest and simplest ways to enhance or customise a hand knit. It also has the advantage of being possible to do at virtually any stage of a project, or even with an existing knit.

Appealing because of their versatility, edgings worked in a luxury yarn, for example, use a small amount of yarn but create the impression of an expensive garment. Trims can be worked in different stitches, making a project seem intricate or complex, but the complex areas are limited to a small part of the knitting. Beads, sequins and other embellishments can be added to spice up a trim. Playing with colour and texture can do wonders to add a little something special to a classic knit.

Edgings can be worked in the same direction as the main knitting or in a different direction. This means borders can be created that go neatly around corners or that follow curves.

Edgings and trims also have practical functions: They can add weight, shape and structure, hide seams and cover untidy edges. They can also be used to repair and revamp existing knits and breathe new life into a favourite, well-loved garment. And, because edgings are small, you can have a lot of fun sampling and trying out different ones to see what works best.

Depending on the project, an edging can be integrated into and knitted alongside the main knitting or added afterwards; however, edgings and trims are commonly added at the end of a project because this gives more flexibility with the yarn, stitch pattern, direction and structure. Edgings may be joined to the main knitting by picking up stitches, placing live stitches on stitch holders during knitting, or from a provisional cast on. They can also be sewn in position.

Stitched-on edgings
Made separately to the main knitting, stitched-on edgings are stitched on at the end. This allows different shapes and patterns to be explored more freely because the main fabric is not used to provide the base for the edging. Stitches can travel in a different direction and yarns with different characteristics (tension, texture) can be used.

There are a number of key differences in the way that picked-up and stitched-on edgings are made and used.

Changing tension and adding structure
Stitched-on edgings are frequently used for buttonhole bands on jackets and cardigans, where the designer wants the stitches to run in line with the main fabric, but a firmer edge is needed to support buttons or fasteners without sagging.

The preferred way to do this is to knit a separate band, often in a rib stitch, on a smaller needle. The rib stitch adds strength and elasticity, and using the smaller needle gives a firmer finish. If the designer were to try to incorporate this into the main garment the differences in tension would distort the edge.

Curves and corners
Knitting a separate band also means that curves can be neatly followed without worrying about untidy edge stitches. Stitched edgings are also useful for making straight edges (mitring) on square corners. Because bands are only worked on a few stitches it is straightforward to try out different shapings until a neat curve or corner is achieved.

Changing direction
An interesting feature of a stitched-on edging is that the knitting can be worked in almost any direction. Providing care is taken with drape, weight and texture, a stitched band can be as narrow or wide as you wish. Because the band is separate, it is possible to experiment with different stitches and to try new techniques such as cabling and colourwork without any risk of spoiling the main knitting.

> **SIZING NOTE**
> The instructions given over the following pages are for making the edgings and trims as they appeared here, as small samples. Practise the technique and then apply it to a real-size sample for your garment.

SIMPLE RIBBED BAND

Knitted in k1, p1 rib on 3.25mm (size 3) needles, this band has been stitched to the main stocking-stitch fabric, which was worked on 4mm (size 6) needles. To keep the edge firm, the band was stitched on while slightly stretched. This provides a good foundation for buttons or other fasteners.

1
Using 3.75mm (size 5) needles and pale green DK (double knit) yarn, cast on 30 sts and work eight rows k1, p1 rib.

2
At the start of the next row, place the first 5 sts on a stitch holder or a length of spare yarn (do not fasten off pale green yarn), change to 4mm (size 6) needles and mid-green DK wool yarn, then work 16 rows stocking stitch.

3 Shaping rows
Rows 1 and 3 Cast off 3 sts, k to end.
Row 2 and all even rows P.
Rows 5, 7, 9 and 11 Sl1, k1, psso, k to end.
Cast off.

4
Return to the stitches on the holder or spare yarn and, using 3.25mm (size 3) needles and pale green yarn, work in k1, p1 rib on just those 5 sts until the band is almost as long as the main fabric. Complete and fit the band following the instructions on page 145.

MITRED GARTER-STITCH CORNER

This striped garter-stitch border is mitred at the corners, and then stitched onto the stocking-stitch fabric. Paired decreases form the corner shape, and contrasting colours in the stripes add fun detail.

1 Main fabric
Using 4mm (size 6) needles and dark pink yarn, cast on 9 sts and work 11 rows stocking stitch (starting k), and then cast off.

2 Band
Using 3.75mm (size 5) needles and dark pink yarn, cast on 29 sts.
Row 1 K12, sl1, k1, psso, k1, k2 tog, k12 to end.
Row 2 K11, k2tog, k1, sl1, k1, psso, k11 to end. Do not fasten off dark pink. Join in pale green.
Row 3 Using pale green, k10, sl1, k1, psso, k1, k2tog, k10 to end.
Row 4 K9, k2tog, k1, sl1, k1, psso, k9 to end. Fasten off pale green. Continue in dark pink:
Row 5 K8, sl1, k1, psso, k1, k2tog, k8 to end.
Row 6 K7, k2tog, k1, sl1, k1, psso, k7 to end. Cast off loosely.

3
Fit and stitch the band to the main fabric following the instructions on page 145. Start the pinning at the corner to ensure a square edge.

GARTER-STITCH BAND

This sample is made entirely in garter stitch. Making the band after the main piece means the stitches can be taken at right angles to the main knitting, adding interest without even using different stitches. Using the long-tail cast on (page 46) makes a neat edge for garter stitch.

1 Main fabric
Using 4mm (size 6) needles and pale green yarn, cast on 30 sts loosely. Work 26 rows of garter stitch and cast off.

2 Band one (bottom edge)
Using 4mm (size 6) needles and DK yarn, cast on 19 sts loosely. Knit two rows in cream, four rows in a contrasting colour (purple is used here), and then two more rows in cream. Cast off.

3 Band two (side edge)
Using 4mm (size 6) needles, cast on 5 sts loosely in pale green, and then work 30 rows of garter stitch. Change to a contrasting colour (mid-green used here), and knit two rows. Knit four rows pale green. Repeat the last six rows, three more times. Knit four rows of pale green and cast off. (Stitch the right edge of this band to the main piece, to hide the strands carried up from one stripe to the next).

4
Pin and stitch the bands following the instructions on page 145.

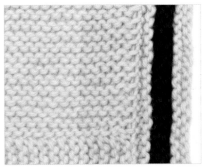

Added extras and exotic touches

Stitched-on edgings are an inexpensive way to incorporate an exotic fibre into your knitting. Because stitched edgings can use yarns with a different tension to your main yarn, you can combine textured yarns with a simpler main fabric. It is even possible to incorporate other techniques, such as I-cords. Again, because the edging is only worked on a small number of stitches, it is easy to experiment until you are happy with the result.

DOUBLE CABLE EDGING

This wide band, worked in a bold, curvy cable stitch, adds dramatic contrast to the simple stocking-stitch fabric.

1 Main fabric

Using 4mm (size 6) needles and pale green yarn, cast on 34 sts loosely. Work 20 rows of stocking stitch and cast off.

2 Band

Using 3.25mm (size 3) needles and pale green, cast on 22 sts.
Row 1 (RS) P2, k8, p2, k8, p2.
Row 2 K2, [p4, k6] twice.
Rows 3–6 Repeat rows 1 and 2, twice more.
Row 7 *P2, place next 4 sts on cable needle and hold at back of work. K next 4 sts. K4 sts from cable needle. Rep from * once, p2.
Row 8 [K6, p4] twice, k2.
Row 9 As row 1.
Rows 10–18 Rep rows 8 and 9 four more times, then work row 8 again.
Row 19 As row 7.
Row 20 As row 2.
Row 21 As row 1.
Rows 22–24 Rep rows 2 and 1, then work row 2 again.
Rep rows 1–24.
Cast off in k and p as set.

3

Pin and stitch the band along the cast-on (long) edge following the instructions opposite.

ANGORA RUFFLE

This sample pairs a handspun angora rabbit yarn with classic Aran-weight pure wool. Differences in the yarns are not crucial if the band is stitched on, because the number of rows and stitches can be varied to give a matching length.

1 Main fabric

Using 4mm (size 6) needles, cast 35 stitches on loosely in purple DK wool. Work 22 rows of stocking stitch (starting k) and cast off.

2 Band

Using 5mm (size 8) needles, cast on 20 sts loosely in angora.
Work four rows stocking stitch (starting k).
Row 5 *K2, kfb, rep from * to last 1, 2, or 3 sts, k to end.
Row 6 P.
Rep rows 5 and 6 three more times and cast off loosely.

3

Pin and stitch the band along the cast-on (long) edge following the instructions opposite. Here the purl side of the band is used as the right side.

I-CORD EDGING

Make a simple stocking-stitch band and use this as your canvas to make a customised pattern in I-cord or French knitting. Add initials, a date or a pattern; whatever takes your fancy!

1 Main fabric

Using 4mm (size 6) needles and dark pink DK wool yarn, cast on 30 sts loosely. Work 22 rows of garter stitch and cast off.

2 Band

Using 4mm (size 6) needles and dark pink DK wool yarn, cast on 10 sts loosely and work 36 rows of stocking stitch (starting k). Cast off.

3 I-cord

Using two 3.25mm (size 4) DPNs and purple DK wool yarn, cast on 3 sts and make an I-cord 30cm (12in) long (see page 215). Cast off.

4

Pin and stitch the band along the cast-on (long) edge, as per the instructions on the right. Pin the I-cord in place, following the pattern as illustrated, then stitch carefully in place.

FITTING YOUR BAND

Taking a little extra time fitting and pinning/tacking your band before stitching it may seem like a fuss but is well worth the effort.

1
To finish your band, don't cast off, but stop knitting when it is slightly shorter than the main fabric. Pin the band carefully in place, slightly stretching it. Use lots of small pins rather than one or two large ones. Placing the stitches on a spare piece of yarn while you pin makes fitting much easier.

2
On large pieces it is often better to pin then tack the band in place before stitching. For tacking use a smooth, contrasting thread so that you can remove it easily afterwards. As with a short edge, stop knitting when the band is a little short but don't cast off. Put the stitches on a piece of spare yarn or a holder to make fitting easier. Pin the band in place. It should be firm but not pulling in. With RS together, tack carefully in place.

3
If after pinning/tacking the band is long enough, put the stitches back on the needles and cast off. If it is too long, rip back some rows, or add more if it is still short. Re-pin or tack if necessary before casting off.

STITCHING YOUR BAND

Once you are happy with the fit, you can stitch the band in place. Overcasting (see page 89) is a useful stitch for bands because it is flatter than backstitch. Ladder stitch is not always suitable because you may not be stitching row-to-row or stitch-to-stitch, so it is difficult to align the stitches neatly. For heavily textured yarns, try a smoother yarn in a matching colour, which will make stitching easier and neater. Stranded tapestry wools can be useful for this as they come in many colours. Combine more or fewer threads to give the correct thickness.

Integral edgings

Certain patterns and stitches can be used to create an edging at the same time as the main knitting is created. Make sure to swatch carefully because any distortion to the main body may only be apparent when a large piece has been knitted. A mistake will mean that the main knitting has to be ripped back as well as the edging. Because there is limited scope to change an integral edging once the knitting is well underway, make sure you are happy with your choice before you begin. Remember, too, to include any buttonholes as you go, because these are difficult to add later.

ROLLED BORDER

This easy edging takes advantage of the fact that stocking stitch naturally curls up when knitted. A row of garter stitch is inserted to stop the curl, creating a well-defined rolled edge. This type of edging is normally used at the cast-on/cast-off edge of a piece and on some necklines. It is ideal for cuffs, round-neck jumpers and hem edges on light- to medium-weight fabrics. It can be used on heavier fabrics but may spread and be too bulky, so swatch it carefully. Rolled borders are good for adding a little extra weight and strength and they work well with both textured and smooth yarns.

1
Using 4mm (size 6) needles and mid-green DK yarn, cast on 30 sts and, starting with a k row, work five rows of stocking stitch.

2
Row 6 K.

3
Starting with a k row, continue in stocking stitch following the pattern.

MOSS-STITCH BORDER

Moss stitch is a flat fabric that doesn't curl. Being similar in tension to stocking stitch, it can often be incorporated into the main knitting without distorting the shape. Moss stitch is ideal for garments where bulky seams or stitching would spoil the garment, particularly babywear. Smooth yarns show off the stitches to best effect. This stitch works well on afghan squares to create a good, firm edge. It can be interchanged with a rib edge and can be used along the side of a garment as well as for the hem/cast-off edge. With care, it can also be used to follow shaping, around a neck edge for example.

1
Using 4mm (size 6) needles and lilac yarn cast on 30 sts.
Row 1 *K1, p1 rep from * to end.
Row 2 *P1, k1 rep from * to end.
Rep rows 1 and 2 twice more.
Row 7 K1, p1, k1, p1, k to end.
Row 8 P to last 5 sts, k1, p1, k1, p1, k1.
Rep rows 7 and 8 as required.

2
To shape for a neckline, such as a V-neck, decreasing may be worked inside the 5 border sts, as shown here:
Decreasing row K1, p1, k1, p1, k1, k2tog, k to end.
Foll row As row 8.
Rep these 2 rows as required.

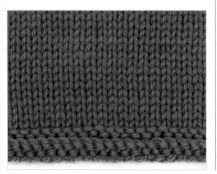

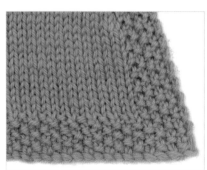

FLARED CUFF

Flared edges are worked by creating increases (or decreases) at intervals. When knitted as part of the fabric, these edgings are usually found on the cast-on or cast-off edge. Increase stitches quickly and regularly for lots of ruffles; space them out for more subtle effects.

The fabric here has been spread out to show how the increases work. The pattern is designed to be knitted from the top down and starts with a small number of stitches, increasing rapidly to create a flared ruffle effect at the cast-off (cuff) edge of the sleeve.

Using 4mm (size 6) needles and lilac DK yarn, cast on 30 sts (or any multiple of 5 sts).
Starting k, work 10 rows stocking stitch.
Row 11 *K5, m1tbl rep from * to last 5 sts, k5. (35 sts.)
Row 12 P.
Row 13 *K5, m1tbl, k1, m1tbl rep from * to last 5 sts, k5. (45 sts.)
Row 14 P.
Row 15 K.
Row 16 P.
Row 17 *K5, m1tbl, k3, m1tbl rep from * to last 5 sts, k5. (55 sts.)
Row 18 P.
Row 19 *K5, m1tbl, k5, m1tbl rep from * to last 5 sts, k5. (65 sts.)
Row 20 P.
Row 21 K.
Row 22 P.
Cast off loosely.

PICOT HEM

Hems are useful when a near-invisible border is needed, for example, in a stocking-stitch fabric where the stocking stitch needs to continue right to the edge without curling. Hems are an ideal way to encase elastic and can be used as a channel for drawstrings and cords. Eyelets can be created in the body of a hem to allow a drawstring to be fed in and out. Use these in adult, sweatshirt-style hooded tops or jackets; however, avoid drawstrings and hood cords in anything that might be worn by children. This technique is also great for duffle bags, laundry sacks and handbags where a neat, hidden closure is needed.

When you want to use stocking stitch but need a firm, flat edge, try this picot hem. The row of holes that can be seen below forms the decorative hemline. The fabric has been folded to the wrong side and neatly slip stitched in place. The eyelets give a good fold line but also add interesting detail. As an alternative to this, you could work a row of garter stitch on the purl side (WS) where you want the fold line to be. This creates a ridge on the RS for a crisp hemline.

1
Using 4mm (size 6) needles and mid-green DK yarn, cast on 30 sts and, beginning with a p row, work nine rows of stocking stitch.
Row 10 K2, *yo k2tog, rep from * to last 2 sts, k2.

2
Starting with a p row, continue in stocking stitch as required by the pattern.

3
To make up, fold the hem to the wrong side of the fabric and neatly slip stitch in place to a straight row of sts. Remember to leave the side edges open if a drawstring or elastic is to be threaded through.

Adding edgings using existing stitches

Existing stitches from the main knitting can be used to create the foundation for a border or trim. These may be stitches that were placed on a stitch holder during knitting (for example, at the neckline of a jumper), or, if a piece has been made using a provisional cast-on technique, the stitches may simply be held in place by waste yarn that, once removed, will allow the stitches to be put back onto needles and used again.

This technique is ideal for straight edges where a seamless join is needed, for example around the neckline of a jumper. Any new stitches will follow the same direction as the original knitting (albeit upside down for the provisional cast-on method); however, different needles and stitch patterns can still be used. This technique is rarely used for curves, because the stitches can easily become stretched and distorted; however, it may be combined with picked-up stitches (see pages 98–101).

Using a provisional cast-on to create an edging

This is another good technique for straight edges. It's usually used at the lower edge of the knitted fabric to add many types of edging. It is particularly useful for pointed edges, scallops, loopy edges, etc., as a neater and less bulky alternative to sewing on a separate edging band.

Picked-up edgings

Picked-up edgings can be created almost anywhere in a knitted fabric: up the sides; at the cast-on or cast-off edge; along an opening for a pocket; or around a curve for a neckline or armhole. Because they are added after the main fabric is knitted, you don't need to decide on your edging until the main fabric is completed. You can try several edgings before you settle on one since they are relatively easy to unpick, or you could even design your own.

FRILLED EDGING

These are ideal for throws and blankets, and lend stability to the outer edges, reducing stretching. They are also useful for hiding any stitching, etc., on patchwork afghans. Frills and trims are also, of course, very decorative and are great for cuffs, hems, collars and jacket edgings. Soft and subtle or outrageously flouncy, frills give any knitted fabric the wow factor!

1
Using 4mm (size 6) needles and mid-green DK yarn, cast on 30 sts, work 24 rows in stocking stitch, then cast off.

2
With RS facing, using the same needles and lilac DK yarn, pick up and knit 29 sts along the cast-on edge.
Row 1 *K1, kfb, rep from * to last stitch, k1.
Row 2 K.
Row 3 As row 1, ending k1 or k2.
Cast off loosely.

3
Repeat for each edge as required.

Suggested variations

You can customise this edging simply by adding extra rows and varying the number of increases for a fuller frill.

FOLDED RIB EDGING

Ideal for firm edgings, particularly on heavier garments such as coats and jackets, working a buttonhole on the inner folded edge creates a band with concealed buttonholes. Here, the rib is folded to give extra strength for buttons. Adding the knit row creates a neat fold line, but it would look equally nice without the fold for a softer look.

1

Using 4mm (size 6) needles and dark pink DK yarn, cast on 24 sts, work 30 rows stocking stitch and cast off.

2

With RS facing, using 3.25mm (size 4) needles and lilac DK yarn, pick up and knit 30 sts (multiple of 5 sts) up one side edge of the piece.
Row 1 (WS) *P2, k3 rep from * to end.
Row 2 *P3, k2 rep from * to end.
Rep rows 1 and 2 twice more.
Row 7 K.
Row 8 As row 2.
Row 9 As row 1.
Rep rows 8 and 9 twice more.
Cast off loosely in k and p as set.

3

Fold the edge at the k row to the WS and stitch down neatly. For the unfolded version, simply cast off in rib after row 6.

FLAG EDGING

Although this pretty flag edging can be made and stitched, or joined, on later, this can give a bulky result and spoil the drape. Here, it's knitted down from a provisional cast on creating an invisible join.

1

Using 4mm (size 6) needles, cast on 31 sts using the provisional cast-on technique (see page 50). Change to dark pink DK yarn, work 30 rows stocking stitch and cast off.

2

Return to the cast-on edge and, with RS facing and working from left to right, carefully remove the waste yarn, placing the newly exposed stitches on your needle ready to be worked (you will be knitting from the top down rather than bottom up and the needle with the stitches is in your LH). 30 sts.
Join in mid-green DK yarn.
Row 1 (and all odd rows) K.
Row 2 K10, turn and work on just these 10 sts.
Row 3 K10.
Row 4 K1, k2tog, k to last 3sts, k2tog, k1, turn.
Row 5 K8.
Row 6 As row 4.
Row 7 K6.
Row 8 As row 4.

Row 9 K4.
Row 10 K2tog, k2tog.
Row 11 K2.
Row 12 K2tog and fasten off.

3

With RS facing, rejoin yarn to main knitting next to the flag just worked and work rows 2–12. Repeat to form third flag.

Suggested variations

There are many ways to vary this simple edging. Decreasing more often will produce a shorter, squatter shape, or you could cast off when there are more stitches on the needle for a squared-off top effect. On a piece with more stitches you can also make the flags wider (or narrower).

Buttons and buttonholes

With so many beautiful buttons on the market, it goes without saying that the buttonhole should do the button justice by being equally beautifully made. If a buttonhole is noticed it should only be because the knitter intended it to be so!

There are a number of ways to make buttonholes, some more effective than others. A buttonhole should first and foremost be the right size: it should keep the garment fastened as desired and it shouldn't gape or sag. Buttonholes can be small and discreet or bold and decorative, and they may be clearly visible or concealed.

Before making any buttonholes it is a good idea to have in mind the buttons you will be using. It is usually preferable to purchase the buttons first and adapt the buttonholes to suit. Within reason it should be possible to make a buttonhole to match most buttons.

Do consider, however, the button in the context of the garment – for example, tiny buttons on a super-chunky jacket may not be suitable. Always buy at least a couple of extra buttons in case you need to adjust the spacing (or you lose one!).

The style and construction of buttonholes will vary depending on where the buttons are to be located. Classic cardigan or jacket buttonholes are set horizontally, often in a separately knitted or sewn-on band. Buttonholes at cuffs, on pockets, and on waistbands, etc., may need different treatment.

HORIZONTAL BUTTONHOLE

This is a good, very neat buttonhole that can be adapted to suit the size of the button and gives a firm edge to avoid any sagging or looseness.

Avoid working buttonholes at the very edge of the band since this can distort the work.

CLIP 13
Working a buttonhole

www.youtube.com/watch?v=9j1vwWr8GZY

1
Knit to the point where the button is to be placed. Bring the yarn to the front of the work and slip the first stitch on the LH needle purlwise (as if to purl) onto the RH needle.

2
Take the yarn to the back of the work and slip the next stitch from the LH needle to the RH needle purlwise.

One stitch
cast off

3
Using the tip of the LH needle, lift the first slipped stitch over the second slipped stitch on the RH needle. Drop the lifted stitch off the RH needle.

4
With the yarn at the back of the work, slip the next stitch on the LH needle purlwise onto the RH needle.

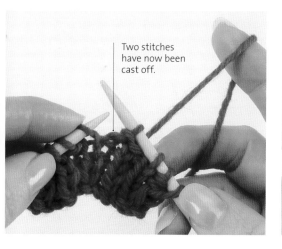

Two stitches
have now been
cast off.

5
Using the tip of the LH needle, lift the first slipped stitch over the second slipped stitch on the RH needle. Drop the lifted stitch off the RH needle.

6
Repeat steps 4 and 5 until the number of stitches required for the buttonhole have been cast off.

Transferring the stitch will give the buttonhole a firm edge.

7
Using the tip of the LH needle, slip the last stitch on the RH needle back onto the LH needle. Turn the work.

8
With the yarn at the back of the work, cast on the same number of stitches as you cast off using the cable cast-on method (see page 55).

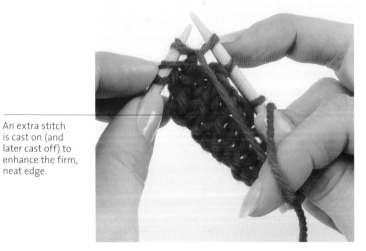

An extra stitch is cast on (and later cast off) to enhance the firm, neat edge.

9
Make an extra cable cast-on stitch but, before you place the stitch onto the LH needle, bring the yarn forward between the needles and hold to the front. Turn the work.

10
Take the yarn to the back of the work, slip the first stitch on the LH needle knitwise onto the RH needle.

If working your band in rib or a similar pattern stitch, check for pattern continuity.

11
Using the tip of the LH needle, lift the last of the cast-on stitches over the slipped stitch on the RH needle. Drop the lifted stitch off the RH needle. Continue knitting as usual.

Deciding on the right buttonhole size

Once you have chosen your buttons, make a small sample of the buttonhole band in the correct stitch. Place the button on top and count the number of stitches (or rows if working a vertical buttonhole) that the button spans over. For most buttons a buttonhole will have the same number or one fewer stitches cast off than the width of the button. This may vary depending on the style of the button, particularly in the case of deep buttons or buttons with shanks.

Practise with a couple of sample buttonholes, varying the number of cast-off stitches until you are happy with the finish. Work several rows before and after the buttonhole in the sample to give a more accurate representation of the finished result.

This style of buttonhole has a neat, firm edge. The size can be varied by adjusting the number of stitches to be cast off and on. It also has the advantage of being reversible.

Different buttons require different shapes and sizes of hole.

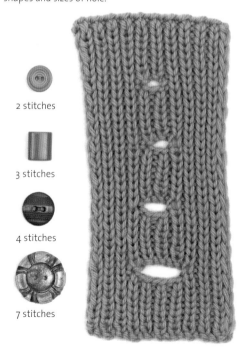

2 stitches

3 stitches

4 stitches

7 stitches

Pockets

Pockets may be functional, decorative or both. Whether you are working to an existing pattern or designing your own garment, a little time spent sampling and planning will help you to choose the best style of pocket for your project.

· ·

Normally stitched in place after knitting the body of a garment, pockets may also be integrated into the design during knitting. A patch pocket will make a statement if it's in a different colour, stitch or yarn to the main fabric. Integrated pockets are more subtle and understated. Complex patterns, colourwork and heavily textured garments benefit from built-in, inset pockets.

KNITTING A PATCH POCKET
This pocket is applied to the right side of the garment and stitched in place.

Use a DPN to pick up the stitches.

1
For a neat lower edge, pick up the required stitches from the main piece of knitting. Begin by slipping a small DPN through a straight line of stitches, picking up the left leg of each stitch, in the position required.

Using a smaller needle will make it easier to pick up the stitches neatly, without distorting the fabric.

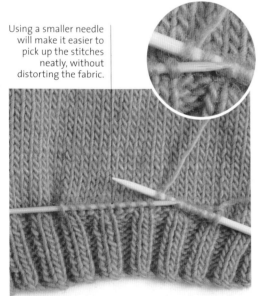

Choose a cast on that will give a firm edge without pulling the fabric. Avoid stretchy cast offs since these can go baggy over time, giving an untidy finish. See pages 130–135 for suggestions.

2
Join in the yarn at the right of the stitches (leave a long tail for assembly) and use a correct-size needle to knit the stitches from the small needle.

3
Knit the pocket to the required length, ending with a few rows of ribbing or other edging, as required, and cast off, leaving another long tail.

When going through the loops be careful not to split the yarn for a neat finish.

A k2, p2 rib has been used to finish the pocket to match the welt and cuffs. Ribs give a snug but elastic top for pockets that bounces back into shape readily, making it suitable for an edge that will get lots of use.

4
Use fine, short DPNs to create straight lines for seaming. Pick up one leg of every alternate stitch along the vertical line at each edge of the pocket. Thread a piece of matching yarn onto a bodkin and join the two vertical seams by going through the edge stitch of the pocket and then through the stitch on the DPN, matching the rows. Work to the top of the pocket edge and fasten off.

5
Repeat for the left edge, working from the top down if this is easier. In this case, you may find it helpful to pin the pocket in place to make sure that it stays aligned with the right side and that the rows match to the main fabric.

WORKING A STRAIGHT-SLIT POCKET

Working in stocking stitch, make a separate pocket lining to the desired size of the finished pocket using the same yarn as for the main fabric. Knit the main fabric to the row where the pocket opening will be (the top edge of the pocket), finishing on a WS row. Knit the next row to the location of the pocket. Cast off the same number of stitches as your lining. (If making a pocket edge, don't cast off but transfer the same number of stitches as used for the lining from the main fabric onto a stitch holder.) Place the lining stitches onto the LH needle with the RS of the lining facing the WS of the main fabric. Knit across the lining stitches and continue knitting the main fabric to the end of the row. Knit across all the stitches as normal (the lining stitches replace the main fabric for the rest of the piece). On the WS, sew down the lining as above.

This straight pocket is hidden behind a deep welt of double moss stitch.

KNITTING A DIAGONAL-SLIT POCKET

A diagonal-slit pocket has a shaped edge, and the only part visible on the front of the garment is the slit, which can be finished in a decorative stitch.

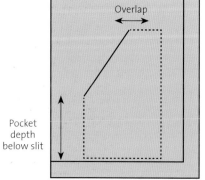

Overlap

Pocket depth below slit

This pocket is shown on the right front of a jacket (on a left front, the slit would slope in the opposite direction).

Work the pocket lining in the same yarn as for the main fabric.

1
First, knit the pocket lining to the depth required below the lowest point of the diagonal slit, ending with a RS row. Break off the working yarn, leaving an 20cm (8in) tail for darning in later, and leave the stitches on a spare needle or transfer to a stitch holder.

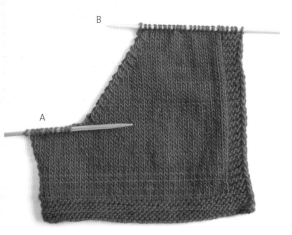

B

A

Draw up the yarn firmly where the lining joins the left side of the main fabric to avoid a hole.

2
Work to the start of the pocket slit. Work the stitches to the right of the slit and place the remaining stitches on a needle (A) or stitch holder. Work the area to the right of the slit, decreasing as required for the slope, until the top of the pocket is reached. Place these stitches on a needle (B) or stitch holder.

3
With the RS of both pieces facing you, rejoin the yarn to the right of the lining stitches. Work across these stitches, then continue to work across the stitches on needle A to the end of the row. Work without shaping on these stitches until the length matches the length of the area to the right of the pocket slit, ending on a WS row. Break the yarn, leaving a long tail.

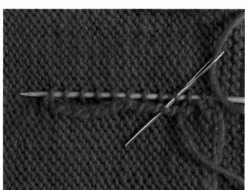

4

Rejoin the front of the slit to the lining by knitting the two fabrics together where they overlap. Deduct the number of stitches decreased to create the diagonal slope from the number of stitches cast on for the lining. This is the number of overlap stitches. With RS facing, work stitches from needle B until the number of overlap stitches remains. Holding B stitches at the front, work two stitches together where B stitches and the lining overlap. Work to the end.

5

Sew the pocket lining in place on the WS of the work as for a patch pocket (see pages 154–155). When sewing the lining in place, check that no stitching is visible from the RS of the work.

TIPS

- **Cast offs and selvedges** are not always neat enough for a pocket edge, so try different edging stitches to preserve the shape and prevent the opening from becoming loose.

- **Pocket edges can often be picked up and added later** if they become saggy over time.

- **Try using contrasting edging colours and different yarns, creating patterned pockets, and adding flaps** for interest. A flap can be added to a horizontal pocket by picking up a row of stitches above the top of the pocket and knitting downwards. Shape with decreases, paying attention to the edges to make sure they don't curl. Alternatively, knit a small flap and sew in place with duplicate stitch (see pages 204–205). Again, make sure the flap is the correct width to match the opening and won't curl when stitched in place.

- **Don't limit pockets to practical handwarming locations.** Consider breast or sleeve pockets for adding stylistic detail.

This diagonal-slit pocket has been finished with a narrow garter-stitch edging (see page 143).

6

The finished pocket blends neatly into the front of the garment. For a matching diagonal-slit pocket on the left front of a garment, work the stitches to the right of the slit along with the stitches from the pocket lining. Then work the stitches to the left of the slit, decreasing for the diagonal slope.

BUTTON UP

Add a button to fasten a pocket. To do this, work a buttonhole near the top of a patch pocket, or just below a straight slit for a pocket, and sew on a button to match. On a diagonal slit, you could work a button loop halfway up the edge of the slit.

Felted/fulled knits

When woollen knits are vigorously washed in hot water and then plunged into cold rinsing water, the fibres mat together and the knitting shrinks, forming a dense fabric suitable for bags and cushions.

One-hundred percent wool yarn works best for felting. Loosely spun wool yarns produce felt with a fuzzy surface in which the individual stitches may be indistinguishable. Yarns that are more tightly spun retain more of the appearance of the individual stitches. Avoid yarns labelled as 'machine-washable'; they have been specially treated to make them shrink-resistant.

MAKING A TEST PIECE

Knit a tension swatch, using your chosen yarns and stitch pattern. Note the numbers of stitches and rows, and the dimensions of the swatch.

1
Wash the swatch on a hot wash in the washing machine with a normal amount of detergent – you can use a half-capacity wash program. Include a large, clean towel or a pair of old jeans to add friction to the wash. Cold-rinse, then dry the swatch flat.

2
Measure the swatch to calculate the tension after felting. Your swatch may shrink by as much as 25% in each direction. The colours usually fade, and blend together in the fuzzy surface of the felt. Use the new tension to plan a project such as a felted bag or cushion.

Striped bag
This bag was knitted in stripes of worsted-weight wool using a slip-stitch pattern at each colour change. The top edge and handle are in garter stitch, finished with a crochet edge. As a rule, assemble a project such as a bag before felting it and run in all the yarn tails. Use the flat seam method to avoid thick, lumpy seams.

Embroider it
Felted knitting makes a great surface for freestyle embroidery because it is firm and non-elastic: it won't stretch and thereby loosen the embroidery stitches. Use a sharp-pointed needle such as a darning needle to work the embroidery. A needle-felting kit can also be used to apply embroidery. As you punch with the tool, five barbed needles (protected by a safety cover) interlace the wool fibres so the design is permanently fixed in place. Woollen yarns give the best results, punched onto a background of felted knitting, as shown.

Needle-felting kit
Follow the instructions supplied with the kit.

SHRINKING

Want a precise size?
You can shrink a garment, such as a hat, to the exact size you want. Find a bowl or pan of the required circumference and felt the hat. Leave it stretched over the bowl or cooking pan until dry.

Moderate the shrinkage
The amount of shrinkage and felting can be controlled by less drastic treatments. Here are two methods:

- Use an old-fashioned top-loading washing machine. Stop the wash every couple of minutes and lift the knitting out with tongs to check how far it has shrunk. When it has shrunk the required amount, rinse well in cool water and leave flat on a towel to dry.

- Prepare two bowls: one of hot, soapy water (about 30°C/ 85°F), and the other of very cold water. You will also need a washboard and a nailbrush. Wear rubber gloves. Wash the knitting in the hot water for a couple of minutes, then lift it out and rub it vigorously on the washboard until it begins to shrink. Brush the surface gently with the nailbrush to fluff up the fibres. Plunge the knitting into the cold water. Repeat the hot/rub/cold process several times if required. Rinse twice more in fresh, cold water, squeeze out excess moisture and leave flat to dry.

advanced knitting
techniques

Now for the more challenging – yet ultimately rewarding – work. From Fair Isle to cables, lace to loop, the more technical stitches will open up a whole new world of knitting. And there are the online films to help you, too, so pick up your needles and prepare to improve!

Working in the round

It is said that what goes around comes around, and in the case of knitting in the round, that would appear to be true. The huge rise in the popularity of hand knitting socks and a burgeoning interest among designers in complex colourwork has seen this technique come back into its own.

Knitting in the round (also referred to as circular knitting), is done using either DPNs (see pages 163–166) or circular needles (see pages 167–168). Circular needles come in a range of lengths. Available in sets of four or five, the most common lengths of DPNs are 12.5cm (5in) and 19cm (7½in), although 25.5cm (10in) sets can also be found.

When choosing whether to use circular needles or DPNs, it comes down to preference mainly. However, DPNs are useful when knitting a small number of stitches, for example, for the crown of a hat. For DPN sizes, consider the projects you are using them for, but also, how nimble your fingers are. For socks and toys, and when you only have a small number of stitches on each needle, 12.5cm (5in) DPNs are a good choice. For hats and similar items, 19cm (7½in) DPNs can also be used. You may find this length more practical for socks, too, although you may need a smaller set for the last few rows when you have few stitches on the needles. The longer length needles are for larger items: bags, jumpers and so on.

Whether you use four or five DPNs is a matter of preference. Initially it is easier to use the number stated in your pattern; otherwise you will have to make adjustments to get the right stitches on the right needles. Buying sets of five needles is always a good idea because you can either knit with the fifth one or keep it as a spare.

Rounds vs rows

When following a pattern using DPNs, patterns refer to rounds rather than rows. One round is the same as a row in knitting: all the stitches on each needle have been worked once.

It can be difficult to tell where a round begins and ends, particularly as the knitting progresses, so markers are used to denote the start and end of each round. Markers are also used to identify pattern changes and repeats, and to denote where shaping takes place. They can be a short loop of contrasting yarn, plastic split rings or you could treat yourself to some beaded markers.

CASTING ON WITH DPNS – FOLD AND DIVIDE METHOD
The fold and divide method uses a DPN to cast on and a set of five DPNs in total. The stitches are cast on to a single DPN; they are then divided onto a second one, folded together and the circle joined. The remaining stitches are divided as they are knitted rather than being slipped off onto new needles. This method makes twisting less likely but is easier when using five DPNs. It is also necessary to be able to get all your stitches onto one DPN.

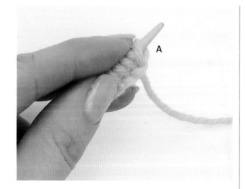

1
Cast on 36 sts on one DPN (A).

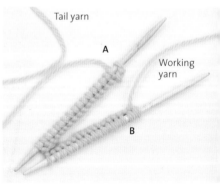

2
Slip half the stitches onto a new DPN (B) and fold the two DPNs together, checking the stitches aren't twisted. The working yarn should be at the tip of the needle nearest to you.

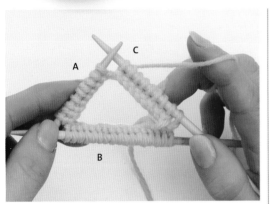

3
With the points of A and B held together, use a third DPN (C) and the working yarn to knit the first quarter of the cast-on stitches (being the first 9 sts from needle A).

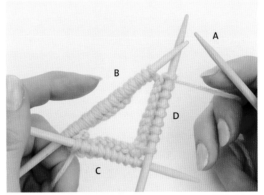

4
Rotate the work, pick up a fourth DPN (D) and knit across the remaining stitches on A. This will leave A empty, ready to knit the next set of stitches from needle B.

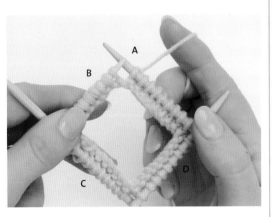

5
Take DPN A and knit the next 9 sts from needle B. This should leave 9 sts on needle B.

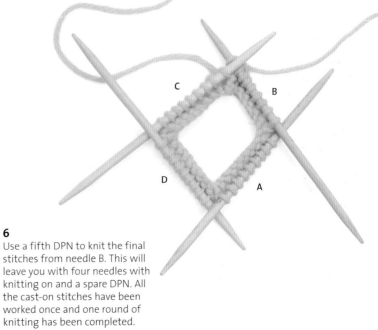

6
Use a fifth DPN to knit the final stitches from needle B. This will leave you with four needles with knitting on and a spare DPN. All the cast-on stitches have been worked once and one round of knitting has been completed.

CONTINUING YOUR KNITTING

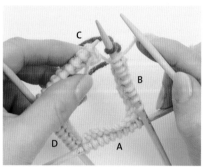

7
Each stitch has been knitted and you have worked one round. Place a marker on B by tying on a slipknot in a contrasting colour of yarn. You will have a spare DPN, which you will use to start the next round of knitting.

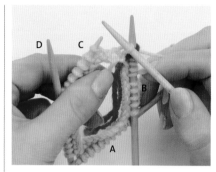

8
Continue to knit using the empty DPN until all the stitches on C have been knitted. As you knit the last stitch, this needle will be empty and now becomes your working needle, so swap it into your RH.

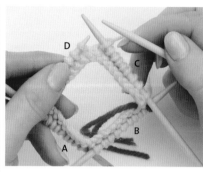

9
Rearrange the needles in your hands, bringing D forward and letting the needle you have just filled (C) drop back. Note that the marker has rotated, too. Knit the stitches off needle D with the spare DPN.

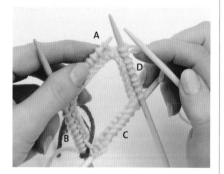

10
Use the new working needle to knit the stitches off A.

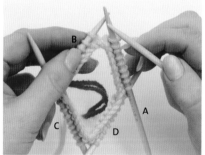

11
When the needle is empty, swap it into your RH, rotate the needles again, let A drop back, bring forward B. Now knit the stitches off B.

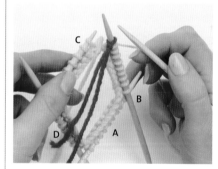

12
You have now worked one complete round. Needle B (with marker) should now be in your RH with the stitches on needle C ready to be worked next. Continue to work in this way. Each time you reach the marker, this denotes one new round completed.

PATTERNS FOR PROJECTS KNITTED IN THE ROUND
Be aware that you are, in effect, always knitting on the RS. So, if you want to knit a stocking-stitch fabric, every round is a knit row. For a garter-stitch fabric, alternating rounds of knit and purl are worked. Don't worry if this seems confusing. Your pattern will tell you which stitches to work.

DIRECT CAST-ON USING A SET OF FOUR DPNS

If you find the single-needle method particularly difficult, there are alternatives you can try. For this method, stitches are cast directly onto the DPNs. This avoids the need to divide the stitches, but can be tricky for beginners and care is needed to avoid loose joins between the needles and twists at the joins. A long-tail or similar one-needle cast on is recommended for this method (see page 46).

1
Cast 9 sts onto DPN A. Supporting A, take a new DPN (B), keeping the working yarn tight as you make the first new stitch. Cast 9 sts onto B.

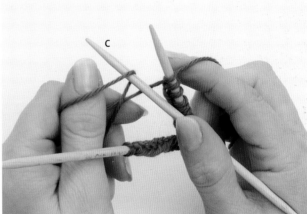

2
Repeat for a third DPN (C).

3
Repeat for a fourth DPN (D).

TOO MANY NEEDLES?
If holding the needles is difficult, drop the needles with stitches on, but be careful to pull joins tight.

If your cord is too long, loop it round on the RH side, as shown here.

JOINING THE CIRCLE

Now that your stitches are divided onto the needles, you may be wondering how you form the stitches into a circle. That's where the 'spare' DPN comes in – it is your 'working' needle, which is used to join the circle and to knit the next stitches. In effect, it is the same as the RH needle in normal knitting, held empty in your right hand, ready to knit the next row. The four needles with stitches already on them are the equivalent of your LH needle, but each of the four holds one quarter of the stitches, waiting in turn to be knitted.

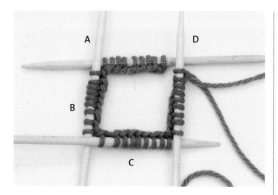

4
Lay your stitches flat and, with the working yarn to the right, check there are no twisted stitches.

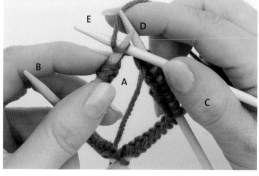

5
Hold D with the working yarn in your RH and A in your LH. Bring A and D together to form a square. Do a final check to ensure that the stitches are not twisted. Pick up a fifth DPN (E) and insert it into the first stitch on A.

6
Holding D in the crook of your RH finger and thumb, knit the first stitch off the LH needle (A) onto the new DPN (E). Pull up the working yarn tightly for a neat join. Knit the remaining stitches from A onto E until A is empty. A will be your new working needle.

Each time you reach the marker, one new round is completed.

7
Repeat, using the empty needle as the next working needle as the stitches are knitted off it, until all the cast-on stitches have been knitted once. Place a marker at the start of the next round and continue to work in this way.

CIRCULAR NEEDLES

A circular needle comprises two short needles joined by a flexible cord. Different cord lengths are available and choosing the right length of cord is important. Ideally, stitches should fit comfortably around the needles and cord without being stretched. Some kits offer interchangeable cords and can be joined together for even longer lengths. For projects with a small circumference, it may be necessary to change between circular needles and DPNs.

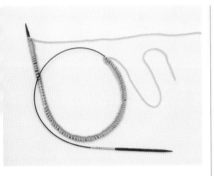

1
Cast on using your preferred technique, holding one needle in each hand, or, for long-tail and other single-needle cast-on methods, holding one needle in the RH as usual. As the needle fills, allow the stitches to slide off onto the cord.

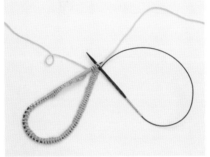

2
With all the stitches cast on, the work needs to be joined to form a circle. Lay the work flat, needle points together. Spread the stitches evenly around needles and cord and check that there are no twists in the cast-on stitches.

3
Place a stitch marker on the RH needle to mark the start and end of the round. Lift the work, holding the needles as usual, with the cord in between, but with the working yarn on the RH needle.

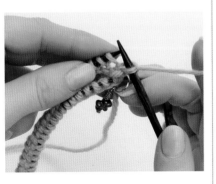

4
Knit the first stitch from the LH needle and draw up the yarn tightly to avoid creating a hole at the join.

5
Continue to knit stitches onto the RH needle. As the knitting progresses, shuffle the stitches around the cord onto the LH needle, ready to be knitted.

6
At the same time, as the RH needle fills up, allow the knitted stitches to slide onto the cord, keeping an even tension around the work as much as possible to avoid distortion.

7
If you have a long cord, when it is time to shuffle the stitches around it, pull the needle through, around the loop. Keep the empty loop to the RH side and continue knitting.

8
When you reach the marker, this completes one round (equivalent to one row in flat knitting). In charted knitting this is represented by one row on the chart. Continue knitting by first slipping the marker over to the RH needle, and then working the next stitch on the LH needle, drawing up the yarn firmly, and knitting around to the marker as before.

Jogless circular knitting

In effect, circular knitting is a subtle spiral, as there is always a slight step between the last stitch of one round and first stitch of the next round. Barely noticeable with fine yarns and plain knitting or multicoloured yarns, this step can be more obvious with stripes. This step is referred to as a jog, and there are several ways to minimise its visibility.

It may seem that there is little difference in the appearance of the three methods (see the swatches opposite). However, which technique you choose will depend on the size of the project, the yarn being used, the number of stripes and the frequency of colour changes. By being aware of the relative benefits and limitations of each method, you will achieve the best result for your project.

SLIP-STITCH METHOD

Although almost invisible, the slipped stitch reduces the height of the work at the round change, pulling up the work. If colour changes are every one or two rounds or on large pieces of knitting, this pulling may be noticeable, in which case the two-strand method may be preferable.

In colour A (white), knit required number of rounds. Place a marker on the RH needle. Change to B (coloured yarn). Knit a complete round to the marker. Slip the marker to the RH needle then slip the next stitch on the LH needle purlwise onto the RH needle. Continue in B until the next colour change, marking rounds with the marker (note that at the end of the first round following the colour change, the slipped stitch in colour A will be knitted in B). Repeat as above, keeping the marker in a vertical line and preserving the start of the round in the same place.

LIFTED-STITCH METHOD

This technique is also virtually invisible, but because it draws up the yarn from the previous round – shortening the work where the stitch is pulled up from below – it is not suitable for frequent colour changes. The shortening can distort the fabric.

In colour A (white), knit the required number of rounds. Place a marker on the RH needle. Change to B (coloured yarn). Knit a complete round to the marker. Slip the marker to the RH needle. Lift the RH leg of the stitch from the previous round (this will be in colour A) onto the LH needle and knit together with the first stitch of the new colour (B). Continue knitting in B until the next colour change and repeat as above.

TWO-STRAND METHOD

This method works best with two similar colours and can be bulky with thick yarns, but is simple and neat. It doesn't shorten the work, so on large garments where shortening would be more noticeable, this method is a good choice.

In colour A (white), knit the required number of rounds. Slip the marker to the RH needle. Change to B (coloured yarn), but knit the next stitch with both A and B. Pull the old colour (A) to the back and continue knitting in the new yarn (B). Having knitted the first stitch with both strands, both will be visible; however, this is dealt with on the next round. At the end of the round, slip the marker to the RH needle. Knit the strand in the old colour (A) together with the new colour (B). Continue knitting as usual. Repeat as required.

TIPS

- **Different yarns and patterns will affect the choice of method for ending and starting rounds when changing colours** (or when working in patterns such as lace or cables) so swatch several samples to see which works best. It is possible to use different methods in one garment, so if your garment is pulling, change to the two-strand method at intervals, to lengthen the fabric at the changeover point.

- **Careful blocking will even out some of the jog effect,** but where possible, locate the ends of the rounds in the least noticeable area, for example, at the underarm sides of a garment or up the inside edge of a sock.

- **Circular needles do vary.** Look for a flexible cord and a smooth join between needle and cord. If choosing interchangeable needles, check how sturdy the join is. Ask to try a pair if possible.

Lace and openwork

Lace knitting has a long and fascinating history. Whereas many knitting styles and techniques are the same the world over, lace patterns can often be traced back to a particular country or region. Shetland, Faroese and Orenburg lace are popular with knitters, and strong lace traditions exist throughout Europe and beyond.

To the first-time lace knitter it can be hard to imagine mastering such apparently difficult patterns; however, most lace stitches are created using straightforward combinations of yarn overs and decreases. The yarn over (also referred to as a yarn forward, yarn in front, or yarn round needle) creates the hole or eyelet that makes the fabric lace, but at the same time it creates an additional stitch. To maintain even edges and keep the number of stitches constant, a compensating decrease must be worked for each yarn over. It is this combination of increases and decreases that create the wonderful patterns seen in so many designs, from gossamer-light shawls to lacy socks, jumpers, accessories and even jewellery.

The keys to successful lace knitting are careful counting, using stitch markers and row counters and knitting in good light. It is important to know that in lace knitting, not every row will have the same number of stitches. In some patterns yarn-over increases will be worked on one row, but decreases may not be worked until a later row. This may be easier to see in charted rather than written patterns, but it is well worth the extra time to check each row in the pattern repeat and note how many stitches you should have in each row before you start knitting.

SIMPLE YARN OVER (YO/YF/YRN) ON A KNIT ROW FOLLOWED BY A KNIT STITCH
Create eyelets in a knit row by first making a yarn over, also referred to as a yarn forward or yarn round needle (yo, yf or yrn).

The yo looks almost like a loop of loose thread rather than a complete stitch.

CLIP 14
Lace knitting, part 1

1
Knit to where the yo is to be made. Bring the yarn under the RH needle to the front of the work. Then take it over the needle and hold at the back ready to make the next stitch.

2
Knit the next stitch as usual. When a yo has been made on a knit row, it is usually worked (normally purled, but in some patterns, knitted) on the following row.

SIMPLE YARN OVER (YO/YF/YRN) ON A KNIT ROW, FOLLOWED BY A PURL STITCH

In some lace patterns a yarn over may be followed by a purl rather than a knit stitch, requiring a slight variation in technique.

The loop of the yo creates the lace eyelet and the purl bump can be seen to the left of the yo.

1
For a yo where a knit stitch is followed by a purl stitch (or two stitches purled tog), bring the yarn under the RH needle to the front, then take it over the RH needle and hold to the back. This creates the yo.

2
To purl the next stitch, bring the yarn under the RH needle again to the front and purl as usual.

YARN OVER, KNIT TWO TOGETHER (YO, K2TOG)

Creating an extra stitch with an immediately corresponding decrease.

The yo looks like a loop of loose thread rather than a complete stitch.

1
Create an eyelet in a knit row by first making a yo as demonstrated in the two steps above.

2
Make a corresponding decrease by knitting the next two stitches together. The yo creates an extra stitch, knitting the next two stitches together decreases a stitch, returning the work to the same number of stitches.

3
As with a simple yarn over, when a yo has been made on a knit row with an accompanying decrease it will normally be worked (usually purled, but in some patterns, knitted) on the following row.

CLIP 15
Lace knitting, part 2

YARN OVER, SLIP ONE, KNIT ONE, PASS SLIPPED STITCH OVER (YO, SL1, K1, PSSO)

Creating an extra stitch with an immediately corresponding decrease. This is an alternative method for making a matching increase and decrease on a knit row by making a yarn over and bringing the yarn from the back under the RH needle to the front of the work.

Don't actually knit the stitch!

1
With the yarn held at the front (this creates the yo), slip the next stitch from the LH to the RH needle as if to knit but without actually knitting it.

Lifting the slipped stitch over and off the needle decreases one stitch.

2
Knit the next stitch in the usual way, leaving the slipped stitch unworked in between the yo and the knitted stitch. As the stitch is knitted, the yo can be seen as a loop of thread over the needle rather than as a complete stitch.

3
To decrease a stitch, use the LH needle to lift the slipped stitch over the stitch just knitted.

This decrease compensates for the stitch increased when making the yo.

4
Drop the lifted stitch off the RH needle. This method is often abbreviated in patterns to yo (or yrn or yf), sl1, k1, psso (yarn over, slip one, knit one, pass slipped stitch over).

5
As with the yo, k2tog, when a yo has been made on a knit row, it will normally be worked (usually purled, but in some patterns, knitted) on the following row.

The yo can be identified as it looks almost like a loop of loose thread rather than a complete stitch.

TIPS

- **Lace patterns look different depending on the yarn.** A smooth yarn, as shown here, will give crisp, clear eyelets and good pattern definition. Fluffy yarns give a softer look.

- **For lacy edgings with waves,** yarn overs are worked on several rows without decreases. The extra stitches create the 'peak' of the wave as the work widens. After several rows stitches are bound off to create a sharp 'trough', returning to the original number of stitches, ready for the next peak.

- **Yarn-over techniques can work very well in bulkier yarns and add interest to textured yarns too.** A simple lace panel on a sock leg is lovely and a good starter project, because it can be worked as one repeat on just one DPN, bordered with plain knitting.

- **Create customised lace charts** with knitter's graph paper. Remember to swatch and match increases with decreases to ensure that the overall shape of the knitting is maintained.

- **Use stitch markers on larger pieces** to indicate pattern repeats within the row.

- **To help you see the eyelets and spot any errors,** place a piece of dark card (or white if using dark yarn) behind your knitting at regular intervals.

- **To help limit the number of rows that need unpicking if an error is made,** many knitters use lifelines. A lifeline is simply a piece of smooth yarn (cotton, for example) in a contrasting colour that is threaded through a complete row of stitches at regular intervals, usually at the start of a pattern repeat. For instructions on using lifelines see page 229.

Cables

Cables create richly textured, dramatic knits. Traditionally featured in Aran jumpers, these patterns are now more widely used in samplers, afghans and accessories. Cabled socks are particularly popular and are combined with lace, bobbles and other stitches to great effect.

Cables may look very complicated but are essentially combinations of knit and purl stitches worked out of sequence. A cable can be a simple, single rope or braid, or a much more intricate combination of honeycombs, plaits and lattices.

Stitches are transferred to a short needle (a cable needle) and these stitches are then held either at the front or the back of the knitting. A number of stitches are then knitted from the main needle. To complete the sequence the stitches from the cable needle are then knitted. This has the effect of creating a crossed fabric. Where stitches are held at the back the cross will be to the right. Stitches held at the front will create a cross moving to the left.

It is possible to add a lovely personalised touch to an otherwise simple knit by adding a cable panel, perhaps down a plain sleeve or along the edges of a knitted throw. However, when working with cables bear in mind that a cable will affect the drape, density and feel of the knitted fabric, so careful swatching is essential.

WORKING INTO REVERSE STOCKING STITCH

Cables are often set on a background of reverse stocking stitch. This is where the purl side of stocking stitch is used as the right side of the work rather than the more usual knit side. This helps the cable stand out more clearly.

CABLE NEEDLE

Choosing a cable needle that is a couple of sizes smaller than the main needles makes cables easier to work. Some cable needles have a kink in the middle, which helps stop stitches from sliding off the needle.

CLIP 16
Cable stitch

www.youtube.com/watch?v=s9wScwZnzfU

Balance the RH needle underneath the cable needle with your ring and little fingers.

1
Work to where the cable begins. Hold the cable needle in your RH like a pen, holding it above and parallel to the RH needle.

This simple cable could be used as a stand-alone panel for a bold effect, or be combined with other cables for a more complex pattern.

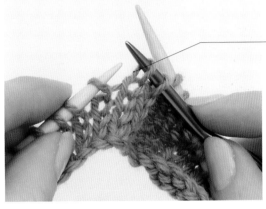

When a stitch is moved to another needle without working it (i.e., when moving onto a cable needle, as here), this may be referred to as slipping a stitch knitwise or purlwise. This means that you move the stitch as if you were going to knit or purl it but without actually working the stitch.

2
Use the cable needle to lift the first stitch off the LH needle. Lift the stitch from right to left, taking the cable needle in front of the LH needle as if you were going to purl the next stitch (purlwise). This stitch isn't worked yet.

3
Lift a second stitch from the LH needle onto the cable needle as before. The cable needle should still be in front of the LH needle, the tip pointing towards your left hand.

4
Lift a final stitch onto the cable needle. Note how the RH needle remains supported in the right hand. This helps to prevent the stitches on either side of the cable from stretching or dropping off the needle.

5
Slide the stitches to the middle of the cable needle to prevent them from sliding off.

Most yarn weights can be used for cables but smooth, untextured yarns will give the best stitch definition and make the cables more prominent.

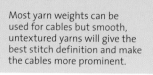

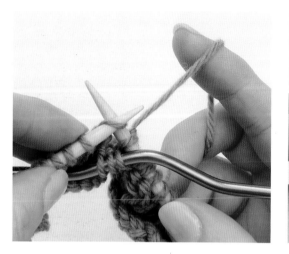

The first and third stitches in particular need to be quite tight to avoid an unsightly hole at the edge of the cable.

6
Allow the cable needle to rest at the front of the work. If the cable needle feels unwieldy, poke the LH end into the knitting, being careful not to split the yarn. Work with the yarn slightly tensioned.

7
Knit the next three stitches from the LH needle. This may feel awkward and the stitches quite tight. This is normal.

Keeping the cable needle parallel and close to the LH needle will reduce stretching.

8
Pick up or untuck the cable needle from the fabric. Keeping the tips of the needles close together and supporting them with the middle and ring fingers will help to keep the cable neat and avoid stretched stitches.

9
Slide the stitches on the cable needle onto the RH end. Hold the cable needle in your LH, in front of the LH needle.

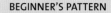

10
Knit the next three stitches one at a time from the cable needle, knitting them from the RH end of the cable needle onto the RH needle.

11
If, as you knit, the stitches feel very tight, check that the cable needle isn't twisted and that you are knitting the stitches in the correct order. You should be knitting the first stitch you slipped first, the second next and so on.

12
When you have knitted all three stitches from the cable needle, set it to one side and return to working the stitches on the LH needle. Draw up the first stitch firmly to avoid a hole.

13
Purled stitches on either side of the cable make it stand out. The cable twists to the left. For a cable that twists to the right, the cable needle is held at the back of the work instead of the front.

Textured patterns

Textured knits may appear to be complicated, but there are many ways to give your garments and accessories that sumptuous, luxurious look without too much difficulty. With the right choice of yarn and a few simple techniques, even beginner knitters can create a designer look.

In addition to cables and lace there are many interesting wrapped, slipped and twist-stitch stitch patterns that can be used to give knitting rich, textural qualities. Wrapped, slipped and twist-stitch patterns are similar to cables but they do not require the use of a cable needle. Instead, they rely simply on working the stitches out of sequence. This can be achieved with all the stitches still on the needles, but in some cases, stitches are simply dropped off the needle until they are required; then they are picked up and returned to the needle, ready to be worked. If the prospect of deliberately dropping stitches sounds alarming, don't worry; it isn't as scary as it sounds!

Bobbles are another fun set of textural stitches. Bobbles follow a straightforward format of working several times into a single stitch, working a number of rows, and then decreasing until only the original stitch remains. This effect looks charming when worked alone, but can also be used effectively in clusters to create highly textured knits.

Textured stitches can be knitted in panels, worked randomly or combined in more complex all-over designs. Once you are familiar with how individual stitch patterns are worked, you will soon be able to create your own combinations and incorporate them into your favourite knits.

TEXTURED WRAPPED RIB
Wrapped stitches make excellent, richly textured ribs. Providing the wrap yarn is not pulled too tightly, good elasticity and softness remain, but the wrap adds depth and interest to your work.

CLIP 17
Textured rib

www.youtube.com/watch?v=ZopW3JF_4K8

CLIP 18
Bobble stitch

www.youtube.com/watch?v=1ZGtSEbLH5o

1
For a simple two-stitch wrap, cast on an even number of stitches, knit one, then purl the next two stitches. (Knitting the first and last stitch of the row keeps the edge even and makes stitching up easier.)

Take care not to pull the wrap yarn too tightly.

2
Keeping the yarn at the front of the work, slip both purled stitches back onto the LH needle.

3
Take the yarn from the front to the back of the work between the needles. Slip the two purled stitches just worked back onto the RH needle. This creates the wrap across the front of the two purled stitches.

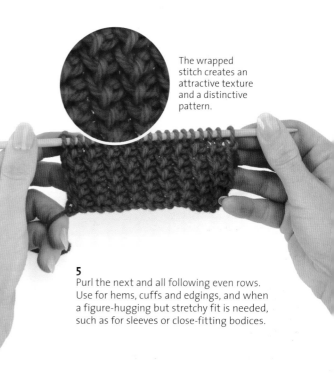

The wrapped stitch creates an attractive texture and a distinctive pattern.

4
Bring the yarn to the front of the work and repeat steps 1 to 3 (ignoring the first knit stitch for the edge) to the last stitch. Knit the last stitch to give a neat edge.

5
Purl the next and all following even rows. Use for hems, cuffs and edgings, and when a figure-hugging but stretchy fit is needed, such as for sleeves or close-fitting bodices.

MOCK CABLES

This mock cable is worked on a reverse stocking stitch background to make it stand out.

1
Cast on 10 sts.
Row 1 P2, take the yarn to the back of the work, sl the next stitch purlwise to the RH needle, k4, sl the next stitch purlwise to the RH needle, p2.
Row 2 K2, bring the yarn to the front of the work, sl1 purlwise, p4, sl1 purlwise, take the yarn to the back of the work, k2.
Rep rows 1 and 2.
Row 5 (the cable row illustrated) P2, take the yarn to the back of the work, and slide the stitch slipped on the previous row off the LH needle, letting it rest at the front of the work.

This slipped stitch will be taken across the next two stitches to create the RH curve of the cable.

This slipped stitch pairs with the first slipped stitch to create a cable-like effect.

2
Knit the next two stitches. Lift the dropped stitch onto the LH needle. Check the lifted stitch is not twisted. If it is, use the RH needle (or your fingers) to return it to the correct shape. If the stitch is small, it can be drawn out gently to allow it to reach the LH needle without distorting the work.

3
For the LH side of the cable, with the yarn held at the back of the work, slip the next two stitches purlwise to the RH needle. Drop the next stitch (the stitch that was slipped on previous rows) to the front of the work. This dropped stitch will form the LH curve of the cable, moving left to right.

4
Return the two slipped stitches on the RH needle to the LH needle. Lift the slipped stitch as before and return to the LH needle.

5
Ensure that the stitch is not twisted, then knit this and the next two stitches to form the LH curve of the cable, moving left to right. Again, use the needle or your fingers to untwist the stitch if needed.

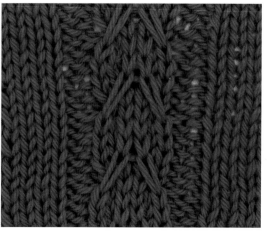

6
This completes the LH cross of the cable. The slipped stitches meet in the centre, completing the mock cable. The slipped stitches should look, smooth, flat and elongated. For the final row, k2, p6, k2, then repeat from row 1.

BOBBLES

Bobbles are clusters of stitches made by increasing a set number of times from a single originating stitch, working a number of rows on these stitches, then decreasing back to just the original stitch.

1
For a simple bobble, knit one stitch, then, without dropping the stitch off the LH needle, wrap the yarn around the needle and knit into the same stitch again.

Three stitches from the one original stitch.

2
There are now three stitches (two increases plus the original stitch) on the RH needle. For larger bobbles, the original stitch may be knitted into several times, or more yos may be used to create more stitches.

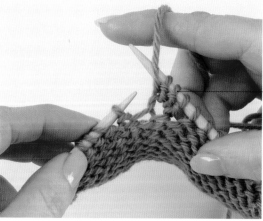

The purled bobble stitches are now on the RH needle.

3
Turn the work so that the three stitches you have just made are now in your LH. Purl these three stitches.

Knit the last two stitches together.

4
Turn the work again, putting the stitches just worked back into the LH. Work these stitches again by knitting the first stitch and then knitting the next two stitches together.

5
Turn the work a final time and purl the first two stitches together.

6
With the bobble now complete, one stitch remains on the RH needle.

7
The clustered stitches should pop out on the front of the work to form a bobble. Keep the bobbles tidy by knitting quite tightly and drawing up the yarn firmly before knitting the rest of the row.

TIPS

- **If you are customising a simple knit,** bear in mind that textured stitches generally use up more yarn than a plain stocking stitch; so remember to allow for this when buying yarn.

- **It's lots of fun to combine textured patterns,** but be sure to create tension swatches for at least two pattern repeats, since there may be differences in tension that could distort your work.

- **If you are swapping a textured rib or edging for a standard one,** make a swatch of each to check tension, drape and elasticity before going ahead. Edgings can often be added later, so if you just 'must have' a particular edging but it has a different tension, why not make it separately and sew or graft it on later?

- **Textured stitches often make a project heavier,** affecting drape and structure. A good-sized tension swatch should help you decide whether your design will be too heavy for your chosen yarn or project.

Loop stitches

Great for adding a funky touch to edgings or trims, or for a boa-like scarf or a flouncy collar, loop stitches are an easy way to add a bit of drama. They are also a super technique for toys and dolls – try them for doll's hair, sheep fleece or a poodle's curly coat.

Loop stitch is also called fur stitch because it is often used to create a shaggy, furry texture for knits. Loops can be varied in size for different effects. They can also be cut for a dense pile texture. Loop stitches do need to be firmly anchored to prevent them from pulling or unravelling. For this reason, loops are rarely worked on every row of knitting, but are interspersed with rows of garter or stocking stitch.

Cut piles and loops are a good addition to housewares. Cushions and rugs made from panels of loop stitches combined with panels of plain or other stitches can give interesting creative effects. Playing with multi-coloured yarns can also create some exciting designs. It is even possible to add beads to loop knits for some real bling!

Loop stitches are formed using the same fundamental technique, which is varied by changing the length, frequency and placing of the loops, as well as varying the background stitches.

LOOPS AT THE FRONT OF THE WORK (ON A BACKGROUND OF GARTER STITCH)

1
Cast on as usual and knit two rows.

2
Knit one but don't drop the stitch from the LH needle.

3
Bring the yarn to the front of the work, between the two needles.

4
Wind the yarn around your left thumb or, for a larger loop, around a piece of card.

5
Take the yarn to the back of the work between the needles, keeping your thumb over the loop to hold it in position.

6
Knit the original stitch again, but this time complete the stitch.

CLIP 19
Loop stitch

www.youtube.com/watch?v=4vpgSNcWFGE

7
Bring the yarn to the front of the work and around the RH needle to make a yarn over (but don't knit the next stitch).

8
Using the tip of the LH needle, lift the two stitches just worked over the yarn over. This completes one loop.

LOOPS AT THE BACK OF THE WORK (ON A BACKGROUND OF GARTER STITCH)

1
Cast on as usual and knit two rows.

2
Insert the tip of the RH needle into the first stitch on the LH needle as if to knit. Wrap the yarn around one or more fingers by taking it in front of the finger(s), around and across the back of the finger(s), bringing it up to the RH needle.

3
Take the yarn around the RH needle as if to knit but don't drop the stitch off the needle.

4
Transfer the part-complete stitch on the RH needle onto the LH needle.

5
Knit into the back of the first two stitches on the LH needle (the new stitch and the original stitch). Continue knitting as usual.

TIPS

- **Vary the spacing of the loops** to create more or less dense fabrics.

- **It is possible to make loops on both sides** of the fabric; however, these should be staggered on alternate rows.

- **For a pile effect,** run a knitting needle through the row of loops and cut the loops one row at a time. Vary the cut length for a fuzzier look.

- **Add a loop-stitch fringe** to scarves, garments, cushions or blankets. Create a reversible scarf with loops on either side of the fabric.

- **Add contrasting yarns** – coloured, sparkly or textured – on loop rows.

- **Loop stitch uses up a lot of yarn,** so allow for this when planning projects.

Entrelac

Derived from a French term meaning interwoven or interlaced, at first glance entrelac looks almost like an optical illusion as the colours and shapes weave in and out, and it is a puzzle how the pieces fit together. Rest assured, however, that the mysteries of this fascinating technique will soon be revealed.

. . . .

Entrelac is made up of a series of triangles and squares that are joined together by picking up stitches and using a combination of simple increases and decreases. Entrelac is most commonly made using stocking stitch, but garter stitch and other stitches can also be used. The sample shown here is a block of three/four squares, each five stitches wide, but this can easily be varied to make larger or smaller squares.

SET ONE: Begin by forming a block of base triangles
This set of triangles is worked once only at the bottom edge of the knitting to give a straight edge and to create a base for the slanting squares that will be knitted on top of them.

1
Cast on 20 stitches in yarn A and work three rows in stocking stitch (knit one row, purl one row, knit one row). Turn the work so that the WS is facing.

2 First triangle
Row 1 Continue with yarn A and, with the WS facing, p2, turn.
Row 2 K2, turn.
Row 3 Sl1, p2, turn.
Row 4 Sl1, k2, turn.
Row 5 Sl1, p3, turn.
Row 6 Sl1, k3, turn.
Row 7 Sl1, p4, DON'T turn the work. (WS facing you.)

3 Completing the block of triangles
Repeat rows 1–7 until all the stitches have been worked. Viewed from the RS, as here, there will be a row of four separate blocks of knitting, five stitches in each block.

CLIP 20
Entrelac, part 1

www.youtube.com/watch?v=Geg16-or4mg

This finished swatch shows the final basket-weave effect achieved by using the entrelac technique.

SET TWO: Make a block of squares that lean to the left

This section is formed from a RH edge triangle followed by a series of LH leaning squares and finishing with a LH edge triangle.

4 To make a straight RH-side edge

A triangular piece of knitting is needed to fill the space and form a base for the next set of squares. Change to yarn colour B and turn work so that RS is facing.

Row 1 K2, turn.
Row 2 P2, turn.
Row 3 K1, m1, k2togtbl, turn.
Row 4 Sl1, p2, turn.
Row 5 Sl1, m1, k1, k2togtbl, turn.
Row 6 Sl1, p3, turn.
Row 7 Sl1, m1, k2, k2togtbl, DON'T turn.

5 To make a block of LH-leaning squares

These squares are formed on top of the base triangles from the previous set.
First LH square
*With RS facing, pick up and k5 sts down the slope you've just come to, turn.
Row 1 Sl1, p4, turn.
Row 2 Sl1, k3, k2togtbl. (This will use up the last working st and the first st of the next group of sts.) Turn.

6

Repeat rows 1 and 2 until all of the stitches from the next group of stitches have been used up. DON'T turn*. Repeat from * to * until you reach the end of the row of stitches. One block of three LH-leaning squares has now been formed.

7

Finish the set with the LH edge triangle. When you reach the end of the row, you will notice that the knitting is not straight, but has a sloping edge. A LH-edge triangle is knitted here to fill this gap and create a straight edge.

CLIP **21**
Entrelac, part 2

8
With the RS facing, pick up and k5 sts down
the slope at the end of the row. Turn.
Row 1 P2tog, p3, turn.
Row 2 Sl1, k3, turn.
Row 3 P2tog, p2, turn.
Row 4 Sl1, k2, turn.
Row 5 P2tog, p1, turn.
Row 6 Sl1, k1, turn.
Row 7 P2tog, DON'T turn (1 st rem).
(WS facing you.)

9
One row of the LH-leaning blocks has
been completed.

SET THREE: Make a block of squares leaning to the right
The next block of knitting will make a series of squares that lean to the right.
These are made on the wrong (purl) side of the work. As the gap on the LH
edge has already been filled, simply make a series of squares as follows.

10
Change to yarn A.
*With WS facing, pick up and p4 sts down
the slope, turn.
Row 1 Sl1, k4, turn.
Row 2 Sl1, p3, p2tog, turn (this will use the
last picked-up st and the first st of the next
square from the previous set).

11
Repeat rows 1 and 2 until all the stitches
from the next square have been used up*.
Repeat from * to * to the end of the row.

12
Repeat sets two and three one more time
(or as stated in your pattern), then work set
two once.

SET FOUR: Final set

When the knitting is the right length, a final set of triangles is needed to fill in the gaps and create a straight top edge before binding off.

13

There should be one stitch remaining from the LH edge triangle. *Working with yarn A and with WS facing, pick up and p4 sts (5 sts total). Turn.

Row 1 K5, turn.

Row 2 P2tog, p2, p2tog, turn.

Row 3 K4, turn.

Row 4 P2tog, p1, p2tog, turn.

Row 5 K3, turn.

Row 6 P2tog, p2tog, turn.

Row 7 K2, turn.

Row 8 p1, p2tog, turn.

Row 9 K2, turn.

Row 10 P3tog. DON'T turn. (1 st remains.)*

14

Repeat from * to * to end of row.

15

At the end of the row, fasten off the final stitch by cutting a tail of yarn, threading through the loop and drawing up firmly but not too tightly.

Here you can clearly see the triangles around the edges and the interlocking rectangles. The basket-weave effect makes an attractive and stretchy cushion cover whether you decide to use one colour or two.

TIPS

- **Traditionally, entrelac is worked in stocking stitch,** but it can look very effective with one colour worked in stocking stitch and the second in a fancy stitch such as moss stitch. Make a tension swatch first, however, to ensure that the different stitch tensions don't make the work distort.

- **It isn't necessary to work entrelac in two colours,** but for a first try it makes it much easier to see how the stitches are forming and how the pieces interlock.

- **Entrelac looks better in a 'grippy' yarn such as wool.** Smooth yarns, such as cotton, can show gaps where the stitches are picked up and at the joining sections.

Slip stitch and mosaic

Slip-stitch patterns are a great way to introduce glorious colours into your knitting projects without the complexities of stranding, weaving in and Fair Isle techniques. Mosaic blocks are slip-stitch patterns that replicate patterns from art and architecture, such as ancient Roman and Greek floor mosaics.

Slip-stitch colourwork is deceptively simple. Because the technique relies on slipped stitches to create colour patterns, only one colour is used per row. To create a slip-stitch pattern, some stitches are knitted or purled, usually in a new colour. Other stitches are slipped purlwise from an earlier row, giving you a row with two colours; the slipped stitches from the earlier row in one colour and the worked stitches in the new colour. On the following row it is usual to slip the slipped stitches and work the stitches in the new colour. By combining knit and purl stitches and by holding the yarn either in front or behind the slipped stitches, interesting textures can be created.

The slipped stitches will be elongated and this can affect tension, so create a sample swatch if you are adding a slip-stitch band or substituting a slip-stitch pattern with a different stitch. Be sure that the yarn held at the front or back of the work is not pulled too tight; otherwise the work may pull in or pucker.

Patterns for mosaic knitting are often shortened. There is usually a foundation row worked in a solid colour (A here). For the pattern repeat, only every other row is written out for each pair of rows. Alternate rows that aren't written or charted are worked in the same colour as the preceding row. This second row of the pair is a repeat of the written row where the knit stitches are worked in the same colour and the slipped stitches from the previous row are slipped. Slipped stitches, however, are worked with the yarn held at the front of the work instead of the back, and are always slipped purlwise to prevent twisting.

SIMPLE STRIPE PATTERN

This dense pattern is good for sock heel flaps or knits that need a sturdy and non-elastic fabric.

Using colour A, cast on an even number of stitches.

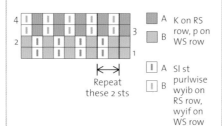

Repeat these 2 sts

A K on RS row, p on WS row
B

I A Sl st purlwise wyib on RS row, wyif on WS row
I B

Row 1 (RS) Using colour B, k1, *k1, sl1wyib, rep from * to last st, k1.
Row 2 Using colour B, p1, *sl1wyif, p1, rep from * to last st, p1.
Row 3 In A, k1, *sl1wyib, k1, rep from * to last st, k1.
Row 4 In A, p1, *p1, sl1wyif, rep from * to last st, p1.
Repeat rows 1–4.

HONEYCOMB

This is similar to the stripe pattern but the stitches are offset to create a honeycomb appearance and a softer, more flexible fabric.

Cast on an odd number of stitches.

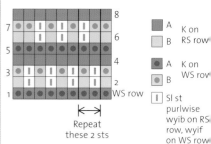

Repeat these 2 sts

A K on RS row
B

A K on WS row
B

I Sl st purlwise wyib on RS row, wyif on WS row

Row 1 (WS) In A, knit.
Row 2 In B, k1, *sl1wyib, k1, rep from * to end.
Row 3 In B, k1, *sl1wyib, k1, rep from * to end.
Row 4 In A, k.
Row 5 In A, k.
Row 6 In B, k2, *sl1wyib, k1, rep from * to last st, k1.
Row 7 In B, k2, *sl1wyif, k1, rep from * to last st, k1.
Row 8 In A, k.
Repeat rows 1–8.

FOUR-COLOUR TWEED

Patterns do not have to be limited to two colours. This pattern uses four different shades, but still uses just one colour per row.

MOSAIC BLOCKS

Mosaic knitting is a form of slip-stitch work with its own conventions for instructions and charts. Patterns are usually geometric and worked with two colours. Many replicate patterns from ancient pottery and weaving.

Using colour A, cast on a multiple of 4 sts, plus 3.

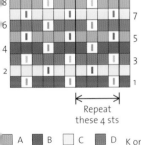

Repeat
these 4 sts

| A | B | C | D | K on RS row, p on WS row |

| A | B | C | D | Sl st purlwise wyib on RS row, wyif on WS row |

Row 1 In B, k1, *sl1wyib, k3, rep from * to last 2 sts, sl1wyib, k1.
Row 2 In C, P3, *sl1wyif, p3, rep from * to end.
Row 3 In D, as row 1.
Row 4 In B, as row 2.
Row 5 In A, as row 1.
Row 6 In D, as row 2.
Row 7 In C, as row 1.
Row 8 In A, as row 2.
Repeat rows 1–8.

Using colour A, cast on a multiple of 14 sts, plus 1.

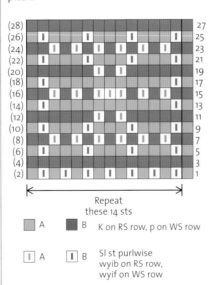

Repeat
these 14 sts

| A | B | K on RS row, p on WS row |

| A | B | Sl st purlwise wyib on RS row, wyif on WS row |

Note: WS rows are not charted separately. Using same colour as previous row, k the k sts and slwyif (purlwise) the sl sts of previous row.

Row 1 In B, k1, *sl1wyib, k1 rep from * to end.
Row 2 and every WS row (not shown on chart) Using same colour as previous row, k the k sts and slwyif the sl sts of previous row.
Row 3 In A, k.
Row 5 In B, k1, *(sl1wyib, k3) 3 times, sl1wyib, k1, rep from * to end.
Row 7 In A, k1, *(k1, sl1wyib) 6 times, k2, rep from * to end.
Row 9 In B, as row 5.
Row 11 In A k1, *k5, sl1wyib, k1, sl1wyib, k6, rep from * to end.
Row 13 In B k1, *sl1wyib, k11, sl1wyib, k1, rep from * to end.
Row 15 In A, k1, *(k1, sl1wyib) 2 times, k1, sl3wyib, (k1, sl1wyib) 2 times, k2, rep from * to end.
Row 17 In B, as 13.
Row 19 In A, as 11.
Row 21 In B, as 9.
Row 23 In A, as 7.
Row 25 In B, as 5.
Row 27 In A, as 3.
(**Row 28** as row 2.)
Repeat rows 1–27.

Fair Isle and stranded colour

Fair Isle may use many colours in a design, but characteristically only two colours are used in any one row, making it easier to master than some other colourwork techniques. The patterns have delightful names such as 'peeries', 'waves and peaks', 'stars' and 'seeding'.

Patterns are worked in stocking stitch from charts, using colours or symbols to indicate colour changes. Once the basics have been mastered, it is easy to design your own patterns.

Yarns

For good pattern definition a fine Shetland wool yarn is traditionally used, being warm, light and durable. Other yarns will work of course, and fun effects can be achieved using thicker and even some textured yarns. Slippery yarns can, however, prove rather challenging for the beginner as there is no 'hairiness' to hold the stitches in place, and it can be difficult to maintain an even tension.

It is possible to work Fair Isle by simply picking up and dropping each colour as required. An alternative is to hold one yarn in each hand, simultaneously utilising both the right-handed and left-handed (Continental) knitting techniques (see pages 197–199). This takes a little practice, but once mastered is quick to do and almost eliminates yarn tangling when changing colours.

Colour changing

When changing colours, the yarn not in use (the float or float yarn) is carried across the wrong side of the work by stranding or weaving in to avoid constantly breaking off and rejoining the yarn.

Reading charts

For Fair Isle patterns, charts are normally used instead of written patterns because they are easier to follow. Charts are read from the bottom, starting at the bottom right. Each square represents a stitch and each row of squares a row of knitting.

In flat knitting, right-side rows are worked from right to left and wrong-side rows from left to right. In circular knitting, all rows are read from right to left and, as a rule with Fair Isle, all rows are knit because the right side of the work is always facing you.

CLIP 22
Fair Isle
technique, part 1

www.youtube.com/watch?v=B3RLCj9di88

CLIP 23
Fair Isle
technique, part 2

www.youtube.com/watch?v=V8VUdQy-o-E

Knit in colour A (background colour) odd rows, purl in colour A even rows

Knit in colour B (contrast colour) odd rows, purl in colour B even rows

Start knitting here

Knit right to left

Purl right to left

Odd rows are knitted, even rows are purled

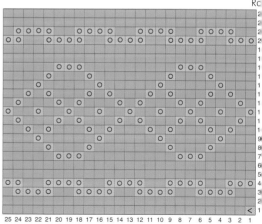

Careful selection of colours enables you to create crisp, clear motifs and repeating patterns in horizontal bands.

STRANDING: KNIT ROW

On both knit and purl rows, this method works well where colour changes are frequent (no more than four or five stitches apart). It gives a less dense, lighter fabric and uses less yarn than weaving in (see pages 194–196).

1
To work the chart shown left, starting at the bottom right and working from right to left, knit in A (magenta) until the first colour change. Make the next stitch by joining in colour B (lime green) as normal. Leave a tail of B for darning in later and don't cut off A.

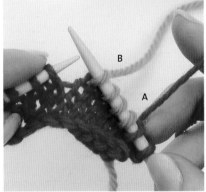

2
Knit in B to the next colour change. Lift yarn A from beneath, under B.

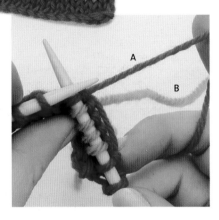

3
Knit with A until the next colour change.

4
Repeat for each colour change, lifting the new yarn from under the working yarn. At the end of the row, check that when the fabric is slightly stretched the floats are not pulling the fabric in.

5
Viewed from the WS, the floats of yarn can be seen stranding neatly across the back of the work. Note also how the yarn working yarns are twisted. These will need to be untangled before starting the next row.

STRANDING: PURL ROW

When changing yarns at the edge of the work, keep both yarns evenly tensioned to avoid untidy edges.

Hold the new colour firmly, but not so tightly it pulls the work in.

1
When making flat knitted pieces, work the next row of the chart from left to right in purl. As with the knit row, lift the new colour from beneath the working yarn at each colour change so that the old yarn lays in front of the new yarn as it faces you. As the first row ended with colour A and row 2 begins with colour B, lift colour B from beneath colour A.

2
Continue to work in purl in colour B until the next colour change. Lift colour A from beneath colour B so that colour B lays across the front of colour A.

The knitted fabric should be flat with some elasticity and the stitches should be even.

3
Repeat until the end of the row.

SEMI-STRANDING
Where there are more than five stitches between colour changes, semi-stranding is used in place of stranding over a large number of stitches. For this technique, the float yarn is caught in every few stitches by working three or four stitches in the current colour, then following the steps for stranding (knitting or purling). Repeat every three or four stitches as required.

Weaving in
What is the difference between stranding and weaving in? Weaving in avoids loose floats across the back of the work and the two colours in the row are neatly entwined at each stitch.

Should I use stranding or weaving in? Both techniques have their place. Stranding is ideal for areas with frequent colour changes within the row and where a lighter, less dense fabric is required.

For firmer fabrics, where the floats would be too long, or where short floats would be likely to snag, weaving in may be preferable. With socks or gloves, for example, when the floats may catch on rings or between toes, this can be irritating and may spoil your knitting.

Sometimes, neither stranding nor weaving in is perfect for the situation. In these circumstances, use a semi-stranding technique (see left) because it produces floats as in stranding, but weaves in the unused yarn at intervals. It is particularly useful where colour contrasts are strong but change infrequently.

The best way to decide which method to use is by making sample swatches. Test each section of the pattern bearing in mind the type of garment/accessory you are making. Where will the pattern be? Will it get lots of wear? Is it likely to be in an area prone to snagging?

Can the techniques be combined? Yes, indeed, with some patterns it may be unavoidable – but take care to create sample swatches. With properly worked samples there shouldn't be any difference in tension, but be aware of the feel of the fabric. Include some rows of single-colour knitting in your samples if they feature in the pattern, because these may also feel different from the coloured sections.

WEAVING IN: KNIT ROW

1
To work in yarn A (magenta), B (lime green) is woven in. Insert the RH needle to begin a knit stitch as normal. Take B over the top of A and wrap round the RH needle as if to knit. Take A around the RH needle as if to knit. B sits behind A on the RH needle.

2
Before completing the knit stitch, bring B back around the RH needle.

Taking yarn B back around the RH needle in this way wraps it around yarn A with minimum tangling.

3
B now lays over A. Leaving B over A, knit the next stitch as normal in A.

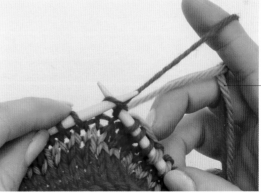

4
With full weaving in, if the next stitch continues in B, bring B up from beneath A and knit the next stitch in B. Otherwise, repeat steps 1–3 until the next colour change. To change to A, bring A up from under B and continue knitting in A.

Yarn B is neatly caught in and knitting can continue in yarn A. Yarn B is held at the back of the work, evenly tensioned, until it is needed.

WEAVING IN: PURL ROW

1
To work a purl stitch in A (magenta), B (lime green) is woven in. Insert the RH needle into the stitch purlwise as normal. Wrap B around the RH needle as if to purl. Wrap A around the RH needle as if to purl.

2
Bring B back around the RH needle so A lays across the front of B. Complete the purl stitch in A.

3
With full weaving in, if the next stitch continues in A, bring A up from beneath B and purl the next stitch in A. Repeat steps 1–3 until the next colour change. To change to B, bring B up from under A.

View from the back

In this swatch, seen from the reverse, the first (lowest) section is stranded because the colour changes are only three or four stitches apart. Four plain rows follow. The second section shows full weaving in with every stitch wrapped (caught in). This fabric is denser and less elastic. The third section shows semi-stranding. There are more than four stitches between colour changes so it is necessary to weave in every three or four stitches to avoid long floats.

The fourth section has long floats that could snag but would give a lighter fabric. The final (top) section shows the effect of alternating between bringing the new yarn up from behind and taking it across the front of the existing yarn at the colour changes. The conventional technique is to work in the same direction (i.e., always bringing the new yarn up from behind). However, by alternating between the two, the yarns don't tangle as each colour change twists, then untwists, the yarns. This puts less strain on the yarns. The fabric is also less likely to bias as each twist is matched by a corresponding 'untwist'. The reverse of the fabric isn't as neat, but the front of the fabric is equally attractive (and it saves a lot of boring untangling!).

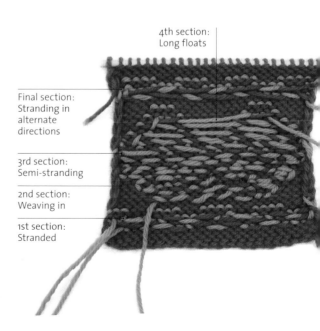

4th section:
Long floats

Final section:
Stranding in
alternate
directions

3rd section:
Semi-stranding

2nd section:
Weaving in

1st section:
Stranded

Holding the yarn in two hands

This method is a combination of the US/Continental European left-handed style of knitting and the right-handed British style, since one strand of yarn is held in each hand and both are used in the same row. Depending on your normal knitting style (left- or right-handed), it is likely that you will need to practise one of the two methods until you are reasonably proficient in both. This may seem like a lot of work, but it is well worth the effort and will have lots of benefits other than just for colourwork!

The big advantage of this method is that the yarns shouldn't become tangled and there is no need to stop to twist/untwist the colours at the colour changes. While it may feel awkward, with practice this will revolutionise your colourwork knitting!

STRANDING ON A KNIT ROW

Hold the yarn not in use evenly tensioned but out of the way of the stitch about to be worked.

Knit the new stitch using yarn B, held in your LH.

The new stitch has been knitted in colour B, without twisting the yarns at the back of the work.

1
When the first colour change is reached, hold one yarn (A) in the RH, the second yarn (B) in the LH.

2
Knit in colour A, using the RH to manipulate the yarn (UK style), until you reach the colour change. Knit in colour B, holding the yarn in your LH and knitting US/Continental style.

3
Repeat at each colour change. Using this method you should find that the yarns do not tangle at the back.

STRANDING ON A PURL ROW

1
As with knit rows, working in A (yarn A in RH), use the RH to manipulate the yarn (UK style), until you reach the colour change. Work in colour B holding the yarn in your LH and knitting US/Continental style.

2
Repeat at each colour change. Using this method you should find that the yarns do not tangle at the back.

WEAVING IN ON A KNIT ROW

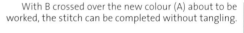
With B crossed over the new colour (A) about to be worked, the stitch can be completed without tangling.

1
To weave in colour B (lime green) on a knit row (yarn B is in the LH), insert the tip of the RH needle into the next stitch knitwise. The RH needle then continues below yarn B, going from front to back.

2
Wrap yarn A around the needle as if to knit.

3
Before completing the knit stitch, take yarn B back around the RH needle. Yarn B crosses over and is caught in place by yarn A.

WEAVING IN ON A PURL ROW

1
To weave in colour B (lime green) on a purl row (yarn B is in the LH), insert the tip of the RH needle into the next stitch purlwise. Wrap yarn B around the RH needle as if to purl US/Continental style.

Yarn A sits in front of B on the RH needle, ready to be purled.

2
Wrap yarn A with the RH to purl UK style.

Yarn A is purled UK style, keeping yarn B evenly tensioned in the LH.

3
Before completing the stitch in A, take yarn B back around the RH needle. Yarn B lays over yarn A.

With the colour change complete, the yarns remain one in either hand and the yarn is secure but not tangled.

4
Complete the purl stitch and continue, changing colours as required, to the end of the row.

TIPS

- **Check floats regularly for correct tension.** As a general guide, floats should have enough 'give' to allow the fabric to stretch and should not pull the fabric in. Test this regularly by gently stretching the fabric (at least every row) during working and if the fabric is pulling in, take the work back and redo.

- **While normal graph paper can be used for charting, bear in mind that knitting stitches are rarely square,** so the proportions of your finished design will be different from the chart. For an accurate representation, use knitter's graph paper. Various websites have free downloadable knitter's graph paper, which allows you to insert your tension and print an accurately proportioned chart. Alternatively, knitting software packages may also include this function.

- **To check your weaving-in technique, look at the reverse of the fabric.** The woven-in yarn should be visible as undulating waves going under and over each stitch until the colour change.

Intarsia

Colour is an exciting part of knitting and there are many different ways to add it to your knits. A technique called intarsia is used for blocks of colour, fun motifs and designs. Intarsia is a neat way to create blocks of colour where stranding or weaving in (see pages 192–199) would look unsightly and be unnecessarily cumbersome.

Intarsia is particularly popular for picture knitting, where a design is worked in a single area (for example, a snowman or a cartoon-character jumper); however, it can also be useful for small areas of colour. Clouds, snowflakes, stars and other small motifs that are randomly placed on a garment are often best made using intarsia.

Why use intarsia?

In the right circumstances, there are several advantages to using intarsia over stranding or weaving in. With intarsia there are no strands at the back of the work to snag or catch. Stranding makes a fabric heavier and thicker, which may not always be desirable, particularly on garments where drape, give or soft textures are needed. Light-coloured main fabrics, finer yarns and open textures may allow stranded yarns to be seen, spoiling the overall effect.

How does intarsia work?

Unlike Fair Isle knitting, where yarns not in use are carried along at the back of the work, intarsia simply uses a separate strand of yarn for each section of colour. One might expect this to result in a tangled mess of yarn. Fortunately, there are a number of easy techniques you can use to keep yarns under control.

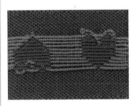

Stranded, WS
The yarns for this simple motif have been stranded across the back. The extra yarn from the strands makes the fabric quite stiff, which is not ideal for projects where a degree of stretch is required. It also uses more yarn.

Intarsia, WS
The reverse of the same motif knitted in intarsia is neater, and less yarn has been used, because no yarn is wasted with unnecessary stranding. With less yarn in the fabric it is softer and more flexible. Note how the yarns have been twisted at the colour change. Twisting the yarns avoids holes at the colour changes.

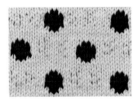

Stranded, RS
With a fine yarn, or when fabric is stretched, strands may be seen from the right side. This can be particularly noticeable if a dark yarn is being stranded across the back of a light-coloured motif, as shown here. Patterns with large motifs or lots of small, random motifs could require extensive, unnecessary stranding.

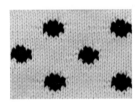

Intarsia, RS
When knitted in intarsia and viewed from the right side, there are no visible dark strands, giving a much more attractive finish. Paying attention to tension at the colour changes, drawing up the threads and checking the shape of the stitches means the motif edges are crisp, neat and well defined.

CLIP 24
Intarsia knitting

www.youtube.com/watch?v=U1TgbHoc04U

MAKING A BUTTERFLY

If only a few stitches are to be worked in a particular colour, wind a small amount onto a bobbin, a small piece of card, or into a 'butterfly', as shown here. Estimating the amount of yarn needed improves with practice, and new yarn can always be joined in if you run out.

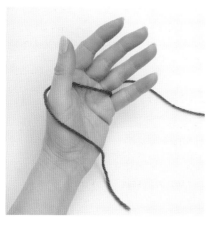

1
To make a butterfly, lay a 12.5cm (5in) tail of yarn across your palm.

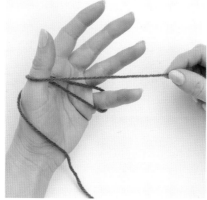

2
Wrap the yarn in a figure-eight around your thumb and little finger, holding the fingers about 7.5cm (3in) apart.

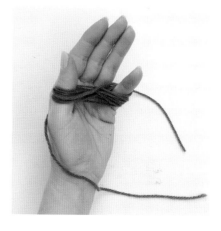

3
When enough yarn has been wound, cut off the yarn leaving a 12.5cm (5in) tail.

4
Leaving the loops on your fingers, pass the cut end up behind the loops.

5
Bring it forward over the loops and tuck it beneath the last wrap. Pull tight.

6
Remove the wrapped loops and draw off the yarn from the centre tail (the end you didn't tie the butterfly with).

TO KNIT AN INTARSIA MOTIF

In contrast to Fair Isle, with intarsia there is no stranding of the yarn at the back of the work. Instead, each time a new colour is introduced a new ball of yarn is used.

1
Knit to the colour change. Leaving 10–12.5cm (4–5in) of new yarn at the back of the work to sew in later, make the next stitch in the new colour. Do not cut off the first colour but leave it at the back of the work.

2
Hold the new yarn firmly and knit in this colour until the next colour is required. At this stage the first stitch may be a little loose. If necessary, pull the tail end gently, enough to stop the stitch from unravelling but not to pucker the knitting.

3
Repeat steps 1 and 2 at each colour change to the end of the row. There will be several butterflies dangling behind the work, one for each colour change. Even if a colour is used more than once in the row, a separate butterfly is used. For large sections, it is normally possible to keep the yarn on the ball.

4
Turn and, leaving the butterflies at the front, purl the second row. For a new colour, add in a new yarn as above (steps 1 and 2). To continue with a colour from the previous row, twist the old and new yarns by holding both yarns at the front of the work and taking the new yarn from front to back beneath the old yarn. Draw up the old and new threads as necessary to keep the stitches even.

5
Continue in the appropriate colour until the next colour change, repeating steps 1 and 2 for new colours and twisting the yarns where the colour changes occur. Gently adjust the tension if the stitches from the first row have become loose.

Hold the old yarn firmly beneath and behind the new yarn.

6

To twist yarns on a knit row, knit the next stitch in the required colour, bringing it up from beneath the current colour, as shown. Draw up the two yarns to prevent a hole. Repeat for each colour change. For a new colour on a knit row, follow steps 1 and 2.

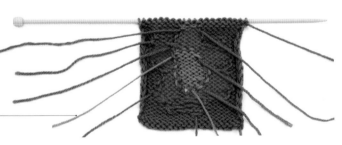

When a section of colour is complete (this may be over a number of rows), leave around 10cm (4in) of thread to allow the end to be neatly woven in and cut off. Any excess can be cut off after weaving in, but too short a thread may allow the work to unravel and stitches to become loose.

7

To tidy up ends, thread the cut yarn onto a blunt-ended tapestry needle and, on the back of the work, carefully weave in and out of neighbouring stitches. Where possible, weave into stitches of the same colour to avoid threads showing through. Check the stitch shape is not distorted or too loose as you work.

TIPS

- **If only a couple of stitches will be worked** in a particular colour, a butterfly or bobbin may not be required, and the yarn can simply be left as a long strand at the back of the work.

- **To prevent the butterflies tangling,** only unwind thread as needed. Keep the threads not in use nice and short. This helps reduce any pull on the yarn and keeps tension even.

- **Stranding can be combined with intarsia** and may be appropriate where, for example, only one or two stitches divide two larger areas of a single colour.

- **Check regularly for yarn tangles** and untangle them sooner rather than later.

- **Don't throw away short lengths of leftover yarn.** They may be useful later in small areas or for sewing up.

- **Weaving in threads as you go** makes the process seem less daunting than leaving them all until the end.

Duplicate stitch

Also known as Swiss darning, duplicate stitch is a great way to enhance knits. Used alone or combined with embroidery, it is effective for adding motifs, creating patterns and adding a splash of colour to garments, accessories or homewares. Duplicate stitch can also be used to cover minor mistakes and strengthen worn areas of knitting.

Duplicate stitch is a means of sewing over an existing knitting stitch or group of stitches. It can be used as a decorative technique to create patterns or motifs, or for functional purposes to cover up a stitch that may have been knitted in the wrong colour. It is also a useful method for reinforcing or repairing knits, for example, sock heels or jumper elbows.

Although the effect achieved is similar to intarsia and can even be used to re-create Fair Isle, because duplicate stitch and embroidery are done once a garment has been finished, they can be used on both newly completed and older garments. Tired or boring garments can be given a new lease of life with a quirky motif or a random scattering of small patterns. Charity-shop finds can be revamped with some funky stitching and zingy colour. And on a practical note, duplicate stitch is particularly useful for covering up small stains or marks on that favourite jumper.

DECORATIVE DUPLICATE STITCH

This step sequence shows you how to create a decorative motif in a contrasting colour using duplicate stitch.

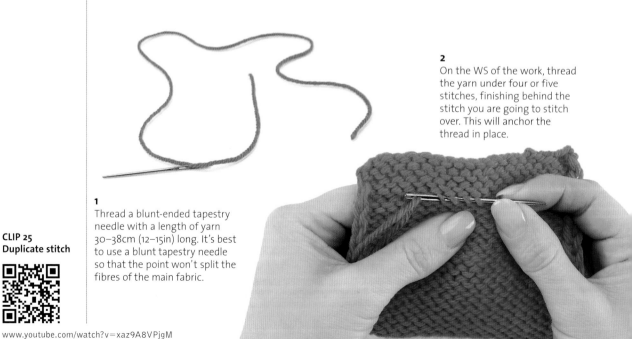

1
Thread a blunt-ended tapestry needle with a length of yarn 30–38cm (12–15in) long. It's best to use a blunt tapestry needle so that the point won't split the fibres of the main fabric.

2
On the WS of the work, thread the yarn under four or five stitches, finishing behind the stitch you are going to stitch over. This will anchor the thread in place.

CLIP 25
Duplicate stitch

www.youtube.com/watch?v=xaz9A8VPjgM

3
A knit stitch is a V shape. Bring the thread to the front of the work at the bottom of the V of the stitch you want to cover.

4
Take the tapestry needle from right to left under the base of the V of the stitch above the one you are working on. Draw up the yarn so that it sits neatly on the surface of the fabric without puckering or hanging loosely.

5
Take the thread back down through the bottom of the V of the stitch you are covering (where you began the stitch). Repeat until you have covered all the stitches required.

6
For sections that are close together, it should be possible to run the thread across the back of the work. However, if the sections are more than a few stitches apart, fasten off the thread at the back of the work by running it through several stitches and then cutting off and restarting.

TIPS

- **When repairing a knit,** start stitching outside the weak area and overlap the weak section by at least a couple of stitches on all sides.

- **If the stitching is to be in an area that could cause discomfort** (a sock heel, for example), it may be appropriate to split the yarn and stitch with a thinned thread so as not to create excessive bulk.

- **Knitted fabrics can be embroidered** with yarns or threads using normal embroidery techniques and stitches.

Beadwork

Adding beads to knitting is fun and easy, and can make the simplest garment look like a million dollars! Homewares too, will look fabulous sprinkled with sparkles. Add beads in a planned way or at random; either way, with these easy techniques and helpful tips you will soon be twinkling the night away.

Beads can be added to knitting in several different ways:

- Pre-stringing: integrating beads into the fabric
- Knitted with a carrying thread alongside the fabric
- Stitched on afterwards
- Crochet-hook method.

Which one you use will depend on the size of bead, the type of yarn, how frequently beads will occur in the pattern and how much patience you have!

Beads can be applied to a wide variety of yarns; however, there are certain limitations, particularly when working with heavily textured yarns. The key to success is in matching the right technique to your chosen yarn. For the pre-strung method the yarn needs to be smooth and fine enough to go through the hole in the bead. It also needs to be strong enough to withstand the friction of beads moving along the yarn. The crochet-hook technique also needs yarn that can be threaded through your beads. However, as beads are only added as and when needed, there is less friction on the fibres, so a textured or more delicate yarn can be used. When adding beads by knitting a carrying thread alongside the main yarn, virtually any yarn can be used, providing the carrying thread is not too obvious (unless you want it to be) and the finished fabric is not too stretchy. For projects where beads are stitched onto the fabric, the style and weight of the beads relative to the fabric are the key considerations.

CLIP 26
Beadwork

www.youtube.com/watch?v=Y2TQCkxhZDQ

Manufacturers generally give two sizes for their beads one in millimetres, the other simply a number – the higher the number, the smaller the bead. These numbers are useful in terms of gauging the overall size of a bead.

Consider how the bead will sit on the fabric. Beads can be heavy and add weight, changing the drape and flow of the fabric. Use this weight deliberately to create, for example, a fringe on a stole, but for lightweight fabrics, smaller beads are a good choice, or lighter acrylic beads if large beads are required. Larger and heavier wooden, ceramic and glass beads stand out on heavier fabrics.

Ultimately it is the size of the bead hole that determines how it can be applied. If you intend to thread the beads onto your yarn before knitting (pre-stringing), the yarn needs to fit through the holes. This technique is explained in more detail below and, if you are new to this type of beading, it is worth reviewing this method before buying your beads.

Pre-stringing

For this method, beads are threaded onto the yarn before knitting begins. This requires careful planning beforehand since the order in which the beads are threaded is crucial to success. Often a chart is provided showing where to place your beads, rather like a needlework chart. Matching the size of the bead hole to the yarn is also important because the beads need to be a snug fit while still being able to move along the yarn without snagging. A beading needle is required for this method. This technique is suited to charted patterns and areas where lots of beads are to be worked.

Silk yarn
This textured silk yarn looks more impressive with these pottery beads as accents.

Seed beads
These 4mm, size 6 seed beads will work well with a fingering (4-ply) to sportweight (DK) yarn.

THREADING BEADS ONTO YARN: PRE-STRINGING

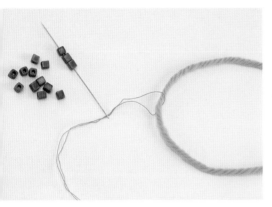

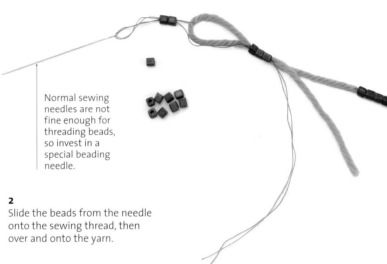

Normal sewing needles are not fine enough for threading beads, so invest in a special beading needle.

1
Using a normal sewing thread and a beading needle, pass the thread twice through the needle, leaving a loop of thread for the yarn. Pass the yarn through the loop in the thread and place the beads onto the beading needle.

2
Slide the beads from the needle onto the sewing thread, then over and onto the yarn.

TESTING BEADS FOR SUITABILITY

Before you begin your project, thread 20 beads onto the yarn using the method described above. Slide the beads along the yarn. If it is a lot of work to pull them along, or if there is any unravelling, try a larger-holed bead or a finer, smoother yarn. If the beads drop straight down the yarn, the hole may be too large. If the beads are too loose they may not stay in place when knitted.

Make a tension swatch as usual, incorporating the beads according to the pattern instructions. Check the fabric for drape, feel and overall look of the beads. Consider changing if necessary.

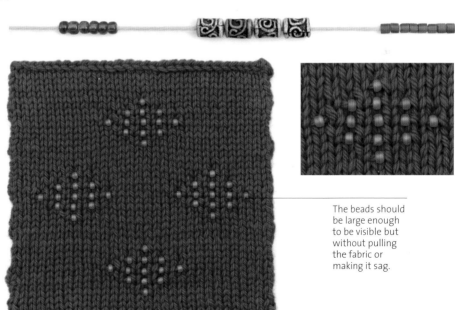

The beads should be large enough to be visible but without pulling the fabric or making it sag.

Preparing the yarn

Once you are happy with your choice of beads, thread the beads onto the yarn, following the order and numbers in the pattern. Your beads will be threaded in reverse order, meaning the first beads to be knitted will be the last ones to be threaded onto the yarn. Now you can knit with your beads. There are several ways of knitting with pre-strung beads. Here are two.

SLIPPED-STITCH METHOD

This method creates a bold effect with the beads clearly visible, sitting horizontally in front of the stitch.

1
When the pattern requires a bead, slide it up along the yarn, bring the working yarn forward (as if to purl) and then slip the next stitch purlwise.

2
Hold the bead at the front of the work, close to the fabric and the RH needle. If the next stitch is knit, take the yarn to the back of the work and knit as usual.

3
For a purl stitch, leave the yarn at the front and purl as usual. The bead is now fixed in place and should be sitting vertically on a 'floating' thread over the slipped stitch.

4
This method places the bead firmly at the front of the work. Up to about four stitches can be worked in a row to form a short chain. More than this may droop and snag. Working slipped stitches in long 'ladders' on top of one another can cause the work to distort. Placing beads on alternate rows, as shown here, should avoid this.

BETWEEN THREADS

The bead sits vertically between two stitches. This is a good choice for reversible or fine fabrics, but is not as bold as the slipped-stitch method.

Place the bead close to the RH needle.

The bead is knitted into the work.

1
When the pattern requires a bead, slide it up along the yarn and snuggle it close to the RH needle.

2
Work the next stitch as usual (knit or purl), pushing the bead forward with the LH finger if necessary.

3
The bead sits securely on the thread between the stitch just worked and the previous stitch. Note that when using this method, the bead may not be as prominent as with the slipped-stitch method, but it can be useful for fine, reversible fabrics, where it may be desirable to see part of the bead on the reverse.

The bead is visible on the reverse of the work as well as on the front.

TROUBLESHOOTING

- **If your carrying thread breaks,** take back your knitting, removing any worked beads as you go, until you have about 15cm (6in) of thread unpicked. Fasten off the carrying thread at the back of the work by making several small stitches and snipping off the spare thread. Return to the carrying thread and thread the beads you have unpicked back onto it in reverse order. Leaving a long thread (about 15–20cm/6–8in), restart your knitting from the correct place in the pattern; ideally, do this several stitches before a bead is needed so that your thread is secured and your next bead will not come loose. After a couple of rows, return to the long thread and stitch it in place on the reverse of the work. Don't pull too tightly but try to keep the tension even. Alternatively, take back the work as above and thread the beads back onto the carrying thread in the correct order. Knot the threads and continue as for a wrongly threaded bead (see page 209). However, as your thread may be fine, don't undo the knot; instead weave in the ends on the back of the work.

ADDING BEADS USING A CARRYING THREAD

This method can be used with a wide variety of yarns, including slubby and textured yarns and a wide range of beads, sequins or other embellishments. Use a fine thread in a colour that matches the main yarn. Ordinary cotton sewing thread can be used, but be careful to ensure that it can support the weight of the bead and be cleaned in the same way as your main fabric.

1
Beads are threaded onto the carrying thread in reverse order as they are for pre-strung beads. Knit with both the yarn and the carrying thread.

2
When a bead is needed, hold just the carrying thread with the bead at the front of the work.

3
Knit the stitch with just the yarn in the usual way.

This is a useful method for adding sequins and other embellishments that have very small holes.

4
With the bead close to the RH needle, continue knitting with both the carrying thread and yarn as before until the next bead is needed. The bead will be sitting at the front of the work with the carrying thread acting as a 'float', supporting it.

CROCHET-HOOK METHOD

The beauty of this technique is that it is very flexible and patterns can be created at random as you knit, or be planned beforehand. You will need a crochet hook with a tip that's small enough to go through the bead. The bead sits horizontally on top of the stitch.

1
To place a bead, slide it onto the head of the crochet hook.

2
Hook the stitch that is to hold the bead off the LH needle and onto the hook. The loop of the stitch should be on the hook with the bead sitting behind it on the hook.

3
Carefully pass the bead over the hook and over the loop of the stitch. Ease into place. The bead should be sitting horizontally over both legs of the stitch, with the loop still on the hook.

4
Return the stitch to the LH needle then slip the stitch purlwise onto the RH needle.

5
Add beads at almost any point in the fabric to create a random or planned pattern.

Stitched-on beads – surface embellishments worked after the knitting has been completed

Another useful beading technique is to stitch beads on once the knitting has been completed. This is a flexible technique that is well suited to freeform patterns because they can readily be placed anywhere on the fabric. It is a nice method for small motifs and for 'sprinkling' beads and sequins over a fabric. Sewing on large numbers of beads can, however, be time-consuming. Stitched beads may not be as firmly fixed to the fabric and they can be more prone to coming loose, since they are not integrated into the knitting. As with a carrying thread, the thread may break if the fabric needs to stretch in use.

Stitch canvas

Turn your knitted fabric into a 'canvas' on which to stitch your designs. Stitch freehand as here, or sketch a design on tracing paper (or trace an image from a book or magazine); then overlay the paper on the knitting. As you stitch over the image, carefully tear away the paper to leave behind a lovely beaded design.

Embellishments

These pompoms are made using cardboard discs. They are sewn onto crochet ties to create an attractive fastening.

Add the final touch to any project: a pompom or tassel on a hat, a fringe on a scarf, cord ties to fasten a jacket or a cluster of knitted flowers on a cushion. It is often the trimmings that can turn an ordinary item into something special.

Pompoms

Add pompoms to hats and scarves, or sew them to the ends of tie fastenings. You can easily make your own from yarn remnants, either using the materials you have at home or with the aid of an inexpensive kit.

KNITTED POMPOM

This method makes a firm pompom that will not fray. Size depends on yarn and needles used. Use long needles of the recommended size for your yarn.

Cast on 135 stitches.

Knit 1 row.

Dec row *Sl2, k1, pass the 2 slipped stitches over the stitch just knitted (2 sts decreased)*, repeat from * to * to end.

Repeat the dec row until 5 stitches remain. Cut the yarn, leaving an 20cm (8in) tail.

Thread the tail into a tapestry needle and slip through the remaining 5 stitches. Gather them tightly and secure.

Try changing colours after the first row. Alternatively, omit the cast off and continue on the last 5 stitches to make a knitted cord as explained on page 215.

MAKING A POMPOM USING CARDBOARD DISCS

You can make your own winders for pompoms using a pair of compasses and thin card.

1
Using the compasses, draw two matching circles on card, each with a small circle at the centre. Cut out the large and small circles and cut away a wedge. Place the shapes together and wind yarn around them as fully as possible. Use several colours if you wish.

2
Carefully insert the point of scissors between the cardboard layers and cut all around.

3
Tie a length of yarn tightly around the centre, between the card layers, then pull away the card. Do not trim the tie ends yet – use them to stitch the pompom where required. Snip off any untidy ends.

Using a pompom maker
Pompom makers are little plastic frames, available in various sizes, with four sections for each size. They have the advantage of being perfectly round and reusable.

Two tassels made in different yarns: turquoise mohair and soft green wool.

Padded tassel
A small amount of wadding is inserted in the centre of the top of the skirt, below the securing knot, before the tassel head is finished. This wadding provides a secure base for embellishment as well as altering the shape of the tassel head.

Tassels

Trim a hat, a bag or the corners of a cushion with matching or contrasting tassels. There are many ways of making tassels, but the method described here is simple and straightforward.

1
Cut a piece of firm card to suit the length of tassel you want. Wind yarn around it to the required fullness.

2
Thread a separate length of yarn into a tapestry needle and slip it under the wrapped yarn at one edge of the card. Tie the ends tightly.

3
Cut the yarn along the opposite edge of the card. Remove from the card and slip the needle down through the top of the tassel, emerging a short distance below.

4
Cast the yarn tightly around the tassel. Pass the needle under the casting and back to the knot at the top. Use this yarn to attach the tassel as required.

Fringes

Add a fringe to a scarf, bag or other accessory. Use yarn to match the project, or choose a draping yarn such as viscose or silk to add swing to a fringe. You will need a piece of firm card, scissors and a crochet hook.

1
Cut a piece of card a little wider than the depth of fringe you want. Wind yarn around it and cut along one edge to make lots of identical lengths of yarn.

2
Take two or three lengths and double them. Insert the crochet hook from the WS to the RS, one stitch (or row) in from the edge of the knitting; catch the loop and pull it through the knitting.

3
Catch the strands again and pull them through the loop. Repeat as required.

4
Place the work flat and trim all the ends to exactly the same length.

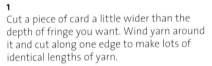

SIDEWAYS KNITTED FRINGE
This fringe has a short knitted border, making it easy to attach to a garment or other item. Use the needle size recommended for your yarn.

Cast on 7 sts (or more for a longer fringe). Work in garter stitch to the length required. The sample shown left was worked with a garter-stitch selvedge. To form the fringe, cast off the first 3 sts, cut the yarn and pull through. Drop the remaining stitches from the needle and unravel them all the way down. Block the fringe (see page 86) to remove kinks, allow to dry and sew in place. Cut through all the loops, or leave them uncut, as desired.

Twisted, braided and knitted cords

Cords are useful as drawstrings or ties, or to attach a tassel to an item, such as a hat. They can be twisted, braided or knitted, according to preference.

TWISTED CORD

1
Cut two or more lengths of yarn, each about three times the final length required. Knot the ends and secure to a firm surface with masking tape or a pin. Hold the free ends and twist between your fingers until the whole length is tightly twisted. Don't let go!

2
Hold the cord at the centre point and bring the two ends together. Release the centre and the cord will twist up around itself. Knot all the ends together and run the braid through your fingers to even out the twists.

Here, twisted cords are used to form a fringe. Thread lengths of yarn through the knitted edge. Twist them into cords, then trim the knotted ends into little tassels.

BRAIDED CORD

Strands of yarn can be braided in the same way as you braid hair. Cut the strands longer than the braid length required because the process will use up extra yarn.

Group strands of yarn into three and braid in the usual way. In the sample at the top, three groups of three strands each form a neat braid, knotted at the end and trimmed into a tassel. In the second sample, each group of strands is a different colour, with a bead added to each group below the knot at one end.

Start small
I-cord is pliable and easy to knit. Knit a short sample first so you can decide how many stitches to work with.

KNITTED CORD (I-CORD)

Sometimes called an I-cord (or idiot-cord, because it's so easy), tubular knitted cord is made on two double-pointed needles, two sizes smaller than recommended for your yarn.

Cast on 4 or 5 sts. * Knit 1 row. Do not turn the work. Push the stitches along to the other end of the RH needle and hold this needle in your LH. Bring the yarn tightly across the back of the work. * Repeat from * to * to length required. Cast off. Pulling gently, run the cord through your fingers to even out the stitches.

I-cord patterns
Lengths of knitted cord can be sewn down to make free-form designs, or to imitate cables.

Flowers and leaves

This ever-popular decorative theme is popular because it is easy to make it look good. Choose a fibre that will produce the desired effect, working in colours sympathetic to the scarf or shawl or in colours that work well with a favourite outfit. Attach the motif shapes carefully so that they can be changed from time to time. The only note of caution is that too many motifs may make the piece too heavy and distort the knitted fabric.

LEAVES

This leaf shape looks wonderful applied in a thick layer along an edge or worked in bulky yarn as a skinny scarf.

Cast on 5 sts.
Row 1 (RS) K2, yo, k1, yo, k2 (7 sts).
Row 2 (and all even-numbered rows) K1, p to the last st, k1.
Row 3 K3, yo, k1, yo, k3 (9 sts).
Row 5 K4, yo, k1, yo, k4 (11 sts).
Row 7 K5, yo, k1, yo, k5 (13 sts).
Row 9 K6, yo, k1, yo, k6 (15 sts).
Row 11 K7, yo, k1, yo, k7 (17 sts).
Starting with a p row, work 7 rows of stocking st, knitting the first and last st of each row.
Row 19 Skpo, k to the last 2 sts, k2tog (15 sts).
Row 20 K1, p to the last st, k1.
Rep rows 19–20 until 3 sts remain.
Row 31 Sl2tog, k1, psso.
Fasten off.

Colours and fibres
When selecting a motif, work the same motif in a variety of fibres and colours.

ROSES

The rose motif is particularly interesting because it is a long coil that can also be extended and sewn to an edge. The easiest way to work this pattern is with two circular needles or a circular needle and a DPN of the same size. The circular needle acts like a flexible stitch holder.

Large rose

Cast on 11 sts.
Row 1 (RS) [K1, p1] to the last st, k1.
Row 2 [P1, k1] to the last stitch, p1.
Sl the first 2 sts worked of row 2 onto a circular needle.
The sts on the circular needle are not worked again until the cast-off row.
Row 3 [K1, p1, yo] to the last stitch, k1.
Row 4 P1, [k1tbl, k1, p1] to the end of the row.
Sl the first 3 sts worked of row 4 onto a circular needle.
Row 5 [K1, p2, yo] to the last stitch, k1.
Row 6 P1, [k1tbl, k2, p1] to the end of the row.
Sl the first 3 sts worked of row 6 onto a circular needle.

Row 7 [P2, yo] 4 times, p2.
Row 8 K.
Slip the first 3 sts worked of row 8 onto a circular needle.
Rep rows 7–8, fitting as many repeats into the odd-numbered row as the number of sts allows, and sl3 onto the circular needle after each even-numbered row, until there are 11 blocks of sts or 32 sts on the circular needle and 22 rows have been worked.
Cast off all the stitches on both needles.
Coil the length around a finger and secure the layers at the base.

Small rose

Work as for the larger rose but rep rows 7–8, fitting as many repeats into the odd-numbered row as the number of sts allows and sl3 onto the circular needle after each even-numbered row, until there are 9 blocks of sts or 26 sts on the circular needle and 18 rows have been worked.

White roses
These neutral motifs tone with the knitted fabric to make a subtle addition.

· ·

NARCISSUS

From the leaf pattern (see opposite) a variety of leaves can be made just by altering the type of increases and the size of the leaf before the stitches are decreased. Or it could be the petal of a flower with a single layer of petals or a double layer.

Cast on 3 sts.
Row 1 (RS) K1, yo, k1, yo, k1 (5 sts).
Row 2 (and all even-numbered rows) Sl1 purlwise, p to the last st, sl1 purlwise.
Work as the leaf pattern above from rows 1–12 but on each even-numbered row, sl the first st purlwise, p to the last st, sl the last st purlwise.
Row 21 Skpo, k to the last 2 sts, k2tog (15 sts).
Row 22 Sl1 purlwise, p to the last st, sl1 purlwise.
Repeat rows 21–22 until 3 sts remain.
Row 33 Sl2tog, k1, psso.
Fasten off.

Spring splendour
The petals of this flower pattern are based on the leaf pattern opposite. The button in the centre is secured and loops of yarn are worked through the buttonholes, secured to the base and cut.

STAR FLOWER

The petals of this flower motif are completed one after the other in one curving piece. This is a useful flower motif when you don't know how big or how full you want the final motif. The stitch pattern also works well as an edging or as a skinny scarf.

Cast on 10 sts.
**Row 1 P.
Row 2 (RS) K1, m1, k to the last 3 sts, k2tog, k1.
Rep rows 1–2 three more times.
Row 9 P.
Row 10 Cast off until 1 st loop remains on the RH needle.
Pick up and k 9 sts along the left selvedge of the piece just completed.
Rep from ** 11 more times.
Fasten off.
Seam the left selvedge of the piece just completed to the right selvedge of the first piece completed.

Curving petals
The number of petals in this flower can be varied to alter the fullness of the motif. A large glass bead has been placed in the centre but a small pompom or a button would work well too.

knitting
SOS

Every knitter comes unstuck at one time or another; it's part of the craft. The key is in knowing how to rescue your knitting from the brink of disaster, and in making sure your successes far outweigh any failures.

Know your knitting

Certain concepts in knitting are second nature when you are an experienced knitter, and knowledge of them is often assumed in patterns, but some newer knitters may not have experience with these concepts.

Pattern shorthand

There are numerous examples of pattern-writing shorthand. This is mostly done to save space but it can be confusing. Here are examples of shorthand instructions commonly used by pattern writers and designers.

'Turn(ing) the work': Stop where you are knitting and swap the needles into the other hand so that you can work in the opposite direction. It may happen at the end of a row or round, but can also happen partway through a row or round, for example when shaping.

'End(ing) with a WS (RS) row': The last row you knit should be a wrong side (right side) row. If you are knitting flat in stocking the WS will be a purl row, so you should finish with a purl row. In this case, the next row you work would be a knit row.

'Continue even until the work measures': Continue working without any shaping or other changes (other than following any stitch or colour pattern) until the work measures the stated length. This term is frequently used during armhole shaping when there are several decrease rows followed by a long stretch of straight rows without shaping.

'Work in k1, p1 (k2, p2) rib until work measures': K1, p1 rib is a pattern stitch where the stitches alternate one stitch knit, one stitch purl, and so on. To create the ribbed pattern, the smooth (knit) stitches need to line up on top of one another. Likewise, the bumpy (purl) stitches should sit on top of one another. With an even number of stitches,

working in k1, p1 rib, the second row will be the same as row 1. With an odd number of stitches, row 1 (and all odd rows) will be worked k1, p1. However, row 2 (and all the even-numbered rows) will start with a purl stitch and be worked p1, k1. For a k2, p2 rib, work two knit stitches, two purl stitches.

'Complete right front, reversing all shaping': This instruction requires you to work out where to put your shaping and which increase/decrease to use. Thankfully this is less common in newer patterns – it can be time-consuming to work out the reverse instructions even for an experienced knitter.

For example, a pattern may read: 'Left front: Dec at neck edge on next and every alt row three times': To reverse this instruction for the right front will require several steps.

'Dec at neck edge': Firstly, determine the location of the neck edge by holding the garment in place as though you were wearing it. Put a marker at the edge where the neck (as opposed to the armhole) will be. Decreases will be made at this edge when completing the right front. Reverse the shaping as follows:
Left front: (RS) Decrease will be at end of row, so, for example, k to last 3 sts, k2tog, k1.
Right front: (RS) Decrease will be at start of row, so, for example, k1, k2tog, k to end.
Left front: (WS) Decrease will be at start of row, so, for example, p1, p2tog, p to end.
Right front: (WS) Decrease will be at end of row, so, for example, p to last 3 sts, p2tog, p1.

'On next and every alt row': This means a decrease on the row you are about to work (row 1) and then on rows 3 and 5. You have then made three decreases as per the pattern. (See pages 126–129 for suggestions as to which decreases to use, because different decreases give a different look.)

'Working in stocking, starting with a k row': Stocking describes a fabric that is one row knit, one row purl in flat knitting. When knitting in the round, to achieve a stocking fabric, every row is a knit row because you are always knitting in the same direction and don't turn the work.

Which are the right and wrong sides will depend on the pattern. In a stocking pattern, the knit side is usually the right side. Reverse stocking is the same basic pattern of stitches but the purl side is the right side.

'Increase on next and every following sixth row': You may find there are differing opinions on this instruction. Some designers will mean increase on row 1, work six rows, and increase again on row 7, then on row 13, and so on. Other patterns mean increase on row 1, then work five more rows and increase on row 6, then on row 12, and so on.

It is more likely that shaping will be done on the same side of the work, so you may wish to take this as a guide. However, in most cases it won't be crucial which approach you follow, providing you are consistent.

FREQUENTLY USED TERMS

Right/wrong side facing
The side of the work that you are looking at when you are holding the knitting, ready to work the next row or round.

Back of work
During knitting the back of the work is at the far side of the needles furthest away from you. This applies even if you are working a WS row. Holding yarn to back, therefore, means hold the yarn so that it is on the opposite side of the work and needles to you. Note that when making up, references to the back of the work normally means the WS or reverse of the fabric.

Wyib (with yarn in back)
This means hold the yarn at the back of the work, furthest away from you (this will look as if you are going to knit the next stitch). The fabric may have either the WS or RS facing you.

Front of work
The front of the work is the side of the fabric nearest to you, in front of the needles. This will apply even if the WS of the work is facing you. Front of work when sewing up, however, is usually the RS of the fabric.

Wyif (with yarn in front)
This means hold the yarn at the front of the work nearest to you (it will look as if you are going to purl the next stitch). This will apply whether the work has the RS or WS facing you.

For more terms, see page 244.

How to recognise key stitches
It is useful to be able to identify whether the stitch you are about to work was knitted, purled, decreased or increased on the last row. It can help you to work out which stitch to work next. It is also useful to be able to recognise when a stitch has been put onto the needles the wrong way round (for example, when dropped or taken back).

Knit stitch
A knit stitch looks smooth when viewed from the front. It has a distinctive V shape. The back of a knit stitch has a bump like a purl stitch. Each side of the V is referred to as a leg; you may see this in patterns when working some stitch patterns or picking up stitches and you are instructed to go into the front/back leg of the stitch.

Purl stitch
A purl stitch looks like the reverse of a knit stitch. It has a bump that forms at the front of the work and is smooth on the back. Although not clear in the fabric of the knitting, purl stitches may also be referred to as having two legs when on the needle. Different stitches and processes will ask you to go into either the front or back leg of the stitch.

Stocking stitch
The smooth face of this fabric and the V-shaped stitches mean that the next row will be a knit row, which will keep the stocking pattern working correctly.

Moss stitch
The moss stitch places a knit stitch above a purl stitch and vice versa. If the next stitch to be worked has a purl bump below it, the next stitch should be knitted. If it has a smooth face, the next stitch should be a purl stitch.

Ribbing
In this rib, the knit stitches should sit on top of the knit stitches, the purls on top of the purls (the opposite of moss stitch). The smooth face and distinctive V-shape of the stitch about to be worked shows that the stitch should be worked as a knit stitch. Viewed from the back of the work, the bump means that this stitch will be purled on the next row.

Garter stitch
Because garter stitch is knit on every row, it forms a series of distinctive ridges. This is because on row 1 the smooth face is on the front, the bump on the back. On row 2 the smooth face is still on the front, but is worked over a row of bumps from row 1; this results in a fabric of peaks and troughs.

Knit stitch mounting

Stitch mounting refers to the way in which the stitch sits on the needle. This is the standard mounting for a knit stitch. The front leg is the right-hand side of the V of the stitch; the back leg is the left-hand side of the V of the stitch.

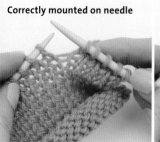

Correctly mounted on needle

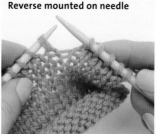

Reverse mounted on needle

With some stitches, or when a stitch has been dropped and taken back, the standard mounting may be reversed. This can be part of the pattern, in which case, proceed as usual; however, if a stitch has been replaced on the needle it may need remounting.

Insert the tip of the RH needle into the back of the stitch from front to back. Slip the stitch onto the RH needle; then insert the tip of the LH needle from right to left into the stitch on the RH needle, going from front to back.

Purl stitch mounting

The standard mounting for a purl stitch with the RH leg at the front and the LH leg at the back of the needle.

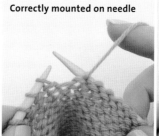

Correctly mounted on needle

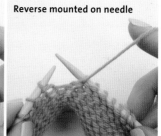

Reverse mounted on needle

As with knit stitches, when a purl stitch has been dropped and taken back, the standard mounting may be reversed. In this instance, follow the instructions for knit stitch mounting, left.

Counting rows

Stocking and reverse stocking

Each V represents one row. Exclude the cast-on row and the row on the needles when counting. Reverse stocking rows are counted in the same way, counting from the knit (smooth) face.

Counting garter stitch

Each pairing of a peak with a trough (see opposite) represents two rows. As with stocking stitch, ignore the cast-on and cast-off rows on the needles when counting.

Avoiding common errors

Even the most experienced knitters make mistakes. But fortunately, if you know how to recognise a mistake it is usually straightforward to correct it with a few simple techniques.

When it comes to errors, the best answer is, of course, to avoid them in the first place, and there are a number of tips and techniques that can help. There are also some simple gadgets that can be useful in reducing errors.

Of course, we are all human, so all the gadgets in the world won't eliminate errors completely. In this case, the next best thing is early identification. The sooner a mistake is spotted the less work is involved in putting it right. However, even a mistake that comes to light late in the day – in some cases, not until a garment is almost complete – can often be corrected without unpicking an entire piece of knitting.

The most common errors arise from misinterpreting patterns and not reading ahead. Once you are knitting, dropped stitches, extra stitches, losing your place and miscounting or misreading a pattern account for most knitting problems.

Interpreting patterns
Frustrating though it may seem, there is no standard set of knitting pattern abbreviations or chart symbols. It is recommended to read all the pattern notes and abbreviations before starting, even if you are an experienced knitter.

Keep a ruler handy to mark your place in the pattern by placing it beneath the row you are working on.

If you're not sure what the designer means by a particular term, don't guess! Check any books you may have or search the internet for explanations of techniques that aren't familiar. In some cases, particularly with online pattern downloads, there may be contact details for the designer. Pattern publishers and magazines are also very helpful in offering support for their patterns. Knitting forums are also a good source of assistance, because there may be other knitters who have had the same problems or queries.

Pattern corrections and errata may also be made available online, and it is always worth checking for these since it can save a lot of time and frustration. An internet search by the pattern and/or designer/publication name with errata in the search is a handy way to track down any pattern changes that have been made post-publication.

Reading ahead

Many errors can be avoided by reading patterns thoroughly and by reading ahead. Of course, it isn't necessary to memorise an entire pattern, but it is worth watching out for unusual instructions and in particular, sections where two or more actions are taking place at the same time. For example, shaping at a neckline will often require stitches to be decreased at both edges of the work, but in different places: 'Decrease one stitch at neck edge on every alternate row. At the same time, decrease one stitch at armhole edge every third row'. It is surprisingly easy to miss the second part of the instruction, and omit carrying out the armhole

Copy and enlarge complex charts so you can mark off rows without spoiling the original pattern.

shaping, meaning you have to undo and reknit the offending section of the work. Reading ahead will point this out, so you are less likely to miss it.

Cable and travelling stitch patterns

Cables and travelling stitch patterns are normally constructed from a series of straight rows followed by a twist row. Complex combinations may have twists arising in different places on different rows.

Common errors with cables occur when counting the number of straight rows between twist rows. Marking up rows on a photocopied or redrawn chart will help to avoid this kind of error. Making sure that twists move in the correct direction is another point to watch out for. Cable directions are normally determined by whether the cable stitches are held at the front or back of the work. The only real way to be sure is to review your knitting after each twist row. Use the pattern picture as well as the pattern instructions as a guide.

Colourwork and stitch patterns

Colourwork and patterns are best checked on a regular basis by comparing the work to the illustration and pattern/chart.

Pattern-reading errors

In complex projects, such as lace or cabling, pattern-reading errors are not unusual, but they can also occur even in simple projects. Pattern repeats and border stitches, sizing differences and multiple instructions can all throw you off track.

There are a number of useful gadgets that can help by acting as 'early warning systems' when it comes to dropped stitches – stitch markers are particularly useful when working a pattern with several repeats.

Using stitch markers

Stitch markers should be used to make sure that you have the correct number of stitches before and after any pattern repeats. They should also be used to check that each pattern repeat has been correctly completed.

Place a marker at the start of the first repeat, at the start of each subsequent repeat, and at the end of the final repeat. Having markers at the start of the first repeat and the end of the last repeat is invaluable. Because knits frequently have different numbers of stitches for each size, there will rarely be an exact pattern repeat for each size. Stitch markers allow you to see any partial pattern repeats at a glance.

Used correctly, stitch markers should limit any stitch-count errors to one row. However, bear in mind that this doesn't necessarily eliminate any pattern errors within the repeat. It is also worth checking that there will be the same number of stitches in each repeat throughout.

Lace patterns and stitch numbers

In a lace pattern, stitches may be increased on one row and decreased on the following or even a later row. This should be made clear in the pattern, but if you are not sure, it only takes a couple of minutes to scan the pattern repeat and identify any differences. Look for key increase stitches such as yarn overs, yarn round needle, yarn forward, make one and increase. Each should be matched by a corresponding decrease, for example, knit two together; purl two together; slip one, knit one, pass slipped stitch over. If the total number of increases is the same as the decreases, expect the same number of stitches in the repeat. Mark up the pattern to indicate any rows with extra stitches or fewer stitches.

TIPS

- **Photocopy your pattern** and note any areas with multiple or unusual instructions.

- **If necessary, write out or chart any rows with multiple instructions.** Use a highlighter pen or soft pencil to mark off rows on your chart as you complete each

row. Avoid crossing out rows using permanent markers in case you need to read it again later.

- **Chart holders** that have a slider or magnetic strip to mark your place in the pattern can be very useful. An inexpensive alternative is to put a sticky note just

beneath the row you are working on, moving it as each row is completed – you could also add notes as you go along!

- **Use row counters** to keep track of your progress – there are various types available – or a simple pen and paper will be fine.

- **When working with complex patterns,** particularly lace patterns, lifelines are a useful way to help with taking your knitting back in the event of an error (see page 229).

Mark sections that form part of the pattern repeat, and any extra stitches at the beginning and end of the row.

10 9 8 7 6 5 4 3 2 1

WRITTEN PATTERN

Reviewing this pattern for the knitting, left, reveals that, after casting on 30 sts, row 2 has 6 decreases but only 3 increases, so there are 3 less stitches at the end of row 2. On row 6 there are 4 decreases but 7 increases, meaning that there are 31 stitches at the end of row 6. Row 8 has additional decreases that are restored to the original 30 stitches on row 12. Being aware of these rows helps to avoid and identify errors.

Multiple 8 sts plus 6.
Cast on 30 sts.
Row 1 (WS) (and all odd rows) P.
Row 2 K2, *k2tog, k1, yo, k1, ssk, k2, rep from * to last 4 sts, k4 (27 sts.)
Row 4 K1, k2tog, k1, yo, *k1, yo, k1, ssk, k2tog, k1, yo, rep from * to last 2 sts, k2 (27 sts.)
Row 6 K3, yo, *k3, yo, k1, ssk, k1, yo, rep from * to last 3 sts, k3 (31 sts.)
Row 8 K5, *k2tog, k1, yo, k1, ssk, k2, rep from * to last 2 sts, k2 (28 sts.)
Row 10 K4, *k2tog, k1, (yo, k1) twice, ssk, rep from * to last 3 sts, k3 (28 sts.)
Row 12 K3, k2tog, *k1, yo, k3, yo, k1, k2tog, rep from * to last 2 sts, k2 (30 sts.)

Stitch markers save time when knitting complex patterns or projects with large numbers of stitches. They help with identifying and locating errors by dividing sections to be checked into manageable chunks.

Note the use of a lifeline (see page 229) as a means of saving time if an error is made. Choose a smooth, fine yarn in a contrasting colour, as here.

CHART

In the charted version of the pattern shown in the panel, right, rows with additional decreases (rows 2 and 8) are indicated by the number of decrease symbols that are later compensated for by the additional increases on rows 6 and 12. The numbers on the left show the total number of stitches in each row.

< Start knitting here

☐ Knit on even rows, purl on odd rows

\ K2tog

O Yo

■ No stitch

ssk Slip, slip, knit

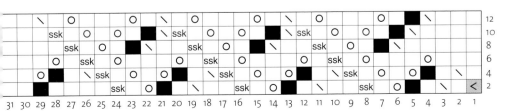

Fixes, fudges and tweaks

If you find yourself on the wrong end of a knitting mistake, the first thing to do is take a deep breath, and then put your knitting down.

Putting your knitting down fulfils two purposes: it gives you a few moments to step back, assess the problem, and plan what you intend to do to put it right; it also limits the risk of any further problems. This can be particularly important with dropped stitches, where moving the knitting before securing the dropped stitch can cause a dropped stitch to unravel further and create a ladder down the work.

Once you have the measure of the error, the next step is to create a plan of action. Ideally, it's a simple question of taking your work back (you may also hear this referred to as unpicking, unravelling, pulling back ripping, frogging or tinking to the beginning of the row, or even just a few stitches). However, mistakes not noticed until a few rows down the line, be they dropped stitches, lost or extra stitches, and pattern errors, may involve a bit more work.

Taking stitches back individually

KNIT STITCHES
Taking back knit stitches is relatively straightforward, but check that the stitch mounting (see page 223) is correct before reworking a stitch that has been taken back.

Check that the stitch mounting is correct before continuing to rework the stitch.

1
Hold the work as usual, with the stitches to be taken back in your RH, and the stitches that haven't yet been knitted on the needle in your LH. Holding the working yarn slightly tensioned, and to the back of the work, insert the tip of the LH needle into the back leg of the stitch on the RH needle, going from front to back just below the needle.

2
Lift the stitch on the RH needle and return it the LH needle. Pull back the working yarn to free the stitch on the LH needle if necessary. Repeat as required until the appropriate number of stitches has been taken back.

CLIP 27
Fixing mistakes

www.youtube.com/watch?v=5TZ8FKGiLFo

PURL STITCHES

Simple purl stitches can be readily taken back and returned to the needles for reworking using the steps below.

Check that the stitch mounting is correct before continuing to rework the stitch.

1
Hold the work as usual with the stitches to be taken back on the needle in the RH and the stitches that haven't yet been knitted on the needle in the LH. Holding the working yarn slightly tensioned, and to the front of the work, insert the tip of the LH needle into the front of the stitch on the RH needle, going from front to back just below the needle.

2
Lift the stitch on the RH needle and return it to the LH needle. Pull the working yarn back to free the stitch on the LH needle if necessary. Repeat as required until the appropriate number of stitches has been taken back.

TIPS

- **When all the stitches are back on the needles,** count them to ensure that none have been lost or gained. If there are extra or missing stitches, individually take back another row. Edge stitches are often the culprit and taking back a row usually reveals any errors at the edges, but should also reveal any dropped or gained stitches.

- **Work in good light,** particularly if you're using dark yarn, or where the colours in a project are similar.

- **Stitches can be put back onto a smaller needle** than will be used for the knitting. This can make it easier to pick the stitches up. Remember to change back to the correct needle size when knitting resumes.

- **The advantage of taking the work back a row after the error** is that pulling back several rows of knitting can cause the final row to be uneven when putting it back on the needles. Taking back the final row stitch by stitch allows the tension to even out.

LIFELINES

Lifelines come in handy when you are learning a new pattern or techniques because they allow you to pull the stitches off the needles and rip back to where you know the work was correct. A lifeline is a piece of smooth, contrasting-colour yarn – a good 50cm (19³/₄in) or so longer than the knitting when fully stretched out – fine enough to go through the stitches without distorting them, but strong enough not to break.

To insert a lifeline, decide where you want your marking point to be – often, the first row of a pattern repeat. Thread your lifeline yarn onto a blunt yarn needle. Thread the yarn needle through the stitches on the knitting needle. Don't split the stitches as you go through, since this may damage the yarn and make it more difficult to unravel the work if needed. Continue knitting your pattern. If you need to use your lifeline, take all the stitches off the

needle and pull back the work to the lifeline row. Insert the tip of your knitting needle (or smaller needle if necessary) into each stitch, following the lifeline exactly, however odd it may look. With the stitches back on the knitting needle, you can restart. Lifelines stay in the work until you are finished, or can be removed once you are happy that a section is correct, placing a new lifeline at the start of the next pattern repeat.

Taking back several rows of knitting at once

If you spot an error after you have worked several more rows of knitting, it would be a time-consuming process to undo the rows stitch by stitch. It is possible to simply pull the knitting off the needles, pull out the desired number of rows, put the stitches back on the needles and continue knitting; however, if the knitting is simply pulled off the needles it can be difficult to keep track of the number of rows being taken back and there is a risk that the knitting may unravel more than intended. It is also possible that stitches may ladder, either while taking back the work or when putting the stitches back on the needles. Nonetheless, sometimes it is unavoidable, so here's how it's done. (Note: this technique isn't recommended for lace or very fine knits.)

Pull yarn firmly but slowly. Tease any stuck stitches loose to avoid runs (ladders).

1
To take back several rows of work, lay the knitting on a flat surface. Holding the knitting with the flat of your hand several rows below the needle, remove the needle.

2
Keeping your hand in place on the knitted fabric, slowly take back the knitting by pulling steadily on the working yarn. If a stitch starts to run or ladder, move your hand directly below the stitch in question and press more firmly until the working yarn pulls away.

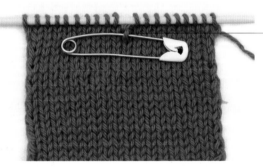

Holding a dropped or run stitch on a marker will allow you to finish the row and come back to it, reducing the risk of creating more dropped stitches as you try to fix it.

3
Take the work back to the row after the error was made, then pick the work up in your RH. With an empty needle in your LH take back the final row stitch by stitch (see pages 228–229). This will return the knitting to the start of the row where the original error was made, allowing you to reknit it and correct the mistake.

4
If a stitch has run or does run during the picking-up process, don't try to put it on the needle. Instead, thread a safety pin or split ring stitch marker through it and follow the process for dropped stitches (opposite).

Dropped stitches

This is a term to strike terror into the heart of the novice knitter, but it is not the end of the world once you know how to deal with the problem.

At this stage it doesn't matter which needle the stitches are lifted onto, it's just important to make sure they don't unravel down the work.

1
If you spot a dropped stitch (or stitches), lay your knitting flat and pass a safety pin or split ring stitch marker through each dropped stitch. Be careful not to pull on the working yarn.

2
Identify whether the stitch has simply fallen off the needles or whether it has unravelled one or more rows down the work (laddered). If the stitches have fallen off the needles but not unravelled into the rows below, use a smaller spare knitting needle or yarn needle to lift the stitches and put them onto the needle.

3
Identify whether the stitches belong on the LH or RH needle by examining the position of the stitches in relation to the working yarn. If the stitches are to the left of the yarn, they should go on the LH needle. If they are attached to, or to the right of the yarn, they belong on the RH needle. If your knitting has come off the needles partway through a row you may have dropped stitches that need to be put back onto each needle.

4
Transfer the stitches onto the correct needle as required. Count your stitches to ensure that you have the correct number. As you knit the picked-up stitches, check first that they are correctly mounted and remount them if required (see page 223), then continue knitting by following the pattern.

Single dropped stitch

If a stitch has fallen off the needle and unravelled into the row or rows below, it can usually still be retrieved if you notice it within the same row or the next row. A dropped stitch that hasn't unravelled more than one row can be dealt with using your working knitting needles in the following ways.

PICKING UP A DROPPED KNIT STITCH THAT HAS DROPPED ONLY ONE ROW

When lifting the dropped stitch, be careful not to allow it to unravel further down the work.

1
Take the knitting back to the location of the dropped stitch (this may be necessary if you inadvertently continued knitting for a few stitches before noticing the dropped stitch). To pick up a knit stitch, remove the stitch from the holding pin. You should see a floating strand of yarn where the stitch was dropped and has unravelled. If this strand is in front of the dropped stitch, lift it to the back.

2
Insert the RH needle into the dropped stitch from front to back, then continue under the floating strand.

Check the stitch mounting to ensure that the dropped stitch is not twisted when it is reworked.

3
Use the tip of the LH needle to lift the dropped stitch over the floating strand and off the needle.

4
Transfer the stitch back to the LH needle, checking the mounting of the stitch and remounting if necessary (see page 223). Continue knitting as usual.

• •

PICKING UP A KNIT STITCH THAT HAS DROPPED SEVERAL ROWS (LADDERED) USING A CROCHET HOOK

1
Remove the dropped stitch from the holding pin. Loosen it a little if necessary and insert a small crochet hook through the stitch from front to back.

2
At the back of the work, behind your crochet hook, you should see a series of floating strands of yarn like horizontal ladders. With the strand behind the dropped stitch, catch the lowest floating strand with the crochet hook and draw it through the stitch to the front.

3
Repeat this process, pulling each floating strand through individually as you work, up towards the top of the knitting. When all the strands have been pulled through, return the stitch to the LH needle, remounting if required (see page 223).

PICKING UP A DROPPED PURL STITCH THAT HAS DROPPED ONLY ONE ROW

1
To pick up a dropped purl stitch that has only dropped one row, take the work back to the dropped stitch. The floating strand should be in front of the dropped stitch. If not, lift it to the front.

2
Insert the tip of the RH needle from back to front into the dropped stitch, then continue under the floating strand.

3
Use the tip of the LH needle to lift the dropped stitch over the floating strand and off the RH needle. Return the stitch to the LH needle, correcting the mounting as required (see page 223), and work to the end of the row.

PICKING UP A PURL STITCH THAT HAS DROPPED SEVERAL ROWS (LADDERED) USING A CROCHET HOOK

1
To pick up a laddered purl stitch, turn the work so that the side facing you is the one where you want the purl bump to be seen. Use a crochet hook to catch and reinstate the dropped stitch (see page 233).

2
Viewed from the knit side of the work, the purl bump is hidden on the WS, leaving a smooth fabric on the RS.

Multiple dropped stitches

If the work has come off the needles and a section has unravelled down by several rows, it is recommended that you run a lifeline along the row below the lowest dropped stitch (see page 229), and take the work back to the lifeline. Achieving a neat fabric where multiple stitches have run is difficult due to the need to even out the floating strands. The end result is often unsatisfactory.

Colourwork errors

Stitches that have been knitted in the wrong colour can often be covered over using duplicate stitch (see pages 204–205). If it is in the current or previous row (or further back, depending on your patience level!), taking the work back is preferable because a duplicate stitch can stand out from the main fabric. However, this is a useful technique if an error is spotted late in the knitting or even after the knitting has been completed.

Pattern stitch errors

A single stitch (for example, a purl worked where there should have been a knit stitch) can be deliberately dropped and unravelled to the incorrect stitch. Place a safety pin or stitch holder through the left leg of the stitch below the incorrect stitch. Unravel the work down to the holder. The incorrect stitch will be the final one to unravel and form a floating strand. Put the stitch on the holder onto a crochet hook, correct the stitch as required and then treat it as a dropped stitch (see pages 232–234).

Combination pattern stitches, for example, cables can be dropped as a unit. Place a safety pin or stitch holder through the left leg of each stitch in the row below the incorrect row. Drop and unravel all the affected stitches down to the holder. Correct the stitches as required using the stitches on the holder as the base row (this may involve using a cable needle to twist the stitches if cable stitches are involved); then use a crochet hook to lift the stitches individually back onto the needles (see page 234).

If several stitches have been worked incorrectly, drop, correct and pick each one up individually.

TIPS

- **When taking back several rows,** make a note of how many rows you have taken back so that you can pick up again at the correct point in the pattern.

- **If you are not sure where you are in the pattern** when you have finished picking up a dropped stitch, take the work back to the start of the row and continue to work from there.

- **If the work is puckered after picking up a stitch,** use the tip of a yarn needle to ease out any puckered stitches. Some puckering will disappear on blocking (see page 86), but if it is severe, it may be better to take the work back by several rows and reknit.

- **Be careful to ensure that you don't split the yarn when pulling the stitches through,** because this will create an unsightly loop or a thin, weak stitch.

- **Put needle point protectors on each needle if you are dealing with a ladder or complex pick up.** This will stop further stitches from coming off the needles. No point protectors? Twist a rubber band around each needle tip to stop the stitches from sliding off.

the
knitting
community

The days of solitary knitting in a rocking chair on your porch or in a secluded corner of your home may still have their place, but online developments and changing perceptions invite you to join a buzzing social scene, and share your skills and enthusiasm.

Finding other knitters

It is very relaxing to spend a few hours knitting alone and enjoying your own company; however, when you do feel the need to connect with other knitters, there are lots of options.

Knitting isn't best known for being a team activity, but that doesn't mean that knitters always like to knit alone. There are lots of advantages to meeting other knitters, whether it's at a regular group, while taking part in a specific project or connecting with people online via knitting forums and social media.

Knitting groups

There are many knitting groups – some small and informal, others large with memberships and more formal meetings. Some groups are simply about sitting and knitting together whereas others arrange meetings with speakers and workshops. It's worth trying out several groups and going along to a couple of meetings to get a feel for whether it's a group setup that suits you. More formal groups with membership

arrangements are normally happy for you to come along as a visitor before you commit to joining. Informal groups are generally open to all and are often free or low cost.

How to find knitting groups in your area

Details of local knitting groups may be available at your local library or information centre. If you have a local yarn shop, be sure to ask there, too. Lots of knitting shops have their own groups, and some offer courses and drop-in sessions.

Search on the Internet for national knitting organisations, such as UK Hand Knitting Association or the Knitting & Crochet Guild in the UK and The Knitting Guild Association (TKGA) in the USA, for details of knitting groups in your area. Magazines and online publications also have information about groups. Forums are another good place to look for details of where to find your fellow knitters.

No knitting group nearby?

If you draw a blank and can't find a local knitting group, you could always set one up. Put up posters in your local library, community centre and craft shop and check out your local newspaper to see if you can put a notice on their listings pages. Publicise your new group on knitting forums and social networks such as Twitter and Facebook. Encourage friends and colleagues to come along and ask as many people as you can to spread the word.

Think about a suitable venue – perhaps a local café, bar, community centre or church hall will let you use their space for free until your group is established. Consider the best time to meet. Evenings are good for working knitters but not so good for knitters with young families; daytime meetings may be more accessible to retired knitters and parents who can attend when children are at school.

TIPS

- **If you are new to online forums,** persevere! It can take a while to get used to the format and find your way around. Look for 'wikis' – help pages that will guide you around a site.

- **If you are thinking of going along to a knitting group,** let the group coordinator know to expect you, so that you know there haven't been any changes to meeting dates/times.

- **Knitting groups cater to knitters of all abilities,** so if you are a complete beginner don't be put off. There will be lots of people present who will be happy to offer help and advice.

- **Take sensible precautions when using an online forum or group.** Be cautious about divulging personal information such as your address or telephone number, and always arrange to meet in an open, public place.

Connecting with knitters online

There are many knitting forums and knitters' networks online and they can be a fantastic way to engage with fellow knitters, particularly if attending a group isn't practical. Forums such as ravelry.com, knittingforums.com, and knittingforums.org.uk offer a wealth of information and support, and have a great community feel to them. There are also a number of groups on sites such as Yahoo or Google. Magazines and some of the larger knitting shops may also have their own knitting forums.

What happens on a knitting forum?

Most online groups and forums are free to join and are friendly and inclusive. You can ask questions if you need help with a particular project, stitch, yarn or technique. You can also answer questions posted by other knitters. Some groups have a gallery where you can share photos of knitting projects. On some forums, knitters

Social hubs
Whether it's a flash-mob knitting event on public transportation or a gathering in a fellow knitter's house, joining up with other enthusiasts can add a welcome social dimension to your hobby.

arrange knitalongs (see page 245). There may also be the facility to buy, sell, swap or trade yarn and other items. As with a knitting group, online groups and forums each have a different feel and will offer different facilities, so it is worth trying out several to see which ones appeal to you.

Other online resources

In addition to groups and forums, the internet holds a rich source of information that knitters will find invaluable. Patterns can be downloaded instantly, often for free or for a small fee. There are also many apps available for smartphones, such as stitch dictionaries, row counters, knitting databases where you can record yarn and project information, as well as guides to tension and yarns. Apps are normally available for a small fee and can often be tried before making a purchase.

Sharing and selling your work

When you've made something special you'll want to share it, and who better to admire your work than your fellow knitters?

Sharing your work with others may be as simple as donning your knit, standing back and waiting for the admiring looks and appreciative comments. You may, however, want to go a step further and sell your work. In this case, you will need to do your research.

Selling your work

With careful planning and realistic expectations, knitting can be turned into a profit-making hobby or even a full-time occupation. As with any venture, even if you only plan to operate your business to fund your hobby, it pays to treat your activity seriously. The ins and outs of starting a business are worthy of at least a full book, but here are some things to consider when getting started.

● **What will you sell?**
You may have finished items to sell or you may prefer to concentrate on selling your designs as patterns.

● **Why do you want to sell your work?**
Are you selling to raise a little extra cash to fund future yarn purchases or do you need to earn a viable income?

● **Where do you plan to sell your work?**
Will you operate online, from your own premises or via a gallery or shop?

● **How much time do you have to invest?**
Be realistic about how many hours you will have to devote to your business. Working all hours in the beginning is all very well, but isn't sustainable in the long term. Make sure you make time for yourself and your family and don't over-commit.

Shops, galleries and craft fairs

There are many outlets for selling finished items. Shops or galleries may buy your products outright or may sell them for a commission, paying you only when they make a sale (sale or return). This can generate a better price for you but you will need a written agreement with the retailer setting out your terms: make provision for who will set prices; who will be responsible for lost, stolen or damaged stock; how often you will be paid; how long the stock should remain on site; and who will insure it. Keep accurate records, so that both parties can keep track of sales and income.

Before approaching shops and galleries, visit them to establish whether your product will fit with their style and ethos. Some owners will be happy with an unannounced visit, but consider calling first and arranging to meet someone to show them your goods. Put your best foot forward with top-notch samples, well presented and flawless. Be enthusiastic and confident about your product, and if you have feedback from happy customers, take it with you. Leave business cards with retailers and follow up visits with a phone call if appropriate.

Craft fairs are your opportunity to interact with your customers. Prices for booths vary and it is recommended to visit a fair before you commit to a booth. Check your booth size and plan your layout to maximise the space. Have clear prices and think about signage and your image – is your style quirky and homespun or slick and chic? Have business cards available and consider a comments book for feedback.

Selling online

There are a number of excellent online outlets for crafts and handmade items such as Etsy, ArtFire and Folksy. These sites allow you to set up your own online shop where you are responsible for all aspects of the process, including photographing and describing your wares, monitoring sales, dealing with inquiries, etc. Online is ideal for starting on a small scale and for testing the water because they give you valuable exposure to a wide customer base that isn't limited by geography. There is little financial risk, and if your product takes off you can move to your own website.

If you are tech-savvy, you may opt to run your own website from the outset. This can be a cost-effective option because you won't be paying commission or listing fees. However, you will need a shopping cart and you should be confident about your web-design skills. You will need to be much more proactive about marketing your product and you will need to work hard to make sure that your potential customers can find you. In addition, you may need to advertise, which can add substantial costs.

Legislation

If you are selling finished items, be careful to make sure that you are not breaching any copyright restrictions. Most patterns, whether in books, magazines or on the internet, are subject to copyright. Copyright restrictions are not limited to photocopying or reprinting patterns for sale; they also apply to making items based on the patterns and selling the finished items. Even if the pattern is free, do not assume that this will allow you to use it to make items for sale. Some authors will allow knitters to

make a small number of items for resale and others will give permission on request if you agree to abide by certain conditions. If in doubt, check, and, wherever possible, obtain written permission from the copyright holder.

A further factor to consider with knits is complying with any legislation that may affect your product. Take particular care with anything that could be construed as a toy, for example, because there are strict rules governing safety. Labelling of yarn and fibre content and the accuracy of product description will also be important. Organisations such as Trading Standards in the UK or the US Consumer Product Safety Commission help you to be aware of any rules you will need to comply with.

Selling your designs

If you have good ideas and enjoy making your own creations but don't want to sell the finished product, you may want to consider selling your designs or patterns. There are many outlets for selling patterns including magazines, books, online pattern shops and craft shops. You could also set up your own website or online shop and sell directly to other knitters.

Deciding on format

Patterns can be sold as a physical hard copy on paper or card; however, increasingly, designers are making patterns available online for download. Patterns that can be downloaded as apps onto smartphones are also becoming popular.

Finding an outlet

If you plan to approach magazines, publishers or pattern sites with your designs, check submission rules. Most publications will have information on their website about how to submit ideas and designs. Follow the required format,

check dates, and send all the necessary information to the correct person.

There are also sites (Ravelry, for example) that allow you to sell your designs via their site for a small commission without any need to have them pre-approved or validated. You set up your own online shop, take your own photos, typeset your designs and set your own prices and download options. This can be a good way to start out, but don't be disappointed if you don't make millions; there is a lot of competition out there! Think about how to make your designs stand out from the crowd, be proactive with your marketing, publicise pictures of finished items your customers have made, and encourage customers to mention your designs in blogs, on social media and in forums.

Legislation

As with finished items, copyright is important when selling your own designs. Not only should you make sure that you haven't copied another person's design, but you also to need to bear in mind that adaptations of an existing pattern may also be considered an infringement of the designer's copyright.

Whether you are selling finished items or designs, don't forget your own copyright and be sure to protect your original designs. Copyright rules and requirements vary from country to country, so check carefully.

Pricing

Cost your product appropriately. As well as the more obvious costs such as raw materials, don't forget to include any hidden costs such as utilities, internet charges and commission fees. Factor in your time – a design, for example, isn't just the cost of the paper; the main expense is your time in producing it and you need to be remunerated for that time or you risk under-pricing your products.

Finances

Whatever you plan to sell, keep records of your income and retain receipts for anything you spend on your business. Ultimately, this is how you will know whether or not you are making a profit. If you don't have a finance background, take advantage of any free advice that is available from local business advisory groups and, if need be, employ an accountant.

Tax will also need to be factored into your business planning. The rules may seem complex, but tax authorities are normally helpful in enabling you to fulfil your tax obligations. Attend to tax sooner rather than later – an unexpected tax bill can quickly turn an exciting profit into a disappointing loss.

Knitting for charity

Knitters are generous people who enjoy sharing and giving back to the community. Whether you have skills, time or materials to share, you can be sure that there will be a group who will appreciate what you have to offer.

If your knitting stash is threatening to take over your home, or if you love to knit but have knitted more scarves and socks than your friends and family could wear in a lifetime, knitting for charity is an option you could explore. It is satisfying, worthwhile and will be greatly appreciated by the recipient.

Large-scale projects

Charity projects generally fall into two categories: the large-scale group project, and individual knits for specific groups of people. Large-scale projects are often designed to raise awareness of a particular topic. The hugely successful global phenomenon that is the Hyperbolic Crochet Coral Reef is one example. Thousands of individuals from around the globe made small knitted or crocheted corals and marine animals that were brought together to create a massive replica coral reef. The completed reef toured the world, highlighting the need to protect the world's marine environment while educating visitors about maths and science.

Other large-scale projects may be used for fundraising and campaigning. Knit a River asked contributors to knit blue squares. These were joined together to form a huge knitted river that was used by the charity WaterAid to highlight the issue of communities living without access to safe drinking water.

Knitted Christmas trees also seem to be particularly popular fundraisers, with new trees sprouting every year.

Drawing attention to a cause
The Yarn Corner Stitches Up City Square initiative in Melbourne, Australia, promotes yarn bombing as a growing art form while promoting the Urban Forest Strategy, which highlights the plight of the city's ageing tree population.

How can I get involved?

To get involved in a charity knitting project, or if you have items to donate, contact a national knitting organisation or ask on an online knitting group or forum (see pages 238–239) and you're sure to find one to suit you.

Projects and requests for donated equipment may also be publicised in knitting magazines, in your local yarn shop or through individual charities. You may also find a home for your unwanted yarns or needles through sites such as Craigslist, Freecycle or Freegle.

Volunteering your skills

If gifting knitted items isn't for you, there are lots of opportunities to share the pleasure of knitting by passing on your skills. Teaching someone to knit is very satisfying and you don't need to be an expert in all aspects of knitting – most people will be delighted to learn the basics.

There are a number of organisations that recruit volunteers to teach knitting. In the UK, UK Hand Knitting Association and the Crafts Council have details of groups who need volunteer teachers. There are also opportunities to teach knitting at after-school clubs, at knitting shows, Scouting and Guiding groups, and with community organisations. Project Sunshine and Care to Knit, Inc. run regular programs in the USA. Some organisations may even offer training in starting and running a knitting club.

Individual pieces

There are many charities around the world that coordinate projects to make and give individual items to people in need. These may be items of clothing, for example, hats for servicemen, clothes for premature babies or blankets for the homeless. Other organisations collect items such as hand-knitted toys for children affected by war, poverty and illness.

Donating wool and equipment

As well as knitted items, some charities, voluntary groups and community groups will be delighted to receive donations of yarn, knitting needles and knitting-related items.

Knitting terminology

These pages feature technical words used in this book, along with some common knitting terms you might come across. Knitters have created their own unique terminology to describe some of the common features of knitting, and some of those words are also included here.

3-ply, 4-ply: Lightweight knitting yarns, sometimes called fingering.

Acrylic: Synthetic fibre.

Angora: Very soft yarn fibre made from the combed fur of the Angora rabbit, usually blended with other fibres.

Aran-weight: Medium- to heavyweight yarn.

Backstitch: Firm sewing stitch, also used to embroider fine lines and outlines.

Bamboo: Fibre from the bamboo plant, used to make a smooth, silky yarn; also the woody stem, used to make knitting needles.

Block, blocking: Treating a piece of knitting (by washing and/or pressing) to set its shape.

Bobbin: Plastic or cardstock holder for a small amount of yarn.

Bouclé yarn: Fancy yarn with a knobbly effect.

Bulky: Heavyweight yarn, sometimes called chunky.

Button band or button border: Separate band, knitted sideways or lengthways, to which buttons are sewn.

Buttonhole band or buttonhole border: Separate band, knitted sideways or lengthways, with buttonholes worked as knitting proceeds.

Cable needle: Small double-pointed needle used to work cables.

Cable: The crossing of two groups of stitches.

Casting off: Fastening off stitches so they will not unravel.

Casting on: Making new stitches on a needle.

Chain stitch: Embroidery stitch, used for medium-width, curved lines.

Chenille: Type of yarn that makes a velvety texture when knitted.

Chevron: Knitted zigzag formation made by increasing and decreasing.

Chunky: Heavyweight yarn, sometimes called bulky.

Circular knitting: Worked with a circular needle, or a set of double-pointed needles, to form a tube.

Collar stand: Extra-short rows worked above a neckline, but below a collar, to improve fit.

Cotton: Natural fibre from the cotton plant.

Counted-stitch embroidery: Worked by stitching over knitted stitches, following a chart.

Crew (neck): Round, close-fitting neckline.

Cross stitch: Stitch used for counted-stitch embroidery.

Decreasing: Working stitches together to reduce their number.

De-stash: Reducing your stash by selling, gifting or swapping yarn.

Double knitting (DK): Medium-weight yarn.

Double-pointed needle (DPN): Knitting needle with a point at each end.

Drape: Feel of yarn or knitting, and how it behaves in use.

Drop shoulder: Formed by a sleeve with a straight top edge, joined to a garment body with no armhole shapings.

Duplicate stitch: Embroidery stitch that copies knitted stitches, also known as Swiss darning or Kitchener stitch.

Dye-lot number: Indicates exact dye bath used, not just shade.

Ease: Difference between body measurement and actual garment measurement.

Fair Isle knitting: Small repeating patterns, knitted with two or more colours.

Felting needle: Tool for embellishing with yarns.

Felting: Shrinking knitting to make a firm fabric.

Fingering: Fine-weight yarn (similar to 3-ply and 4-ply).

Flat seam: Method of joining knitted pieces.

Float: Strand of yarn left at the wrong side of the work when stranding.

Freestyle embroidery: Worked by following a drawn or traced outline.

French knot: Embroidery stitch forming a small rounded knot.

Frog/frogging/frogged: Unpicking knitting when things go wrong. So called because you are ripping the work back (i.e., had to 'rip-it').

Fully fashioned shaping: Shaping emphasised by working decreases (or increases) two or more stitches in from the edge of the work.

Garter stitch: Formed by working all stitches as knit on every row.

Grafting: Seamless method of joining knitted pieces.

Hank: Coil of yarn.

I-cord (idiot cord): Tubular knitted cord made with two double-pointed needles.

Increasing: Making extra stitches.

Indie dyer: Individual or small company that specializes in the production of hand-dyed yarn.

Intarsia: Another name for picture knitting.

Invisible seam: Seam stitched with ladder stitch.

KAL – knitalong: Fun event carried out between members of a knitting group or by an online group, in which participants all decide to complete a particular design/project and share their version at their knitting group or in an online community forum.

KIP – knit/ting in public: When knitters get together in groups and knit in public places such as parks, museums or galleries. Can also refer to individuals knitting in waiting rooms, on trains, etc.

Knitwise: As when knitting a stitch.

Ladder stitch (also known as mattress stitch or invisible seam): Neat method of joining knitted pieces.

Lazy daisy: Another name for single chain stitch.

Linen: Natural fibre derived from the flax plant.

Lurex: Metallic fibre used to make yarn, either alone or blended with other fibres.

Mattress stitch: Another name for ladder stitch.

Medallion: Unit for knitted patchwork: square, round or hexagonal (or other regular shape).

Metallic: Yarn or fibre with a metallic effect.

Mitre: Shaped corner formed on a border.

Mohair: Natural fibre, hair from the Angora goat.

Mosaic knitting: Repeating patterns in two or more colours, knitted using one colour at a time by means of slip stitches.

Moss stitch: Stitch pattern with a dotted appearance.

Natural fibre: Fibre naturally occurring as an animal or vegetable product.

Needle tension: Small gadget for checking the size of knitting needles.

OTN – on the needles: As it suggests, this refers to any project that you are currently working on. Usually this will be a project that is actually current (not gathering dust in a cupboard).

Pattern: Stitch pattern, or a set of instructions for making a garment.

Pearl cotton: Slightly glossy embroidery thread suitable for use on knitting.

Picker: Knitter who knits with the yarn in the right hand but keeps hold of the needle and the yarn when wrapping round the needle.

Picot: Nub formed with knit or crochet stitches, normally repeated along an edging.

Polyamide: Synthetic fibre.

Polyester: Synthetic fibre.

Purlwise: As when purling a stitch.

Raglan: Sleeve and armhole shaping that slopes from the armhole to the neck edge.

Ramie: Fibre from the ramie plant, used to make a smooth yarn.

Reverse stocking stitch: Stocking stitch worked with the purl side as the right side.

Rib stitches or ribbing: Various combinations of knit and purl stitches, arranged to form vertical lines.

Ribbon yarn: Fancy yarn made from flat tape.

Right and left (when describing parts of a garment): Describe where the garment part will be when worn, e.g. the right sleeve is worn on the right arm.

Right side: Side of the work that will be outside the garment when worn.

Ring marker: Smooth ring of metal or plastic, slipped onto a needle to mark a particular position along a row, and slipped from row to row as knitting proceeds.

Rip/ripping: Unpicking your work when things go wrong.

SABLE – stash accumulation beyond life expectancy: Or, more yarn than you could ever knit in a lifetime. Not an uncommon problem.

Seam: Join made when two pieces of knitting are sewn together.

Selvedge stitch: First or last stitch(es) of a row worked in a different way to the rest of the row, to make a decorative edge, or a firm, neat edge for seaming.

Set-in sleeve: Sleeve and armhole shaping where the armhole is curved to take a curved sleeve head.

Shank: Pierced stem on the back of a button, used for attaching it; and a similar stem made with sewing thread.

Shaping: Increasing or decreasing the number of stitches to form the shape required.

Shawl collar: Large collar that wraps around the neck like a shawl.

Shetland wool: Loosely spun sheep's wool from the Shetland Islands.

Short-row shaping: Working incomplete rows to shape the knitting.

Silk: Natural fibre from the cocoon of the silkworm.

Single chain stitch: Embroidery stitch used for flower petals, etc.

Skein: Loosely wound coil of yarn or embroidery thread.

Slip stitch: Stitch slipped from one needle to the other without working into it.

Slub yarn or slubby yarn: Yarn of uneven thickness.

Soft cotton: Heavyweight embroidery thread suitable for use on knitting.

Sport-weight: Medium-weight yarn.

Stash: Yarn you haven't started knitting with yet, e.g. yarn you have plans for, yarn purchased on impulse or yarn you've been given.

Abbreviations

Stem stitch: Freestyle embroidery stitch.

Stitch holder: Device for holding stitches temporarily.

Stitch marker: Split ring of metal or plastic, slipped onto a knitted stitch to mark a position.

Stocking stitch: Formed by working one row of knit stitches, one row of purl stitches, and repeating these two rows.

Stranding: Method of dealing with floats in two-colour knitting.

Swiss darning: Another term for duplicate stitch.

Synthetic fibre: Manufactured fibre, not naturally occurring.

Tapestry needle: Sewing needle with a blunt tip and a large eye.

Tapestry wool: Wool sold in small skeins for embroidery.

Teasel brush: Small, stiff brush.

Tension: The number of stitches and rows to a given measurement.

Thrower: Knitter whose knitting style is to tuck the yarn under one arm while knitting and use the free hand to 'throw' the yarn around the needle without holding the needle with the hand.

Tink/tinking: Unpicking your work when you've made a mistake. Derives from 'knit' read backwards.

Tucker: Knitter who tucks one needle under their arm when knitting.

Tweed yarn: Yarn spun with flecks of contrasting colours, to resemble tweed fabric.

Twisting: Method of dealing with floats in two-colour knitting.

UFO – unfinished object: A project that hasn't been finished, and isn't likely to be in the near future. This is a likely candidate for repurposing. Knitters also like to discuss the number of UFOs they may have at any one time.

Viscose rayon: Man-made fibre derived from cellulose.

Weaving: Method of dealing with floats in two-colour knitting.

WIP – work in progress: Any project you haven't finished, or have recently (or not so recently) started. Knitters often refer to the number of WIPs they have on the go at any one time.

Wool: Natural fibre from the coat of sheep.

Worsted: Medium-weight yarn.

Wrong side: Side of the work that will be inside the garment when worn.

Yarn bombing: Public event where knitters promote their craft or a topical subject by decorating public places with knitting.

Yoke: Neck and shoulder area of a garment, especially where this is made all in one piece.

Always read the list of abbreviations used in any knitting pattern – different suppliers may use different abbreviations. Here are some of the most commonly used.

alt	alternate
approx	approximately
B	bobble or bead
BC	back cross; back cable
beg	beginning
bet	between
BH	buttonhole
C	cable; cross
CC	contrast colour
ch	chain
col	colour
cm(s)	centimetre(s)
cn	cable needle
CO	cast on
cont	continue
dc	double crochet
dec(s)	decrease(s), decreasing
DK	double knitting
DPN(s)	double pointed needle(s)
EOR	every other row or round
ER	every row or round
est	established
FC	front cross; front cable
foll	follow(ing)
g; gr; gm	gram
grp(s)	group(s)
g st	garter stitch
hk	(crochet) hook
in(s)	inch(es)

inc(s)	increase(s), increasing		**pwise**	purlwise
incl	include, including		**RC**	right cross; right cable
k	knit		**rem**	remaining
kb; k1b	knit stitch in row below; knit stitch through back loop		**rep**	repeat
kbf	knit into back and front of same stitch		**rev St st**	reverse stocking stitch
kfb	knit into front and back of same stitch		**RH**	right hand
k2tog	knit two together		**rib**	ribbing
kwise	knitwise		**rd(s) or rnd(s)**	round(s)
LC	left cross; left cable		**RS**	right side (of work)
LH	left hand		**RT**	right twist
lp(s)	loop(s)		**sk**	skip
LT	left twist		**SKP; skpo**	slip 1, knit 1, pass slip stitch over
M	marker		**sl**	slip
m	metre(s)		**sl st**	slip stitch
MB	make bobble		**sm**	slip marker
MC	main colour		**sp(s)**	space(s)
meas	measure(s)		**ssk**	slip, slip, knit
mm	millimetre(s)		**ssp**	slip, slip, purl
m1	make one		**st(s)**	stitch(es)
m1tbl; m1b	make one through back loop; invisible increase		**St st**	stocking stitch
ndl	needle		**tbl**	through back loop(s)
no	number		**tch**	turning chain
oz	ounce		**tog**	together
p	purl		**tr**	treble
pat; patt	pattern		**WS**	wrong side (of work)
pb; p1b	purl stitch in row below; purl stitch through back loop		**wyib**	with yarn in back, as if to knit
pbf	purl into back and front of same stitch		**wyif**	with yarn in front, as if to purl
pfb	purl into front and back of same stitch		**yb or ybk**	yarn to the back between needles
pm	place marker		**yd**	yard
pnso	pass next stitch over		**yf or yfwd**	yarn to the front between needles
psso	pass slip stitch over		**yo or yon**	yarn over needle to make extra stitch
ptbl	purl through back loop		**yrn**	yarn round needle to make extra stitch
p2tog	purl two together			

Useful references

Knitting spans across continents and sometimes seems mathematical in its approach, so here are some indispensable conversion and reference charts to help you keep up.

. . . .

Measurements

Metric and imperial

Centimetres x 0.394	Inches
Inches x 2.54	Centimetres
Grams x 0.035	Ounces
Ounces x 38.6	Grams
Metres x 1.1	Yards
Yards x 0.91	Metres

Equivalent weights

20g	$^3/_4$ oz
28g	1 oz
40g	1 $^1/_2$ oz
50g	1 $^3/_4$ oz
60g	2 oz
100g	3 $^1/_2$ oz

Sizing

To fit bust/chest	81cm 32in	86cm 34in	92cm 36in	97cm 38in
Actual measurement	92cm 36in	97cm 38in	102cm 40in	107cm 42in
Length	50.2cm 20in	56cm 22in	58.5cm 23in	59.5cm 23^1/$_2$in
Sleeve length	40.5cm 16in	43cm 17in	44.5cm 17^1/$_2$in	46cm 18in

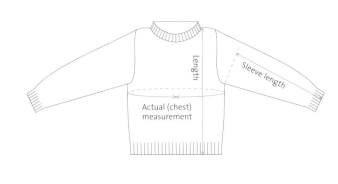

Length

Sleeve length

Actual (chest) measurement

Needles

Choosing the correct size (diameter) of needles is crucial to obtaining correct tension. Needles are sized in Europe from 2mm to 15mm or more and in the US from 0 to about 20. There is not an exact match between the two systems. You can use needles sized by either system, provided you check your tension carefully.

Equivalent needle sizes

Europe	US	Europe	US
2mm	0	5.5mm	9
2.75mm	1	6mm	10
2.75mm	2	6.5 or 7mm	10.5
3mm	3	8mm	11
3.25mm	4	9mm	13
3.5mm	5	10mm	15
4mm	6	12 or 13mm	17
4.5mm	7	15mm	20
5mm	8		

Yarn, tension, needles and WPI

Yarn weight symbol and category names	0	1	2	3	4	5	6
Types of yarns in category	Fingering 10-count crochet thread	Sock, fingering, baby	Sport, baby	DK, light worsted	Worsted, Afghan, Aran	Chunky, craft, rug	Bulky, roving
Knit tension range in stocking stitch to 10cm (4in)	33–40 sts	27–32 sts	23–26 sts	21–24 sts	16–20 sts	12–15 sts	6–11 sts
Recommended needle in metric-size range	1.5–2.25mm	2.25–3.25mm	3.25–3.75mm	3.75–4.5mm	4.5–5.5mm	5.5–8mm	8mm and larger
Recommended needle in US-size range	000–1	1–3	3–5	5–7	7–9	9–11	11 and larger
Wraps per inch (WPI)	16–18 WPI	14 WPI	12 WPI	11 WPI	8–9 WPI	7 WPI	6 or fewer WPI

Web resources

Below is a selection of some useful Web contacts for knitting suppliers, communities and guilds.

Selected suppliers

- www.buy-mail.co.uk
- www.cascadeyarns.com
  (features list of US stockists of Cascade yarns)
- www.coatscrafts.co.uk
- www.colourway.co.uk
- www.coolwoolz.co.uk
- www.designeryarns.uk.com
- www.diamondyarn.com
- www.ethknits.co.uk
- www.e-yarn.com
- www.hantex.co.uk
- www.hook-n-needle.com
- www.kangaroo.uk.com
- www.karpstyles.ca
- www.knitrowan.com
  (features worldwide list of stockists of Rowan yarns)
- www.knittersdream.com
- www.knittingfever.com
- www.knitwell.co.uk
- www.letsknit.com
- www.mcadirect.com
- www.only-knitting.co.uk.
- www.patternworks.com
- www.patonsyarns.com
- www.paviyarns.co.uk
- www.personalthreads.com
- www.shetlandwoolbrokers.co.uk
- www.sirdar.co.uk
- www.spinningayarn.co.uk
- www.theknittinggarden.com
- www.upcountry.co.uk
- www.vogueknitting.com
- www.yarncompany.com
- www.yarnexpressions.com
- www.yarnmarket.com

Online knitting communities

- www.ravelry.com
- www.stitchnbitch.org

Index

Credits

I would like to thank my Gran, for having the patience of a saint when teaching me to knit, and the many knitting friends who have shared their skills and knowledge along the way. Thanks also go to the knitting students whose contributions and feedback have been invaluable in improving my teaching skills and in helping me to understand how best to share my knowledge with them.

Grateful thanks to Betty Barnden for much appreciated assistance with swatches and pattern checking, and to all the team at Quarto for being great people to work with.

And last but not least, to my family and friends for their unstinting support, encouragement and help with chores, especially in the small hours when deadlines were tight!

References

- *300 Knitting Tips, Techniques & Trade Secrets* Betty Barnden
- *The Very Easy Guide to Knitting Scarves* Marie Connolly
- *How to Use, Adapt, and Design Knitting Patterns* Sam Elliott & Sidney Brian
- *The Very Easy Guide to Cable Knitting* Lynne Watterson

Quarto would like to thank:

- **Loop**
www.loopknitting.com
15 Camden Passage, Islington, London N1 8EA

- Films: Voiceovers by **Meghan Fernandes**.

Page 21 Chart credits
- **Craft Yarn Council**: www.craftyarncouncil.com/weight.html
- **HandKnitter.co.uk**: http://handknitter.co.uk/yarn_guage_wraps_per_inch.html

Page 29
- T-shirt yarn balls supplied by **Paula Ferreira**: cards-by-paula.blog.co.uk
- Newspaper yarn ball and flags supplied by **Kate Burrows**: flyhoof.blogspot.co.uk

Pages 216–217
- Thanks to **Luise Roberts** for the flower swatches.

Page 241
- Photographer: **Sarah Bell** , Model: **Celine Hughes,** Styling and knitwear: **Sorrel Wood**.

All step-by-step and other images are the copyright of Quarto Publishing plc. Whilst every effort has been made to credit contributors, Quarto would like to apologise should there have been any omissions or errors – and would be pleased to make the appropriate correction for future editions of the book.